Sir Gawain
and
Pearl

Sir Gawain
and
Pearl

❧[CRITICAL ESSAYS]❧

Edited by
Robert J. Blanch

Indiana University Press
Bloomington & London

To my wife
MARGIE
with adoration and admiration

Preface

With the resurgence of critical interest in *Pearl* and in *Sir Gawain and the Green Knight,* a definite need has been established for the undertaking of a *Pearl*-Poet anthology, an anthology which would serve to acquaint undergraduate and graduate students alike with the best of current criticism drawn from the scholarly journals in the modern language field.

The fourteen essays in this volume, five on *Pearl* and six on *Sir Gawain and the Green Knight,* have been selected in part because they represent a broad spectrum of criticial opinion based upon biblical exegesis, literary history, social history, myth-and-ritual interpretation, or formal textual explication.

The first essay on *Pearl,* that by Wellek, provides a perceptive review of early critical treatments of *Pearl* up to 1933, and then attempts to resolve "the dilemma between the elegiacal interpretation and the allegorical interpretation," to elucidate "the theological contents of the Pearl's instruction," and to examine "the question about the actual meaning of the symbolism of the Pearl."

Hamilton, in the second essay, views *Pearl* theologically as a *Paradise Lost* and *Paradise Regained* and employs medieval biblical exegesis in order to explain the spiritual motifs underlying the terrestrial garden scene. Luttrell, on the other hand, offers a detailed humanistic study of the garden setting of the opening of *Pearl*—"within the context of the life and literature of the period."

The last two essays on *Pearl* shed light upon the current of symbolism running throughout the poem. Blanch, basing his interpretation of precious metal and non-pearl gem symbolism upon medieval lapidaries and modern authorities of gemology, views the author of *Pearl* as employing these symbols in order to suggest the complete virtue whereby the poet-dreamer may attain spiritual peace. Spearing examines the pivotal symbol of the pearl and its relationship to the development and meaning of the poem. Revealing the pearl symbol as a dynamic force which "develops in meaning as the poem extends itself in time," he argues convincingly for a "nonallegorical reading of the pearl symbolism."

The second section of this volume, devoted to *Sir Gawain and the Green Knight,* opens with Burrow's essay, which concentrates on an often neglected aspect of *Gawain,* Gawain's "fault" and the theme of penance. Friedman investigates Morgan le Fay's role as magical creator of Gawain's "test." Markman, ignoring the penchant of modern criticism for symbolic and mythological approaches to *Gawain,* discloses, within the framework of romance, the moral test of a real human being—"the ideal feudal Christian knight who . . . represents the very high reaches of human behavior."

The next two essays focus upon the structural elements in *Gawain.* Green perceives a definite parallel in structure between the seasonal and liturgical cycles of *Gawain,* thereby pointing to "the passage of time from the First Coming to the second, from man's undertaking the journey of life to the judgment which is its inevitable conclusion." Howard, on the other hand, examines the parallel contingent upon the juxtaposition of two symbols, the shield and the green girdle. "The symbolism of shield and girdle suggests an essential . . . conflict between chivalry and Christianity."

The last essay represents an interpretive view of *Gawain* as an artistic whole. Expressly a rebuttal to a controversial essay by Speirs appearing in his book, *Medieval English Poetry: the Non-Chaucerian Tradition,* Moorman's essay construes *Gawain* as a *rite de passage,* an archetypal journey of the hero from innocence to experience.

All essays are reproduced uncut in their text and notes. To aid the student bibliographical references for further study are provided, when necessary, at the bottom of the first page of the essays.

I am grateful to the medieval scholar-advisers of Indiana University for their helpful comments on the selection of essays and for their encouragement. The two illustrations from the Cotton MS. are reproduced with the kind permission of the Trustees of the British Museum. I am especially indebted to the contributors and to their publishers for the permissions which made this anthology possible.

R. J. B.

Buffalo, New York
December 7, 1965

Contents

Pearl

Cotton MS. Nero A. x., folio 37a

··◦]‖ 1 ‖[◦··

The *Pearl:* An Interpretation of the Middle English Poem

RENÉ WELLEK

I

A lucky chance has preserved to us two English poems of the fourteenth century which rank not far below the best we have from Chaucer's master hand. MS Cotton Nero A. X. (now A. X. 4) in the British Museum contains the only known text of both *Sir Gawain and the Green Knight* and the *Pearl*. Since Richard Morris's first edition in 1864 the *Pearl* has found an ever increasing number of editors, translators, interpreters and admirers. The aesthetic qualities of the poem—its finished grace, the unearthly loveliness of its descriptions, the heavy brocade of its strange diction, the depth of feeling expressed—have become universally recognized. The linguistic and textual problems it offers have attracted an unusual number of Middle English scholars, and the wide perspectives it opens for speculations in biography, interpretation, comparative literature and

Reprinted, with some revisions by the author, by permission of the author and The Charles University from *Studies in English by Members of the English Seminar of Charles University,* IV (1933), 5-33.

history of thought have made this short poem a focus of combat and polemics, in which few Middle English scholars have failed to join. It may be time to look back at what has been achieved: to survey the state of research and to sift the chaff from the wheat and then to give a new interpretation, which would use the reasonable results of the labors done by others in a spirit of gratitude and add a few new points of view and hitherto unnoticed illustrations, which throw a little more light on this sparkling jewel.

The preparatory work, which scholarship has to perform, has been done well and fairly completely in the case of the *Pearl*. As we have only one MS to go upon, editing does not give us puzzles similar to the amazing MS labyrinths of *Troilus and Criseyde,* so sagaciously solved by Professor Root, or of *Piers the Plowman,* still waiting for a final edition. Nevertheless just because only one MS has been preserved, another type of textual problem is more numerous and free scope is given to emendation of the scribal errors and corruptions and the interpretation of difficult words and passages.

Sir Frederick Madden was the first to give a detailed description of the Cotton MS in his "Syr Gawayne: A Collection of Ancient Romance Poems"[1]—he was at least the first who distinguished between the four poems contained in the MS *(Pearl, Purity, Patience* and *Gawain). Richard Morris,* in 1864, published the first edition of the *Pearl* for the Early English Text Society.[2] To Morris we owe a fair text, which has actually been improved only in details since. *Sir Israel Gollancz* was the next editor in 1891,[3] but his edition, though it meant in some respects a real advance beyond Morris, was vitiated by unnecessary and fanciful emendations. A number of minor contributions in periodicals (by Kölbing, Morris, Holthausen[4]) followed in the next years up to the publication of *C. G. Osgood's* new edition, which came out in 1906[5] and which meant again a distinct advance in the interpretation and illustration of the text, even if some of his conjectures do not commend themselves to a closer scrutiny. In 1921 *Sir Israel Gollancz* reissued his edition in an entirely recast form,[6] which did away with most of the deficiencies of his earlier work. He uses also Osgood's improvements, though he unjustly denies to him any merit in the advance of textual interpretation.[7] Gollancz's edition, in spite of new and ingenious emendations which mean the solution of many puzzles, still leaves some points of dispute open and is not always consistent and logical in its handling of some textual problems.[8] Larger parts of the poem were edited by *A. Brandl* and *O. Zippel*[9] and by *K. Sisam*[10] and a number of important contributions to textual problems were published by *A. S. Cook*,[11] *O. F. Emerson*,[12] and *E. Tuttle*.[13] Still, there is room for a new and final edition which would incorporate these new results, pay more attention to the evidence of the meter and avoid the arbitrary conjectures of Gollancz. To Gollancz finally we owe a Facsimile reproduction of the MS for the Early English Text Society, though unfortunately the reproduction is technically not quite as perfect as we would wish it to be.[14] Recently *J. P. Oakden*[15] has made an attempt to show that the single scribe of the MS has based his transcription on a MS in which it is still possible to recognize three individual scribal hands, but, it seems, his elaborate theory is unnecessary to account for the phenomena he lists. Translations which can also be called contributions to textual interpretation include prose-versions in modern English, free adaptations and attempts to reproduce the exact rhyme and stanza scheme of the original and even a German and an Italian verse-translation.[16]

The establishment of the text naturally involves the question of the author's dialect and language and the place of provenance of the MS. The MS is undoubtedly written by a hand dating from the late fourteenth or early fifteenth centuries. The evidence found by *J. G. Gilson*[17] points to the fact that it came from the monasteries of the North. The early dialectical research of *R. Morris, F. Knigge, W. Fick,* and *Schwahn*[18] pointed to the conclusion that the poem comes from the extreme North West Midlands, probably from Lancashire. This conclusion has been contested by *J. R. Hulbert,*[19] who judges "that the poems may be from the West Midland, but no significant evidence has yet been given to prove that location." He is altogether sceptical as to whether it is possible to assign a definite locality to the poems considering the state of our knowledge of Middle English dialects. "There is no good evidence to connect alliterative romances with the West; their language should not be called West Midland; and until new facts are found the only safe statement of the location of these poems is that they were probably written in some place which possessed a mixed Northern and Midland dialect."[20] As a solution Hulbert suggests a sort of $\kappa o\iota\nu\acute{\eta}$, a conventional language "which had for its basis perhaps some particular dialect (possibly traditionally associated with alliterative verse)" which the writers altered "in the direction of their own native dialect."[21]

But *Karl Luick* in his monumental "Grammatik" has analyzed Middle English dialects much more thoroughly and assigns the poems of the Cotton MS to the type of dialect found in the Ireland MS, written at Hale Hall in Southern Lancashire,[22] and also quotes *Gawain* frequently as having definite West Midland characteristics.[23] Using Luick's results, *R. J. Menner* assembled the evidence for the Northwest. Although he admits the justice of Hulbert's criticism of the older arguments for West Midland, he proves that we actually "possess certain phonological and inflectional characteristics which we have a right to consider West Midland rather than East Midland."[24] But he is careful to state that it would be dangerous to assign these poems to any particular county.

Recently *J. P. Oakden*[25] attempted to narrow down the area even further. On the basis of a complicated map of dialectical boundaries constructed by him, he assigns the *Pearl* to South Lancashire and North West Derbyshire with no preference for either. Because of the strong Scandinavian element in the vocabulary preference is given to South East Lancashire, extreme North West Derbyshire and possibly extreme South West Yorkshire. To make this location even more definite, Oakden makes an elaborate attempt to identify the castle of the Green Knight with the castle Clitheroe near the Ribble, which belonged to John of Gaunt from 1360 to 1398. But the alleged similarity of position is extremely vague and the accuracy of the map of dialect boundaries is also open to grave doubts.[26] Miss *M. S. Serjeantson*[27] recently made another very elaborate attempt to define the region of the *Pearl* more closely. She comes to the conclusion that the *Pearl* may have "originated in an area rather to the east of that in which Sir Gawayne was written." "On the whole, Derbyshire seems the least improbable area to which the Nero MS may be assigned, whatever the original dialects of the poems may have been." But the question does not seem to be settled and, perhaps, it is not possible to settle it with the means at our disposal. In the meantime, we have to rest content with the more cautious conclusions of Menner, especially as the importance of the dialectical evidence is extremely overrated. Though North West Midland must be regarded as the region of provenance, the existence of a special literary language which obscures more definite local traces should not be denied.[28]

The question of the authorship of our poem has naturally attracted many minds. It would be a wonderful find if we should be able to hit on the name of the author of such a large and important body of poetry as the *Pearl, Gawain, Purity,* and

Patience. The evidence of common authorship of these poems is very strong indeed and should be absolutely beyond any doubt as regards the *Pearl, Purity,* and *Patience.* The evidence as to the common authorship of these poems and *Gawain* seems to me a little less convincing, though the metrical similarities and other links make also this identification highly probable, and the difference in tone and atmosphere can be explained by the French source of *Gawain.*[29] Probably *St. Erkenwald,* that curious legend of London, is also the work of the *Gawain* poet, a view which was forwarded as early as 1881 by *C. Horstmann* and has recently been very ably defended by *H. L. Savage* in his edition of the legend.[30]

But the attempts to connect a name with these poems have hitherto failed completely. There is not a shred of evidence for either *Huchown* or *Strode,* who have been suggested by eminent scholars. On the contrary, enough evidence can be brought against these theories to rule them out of any serious consideration. Huchown of the Awle Ryale can lay claim to nothing except the "Pistel of the Swete Susane," and both the *Pearl* and *Gawain* cannot be by the author of the "Pistel" if only on the ground of the striking dialectical and stylistic differences.[31] Equally flimsy is the case for Ralph Strode, whose authorship has been defended by C. Horstmann and Sir Israel Gollancz. There was, it is true, a poet Ralph Strode who wrote a "Fantasma Radulphi" before 1360, but there is not the slightest evidence that this Fellow of Merton College, Oxford, was a Northerner or that he even wrote in English or that "Ralph's Spectre" is in any way identical with the *Pearl.* Moreover, it has been shown that this Strode was probably not identical with the logician Strode, who played some part in the history of scholastics.[32]

Finally *Oscar Cargill* and *Margaret Schlauch* made a new attempt to identify the poet of the *Pearl.*[33] Though they have no positive evidence to go upon, they identify the child mourned in the poem with Margaret, daughter of John Hastings, Earl of Pembroke, and his wife Margaret, a daughter of Edward III. But they cannot even prove that the child died at the age of two; they have to quote a document dating from 1371, when the girl, born in 1367, was four years old and is unmistakably spoken of as a living person. Another document dated 1369, which makes provisions *in case* her father should die without issue, is certainly no proof—as the authors curiously take it to be—of the child's being actually dead by that time. Also the attempt to press the word "countess" in stanza 41 of the *Pearl* into a literal and earthly significance and to read some importance into the fact that the King has actually given pearls to the supposed mother of the girl are completely unsuccessful. On top of this airy structure Cargill and Schlauch erect a theory about the authorship of the poem. Of five servants of the household of John Hastings, who later came to the Court, they pick two, John Donne and John Prat, as the likely authors without deciding between them. John Donne was apparently chosen because of his name and not for any other reason, since he is mentioned in a document as "valet of the king's kitchen," and John Prat's case is not much stronger, as we have absolutely nothing to connect him with any definite piece of poetry. It is true that he is called the "King's minstrel" in 1370, but "minstrel" is a term for any fiddler and rope-dancer.

II

These airy theories disposed of, it will be best to turn to the text of the poem and to ascertain its actual meaning and purpose, as the external evidence has failed to render anything really significant. The history of the *Pearl* research shows that this is not an easy task, as opinions vary with almost every

writer on the question. We shall give a brief but critical review
of the main interpretations offered and then discuss the poem
independently.

All the early editors and interpreters agree in regarding the
Pearl as an elegy for the death of the poet's daughter. *Bernhard
Ten Brink* and *Sir Israel Gollancz* have elaborated this theory
in the greatest detail, and hence it has been taken over by
almost all handbooks and literary histories.[34] Ten Brink was,
I think, the first to construct an imaginary biography of the
poet on the base of this interpretation: "Der Dichter," he
fancies, "hatte sich verheiratet. Ein Kind, ein holdes, im Reiz der
Unschuld strahlendes Mädchen beglückte diese Verbindung.
Auf dieses Kind konzentrierte sich die ganze Zärtlichkeit des
Vaters mit einer Ausschließlichkeit, welche uns vermuten läßt,
daß die Mutter die Geburt desselben nicht lange überlebt hatte.
Da raffte sie im zartesten Alter die Hand des Geschicks un-
barmherzig hinweg. Wie dem Vater da zu Mute war, sagt
uns seine Dichtung; zugleich aber auch, wie er zur Fassung
gelangte."[35] Ten Brink bases his fancy about the mother's death
in childbirth on the mere fact that she is never mentioned in
the poem, but even he seems nearer to asserted facts, if we compare him with Gollancz, who elaborated Ten Brink's idea in
the introduction to his edition in 1891 and repeated his opinions, unshaken by any arguments directed against them, even
in the chaper on the *Pearl* in the Cambridge History of English
Literature (1901) and in his edition of 1921. Gollancz knows
that the author of the *Pearl* was certainly no priest, he knows
that his "wedded life was unhappy; the object of his life had
disappointed him, and had perhaps proved unfaithful."[36]
Nevertheless "his wedded life had brought him happiness—an
only child, his 'little queen.' He perhaps named the child Margery or Marguerite. But his happiness was short-lived; before
two years had passed the poet's home was desolate. With the loss

of his dearest possession a blight seems to have fallen on his life, and even poetry may have lost its charm for him. The lyrist became the stern moralist of the 'Cleanness' and 'Patience'."[37] " 'Cleanness' and 'Patience' were probably written not long after the 'Pearl.' But the vivid descriptions of the sea in these two poems perhaps justify the inference that the poet may have sought distraction in travel. It would seem that late in his life the poet may have found occupation in the City of London, in some secular office" and so on in the most fanciful strain. The text of the poems is utterly silent on the mother, on the name of the child, and flatly contradicts the idea that *Patience* and *Cleanness* could have been written later, as the metrical and artistic advance goes surely the other way round from the earlier homiletic poems to the much more finished *Pearl*.

In 1904 Professor *Carleton Brown* wrote his epoch-making article "The Author of the Pearl Considered in the Light of his Theological Opinions,"[38] where for the first time the actual contents of the poem are taken seriously enough to allow an investigation of its very center, the theological discussion, no longer regarded a mere digression. Professor Brown tries to prove that the poet was an ecclesiastic, as he seems particularly well acquainted with the Bible and the theological controversies of his time. He shows in detail that the poet of the *Pearl* agrees with his contemporary, Thomas Bradwardine, in his fundamental doctrine, directed against the Pelagianism then current, that "salvation is bestowed through the free grace of God, instead of being achieved by any merits." But even further, the author of the *Pearl* "goes beyond Bradwardine in the boldness with which he pushes the doctrine of free grace to its logical conclusion." The assertion that the baptized infant will receive equal reward with the adult is directly opposed to the established opinions of the theologians. The author of the *Pearl* defends the complete equality of the heavenly rewards, a heresy descended from the fourth-century heretic Jovinian. Like Jovinian the poet uses in support of his doctrine the parable of the Vineyard, which he explains literally, implicitly rejecting the scholastic interpretations which tried to smooth over the difficulty. "On the whole, it is evident that our author's attitude towards religious matters was evangelical rather than ecclesiastical." His silence on Holy Church, the absence of any references to apocryphal and legendary matter, his disregard of patristic and scholastic authority, his deep ethical fervor and his assertion of a true equality of the elect are quoted in support of this striking thesis. Professor Brown goes even so far to see, at least in this last respect, a "most interesting and remarkable anticipation of sixteenth century Protestantism."[39]

In the same periodical and in the same year Professor *W. H. Schofield* published an article on "The Nature and Fabric of the Pearl,"[40] which makes a frontal attack on the older interpretation of the *Pearl* as an elegy and tries, besides, to give an allegorical interpretation of the whole poem. He first shows how flimsy is the evidence for the elegiac interpretation and examines further Brown's theory that our author was an ecclesiastic. "An English ecclesiastic in the fourteenth century could not possibly have had any but an illegitimate child and it stands to reason that a priest would not deliberately go out of his way to call people's attention to his child of shame, and then without apology proceed to exalt above all else purity of life." But the poem does not necessitate such a hypothesis, as it is nothing more than an "artistic arrangement of a situation by which certain theological and religious opinions could be effectively presented." The child in the poem is not the daughter of the poet: no kinship is asserted to exist between the two. "One cannot even affirm that it is an imaginary vision of a father without going beyond the information in the text." The Pearl is, in truth, merely an allegorical figure, a being purely and simply of the poet's imagination. The child never had any physical shape on earth. It was the form of a maiden unknown to him, except in his dream, that the poet bodied forth to our view. His poem is no elegy, no lament, no dirge, no *In Memoriam*. What is then the meaning of the allegory? Schofield answers that the vision of the *Pearl* is intended above all to exalt the purity of the maiden, clean virginity. She is merely a symbol of pure maidenhood, a representative bride of the Lamb. However, Schofield's belief in such a one-to-one relation between allegory and its meaning is a little wavering and he quotes the Chaucerian "Testament of Love"[41] to show that the Pearl was a symbol of various connotations. His conclusion is that the Pearl is a purely allegorical figure, similar to those damsels representing Philosophy or Nature or Reason in medieval visions. The poem merely combines the traditional vision of the other world with an equally traditional debate. He asks also, how is it possible that the girl in the vision does not demean herself as a babe of two years and how we can explain "her absolute lack of tenderness in her treatment of her father, her coldly stern rebukes, her never-changing austerity."[42] "Plainly, viewed as an elegy, the poem is ineffective. Unlike the Lady in *Comus,* unlike the Beatrice of Dante, his Pearl, so far as human knowledge can attest, has no stimulating suggestion from a real presence."[43]

In the appendix of his paper, Professor Schofield communicates the interesting discovery of a close parallel to the *Pearl* in Boccaccio's earlier eclogue *Olympia*. Schofield recognizes Boccaccio's eclogue as the starting-point of our author's conception, but, though he does not express any doubt about the elegiac character of Boccaccio's poem written for his daughter Violante, he oddly enough considers this rather a confirmation of his theory. "The Eclogue not only explains the presence of the would-be elegiac atmosphere of the *Pearl,* but accounts also

for its unreality." "If as some might possibly argue, the author
of the *Pearl* had suffered a loss like Boccaccio's and was led to
imitate his poem on that account, he would surely have substituted some of his own for Boccaccio's personal touches. As a
matter of fact, however, there is no single remark in the *Pearl,*
that by any chance could be autobiographical which is not ex-
plicable as an echo of Boccaccio's plainly stated experience."

C. Brown's and Schofield's revolutionary opinions were,
however, not accepted by most other scholars, though they
forced them to consider the allegorical and theological contents
of the poem, which had been hitherto neglected. Professor
Ch. G. Osgood's edition of 1906 gives a most thorough consideration to these problems, quoting a great deal of new illustra-
tive material, while still holding firmly to the elegiac interpretation. "The poem," he decides, "is first of all an elegy."[44]
Professor Osgood is not convinced that the poet is an ecclesiastic, as he may well have been a lay-poet with strong religious
interests. The dilemma concerning the illegitimate child is not
a real one, as he might very well have been married before taking orders. Several references in the poem exclude a purely
allegorical interpretation, nor is the identification of the Pearl
with maidenhood very convincing, as the Pearl had dozens of
meanings; and, besides, the interpretation given by Schofield is
nowhere given or even suggested by the poet.[45] "Considering the
poet's work as a whole, it is clear that he is not only no alle-
gorist, but he rather tends to avoid symbolism, even when it
lies in his way." Professor Osgood grants, that, though the
Pearl is not primarily an allegory, it contains certain allegorical elements. But, on the whole, the poet had no preference
for allegory and only now and then imparts a certain allegorical
cast to his work. The symbolism is merely latent and any such
emblematic result was perhaps reached unconsciously, or at any
rate did not constitute an important part of the poet's original

design.[46] In addition to the allegorical elements Osgood recognizes also the popular medieval theme of the vision of an other world in the *Pearl.* As to the theology propounded, Professor Osgood accepts Brown's conclusion, though he stresses the point that the Jovinian doctrine is only one detail of heresy in a man who, in all other known aspects, was enthusiastically and loyally orthodox. The belief in the equality of heavenly rewards is certainly at variance with the poet's social ideas.[47] It seems, furthermore, to have been of acquisition more recent than the composition of *Purity,* for the orthodox view is there clearly implied.[48] Now this is rather a further indication of the elegiac character of the poem. An isolated point of heresy seems naturally not to have been achieved by reason, but is the reflex of violent emotional experience, the consequence of the poet's affliction by the loss of his daughter. The parallel with *Olympia* Professor Osgood regards rather as based in the general method of treating an elegiac theme, and perhaps in the actual choice of theme, than in the appropriation of poetic details from the eclogue.

Even more thorough is the rejection of Professor Schofield's hypothesis in other papers published in the following years. *C. G. Coulton,* the author of a tasteful translation of the *Pearl,* wrote in its defense.[49] Coulton shows that the supposition that an ecclesiastic could have had only an illegitimate child is not even well founded because he might have married before taking orders and also because lower orders did not prevent matrimony at that time. Coulton also combats with many telling sarcastic questions Schofield's interpretation of the symbolism of the *Pearl* as denoting maidenhood and notes judiciously that the comparison with Boccaccio's *Olympia* speaks rather against Schofield's thesis than for it.

Similar views are upheld by Professor *Clark S. Northrup,*[50] who points the way out of the unreal dilemma between elegy and allegory. "That the framework of the poem is that of a vision and that the debate effectively expounds and defends the equality of heavenly rewards, no one will doubt; but that this excludes the possibility that the poem is based on a personal experience is still, we think, an open question." The use of the conventional vision is no more strange than "Boccaccio's use of the eclogue in writing of his five-year-old daughter Violante, or Milton's use of conventional pastoral figure in writing of Edward King. Both Boccaccio and Milton managed to express genuine feeling; so, to our thinking, did the author of the *Pearl.*" Also *Gollancz* repeated his earlier opinions, embellishing them with even more fantastic speculations such as the curious suggestion that the Pearl was "perhaps a love-child, hence his *privy* pearl."[51] More judiciously he states against the allegorical interpretation: "The attempt to read the poem as a theological pamphlet, and as a mere symbolical allegory, ignores its transcendent reality as a poet's lament. The personal side of the poem is clearly marked, though the author nowhere directly refers to his fatherhood . . . the jeweler indicates clearly enough the reality of his loss."[52]

No wonder that Professor *Schofield* wanted to reassert and to explain his theory, when he saw its ill success. The Paper "Symbolism, Allegory and Autobiography in the Pearl"[53] is a labored, almost line-by-line interpretation of the poem in the light of Professor Schofield's theory. He shows well enough that the opening stanza has been hitherto thoroughly misinterpreted, that it contains no mention whatsoever of the maiden and that its style rather resembles that of contemporary lapidaries. But later on his effort to deny all personal references becomes very strained, although he avoids the simplified interpretation of his earlier paper and states now rather surprisingly that the final and chief teaching of the work lies in the line saying that those who dwell with Christ in heavenly joy are pearls, spotless in his sight.[54] Professor Schofield seems right in asserting against Osgood that the allegorical cast of the poem does not appear now and then, but pervasively, wherever it could appear, from the beginning to the end of the work. The emblematic result is an absolutely fundamental part of the poet's design and not an accidental superaddition as Osgood would have us believe. "Take this away and the structure of the poem falls to pieces. On the other hand, take away the would-be 'personal references' and their absence is hardly noticeable."[55]

While Schofield's handling of the symbolism is a little embarrassed and undecided, and, in the second paper at least, fairly non-committal, the allegory of the *Pearl* found bolder interpreters later, who build on Schofield while they reject his detailed application. Professor *R. M. Garrett* is the author of a little pamphlet: "The Pearl: an Interpretation,"[56] where he claims to have found the sesame. The Pearl, according to Garrett, means nothing but the Eucharist. "I have an idea that the whole poem arose from gazing at the Elevated Host in the hands of the Priest." "I believe the poet conceived the poem as taking place within the church, where the Pearl might be buried, quite regardless of the convention of the arbor and the grass." He suggests that the reference to the smell of flowers on the grave-mound is only a quasi-pastoral device, which really hints at the incense in the church. He recapitulates: "Within the frame of the great Pearl the poet see his lost pearl in the presence of the Lamb of God, a very member incorporate in the mystical body of Christ: and she teaches him that through the grace of God as granted in the Eucharist it is given to him to become a member of this body, thus to be forever united with his Pearl as parts of the great Pearl, the mystical body of Christ."[57] However, the only instance of a parallelism between the Pearl and the Eucharist, which Professor Garrett was able to find in the writings of the Western church, is from an obscure hymn by Venantius Fortunatus. The verses in which the poet refers to the Eucharist[58] do not have the meaning which Professor Garrett's curious mistranslation suggests.[59] The whole is merely a string of more or less interesting quotations; the main thesis, however, must be pronounced as unproven.

Professor *Jefferson B. Fletcher's* comparatively short paper "The Allegory of the Pearl"[60] strikes us as the sanest and most convincing solution of the main questions, and it is a pity that his suggestions have not become the common property of scholarship. First, Professor Fletcher shows that Carleton Brown's interpretation of the theology of the poem is wrong in the essential points: the *Pearl* poet does not actually assert "a flat democracy, or rather oriental despotism of an absolute royal family ruling a dead level of subjects," but he recognizes rank in heaven when he mentions the "aldermen right before God's chair."[61] "The presumption is against a devout fourteenth century Catholic acting the heretic; and if he were to do so, he would certainly try to bolster up his position as strongly as possible." Professor Fletcher shows also that according to the teachings of the Church it is entirely possible to reconcile the equality of the heavenly rewards expressed by the denarius with the subjective variety of the enjoyment of this beatitude. Also the dilemma between *Pearl* as an elegy or an allegory is justly exposed as a false one. It is possible to grant all the allegorical interpretations which the critics have proposed, and still "believe in the historical existence of the child, just as, for instance, Albertus Magnus in his praise of the Virgin Mary described all the symbolic properties, delights, scents, meteorology, flora and fauna of Mary quâ Garden without ever doubting her historical reality." Also the symbolism of the *Pearl* cannot be interpreted mechanically by one correspondent abstract as maidenhood. "Though each fact may reflect but one object, the symbol as a whole may at the time reflect many objects."

Sister *M. Madeleva* has devoted a whole book to a new allegorical interpretation. The subtitle of her book *Pearl: A Study in Spiritual Dryness*[62] indicates the surprising conclusion that the poem is a "purely subjective study in spiritual dryness, interior desolation, a lament for the loss of the sensible sweetness of God."[63] The poem "opens with a real case of spiritual 'blues,' followed by a consideration of God's grace, brought to a perfectly consistent climax, the contemplation of heaven."[64] "As to wife, and child, and bereavement, I say that there was no wife, there was no two-year-old daughter and consequently no bereavement."[65] The spot where the poet mourned his pearl is expressedly not a graveyard, but a typical monastery garden.[66] The child could have never been taken into the procession following the Lamb, a child could never have talked in the way the visionary figure is speaking. The Pearl child rather represents "the poet's own soul, as it might be in a state of perfection at this particular time of life."[67] "The Pearl is a token, a symbol of peace; the poet is not seeking a child but a state, a condition of peace, symbolized by a pearl."[68] All this is illustrated or rather darkened by plentiful quotations from medieval literature on mysticism, on spiritual dryness in general, etc., but the actual argument is quite amateurish and frequently enough flies directly into the face of all evidence of the text.

Another revival of the purely allegorical interpretation is represented by *Walter Kirkland Greene's* article: "The Pearl—A New Interpretation."[69] Like Schofield he asserts that the poem is not autobiographical, but parabolical. It does not refer to the actual loss of a child, but the discussion between the dreamer and the maiden is a literary device for imparting a spiritual teaching. The dreamer's function consists solely in introducing the maiden and allowing her to utter her revelations in regard to divine grace and the heavenly rewards. Greene draws a close parallel to Boccaccio's *Olympia* and makes an unconvincing attempt to establish a parallel with Dante's *Purgatorio*.[70] Greene seems to be still convinced of the justness of Professor Brown's description of the poet's heretical theological opinions, but objects to Schofield's interpretation of the Pearl as a symbol of maidenhood as this would not explain the poet's real or apparent grief and subsequent joy. But the way out found by Greene, that the figure of the child is used merely as a literary device to impart the spiritual lesson of divine grace, is surely a blind alley, even though the article has its merit in insisting on the problem of divine grace as the central theological question of the poem.

Finally, an important parallel was first quoted by Miss *Elizabeth Hart* in her article "The Heaven of Virgins."[71] She disproves Sister M. Madeleva's argument that a two-year-old child could not be among the procession of the hundred and forty thousand by pointing to a passage in Chaucer's *Prioress's Tale*[72] and drawing attention to the liturgical use of the passage describing the procession in the Apocalypse in the Mass read on the Feast of the Holy Innocents. Curiously enough, Miss Hart has no quarrel with Sister Madeleva's main thesis.

It remains for us to reintegrate these interpretations which have passed before our mental eye in a chronological order into one consistent picture which will use the results gained by the study of the literature and will add a few new points of view and illustrations of our own.

III

The study of the literature showed that several questions about the *Pearl* are still undecided. First of all, we have the dilemma between the elegiacal interpretation and the allegorical interpretation; secondly, there is the moot question about the theological contents of the Pearl's instruction; and thirdly, there is the question about the actual meaning of the symbolism of the Pearl.

The debate which is pervading all literature on the *Pearl,* a debate between elegy and allegory, is very poorly formulated at the outset. There cannot be any doubt that the poem is not an elegy in any sense of the word. The mourning of a beloved object which might conceivably be termed elegiac is merely the starting-point of the poem, which obviously is mainly a vision bringing consolation to the mourner. The point of issue should be rather expressed by a dilemma between a personal interpretation and a purely allegorical one. Professor Fletcher has shown very convincingly that even this dilemma is a false one. We can very well grant the reality of the loss of the child and its historical existence, while we are under no necessity whatever to deny the allegorical intent of the whole. However, it is clear that Ten Brink's, Gollancz's and Osgood's interpretations of the personal background go a good deal beyond the real evidence. We do not know anything about the child mourned, except the fact that it died at two years of age. We do not even know that she was the poet's daughter, though this interpretation is plausible enough. The only definition of the relationship—and its particular form might have been necessitated by the exigencies of rhyme—can be found in line 233 and asserts merely:

> Ho watȝ me nerre þen aunte or nece,

so that the possibility of a young sister is left open. We know nothing whatsoever about the child's name—there is no need to see an allusion to Margarete or Margery in the pervading symbolism of the Pearl. Nor do we know anything at all about the mother, who is never mentioned by the poet. Death in childbirth, unfaithfulness, or the illegitimacy of the relation cannot be deduced from the single passage which says:

> Art þou my perle þat I haf playned
> Regretted by myn one, on nyȝte,[73]

which means nothing else than that the poet has mourned her in the loneliness of the night. Gollancz derives from these lines even the notion that the child was an only child and interprets the adjective "privy" applied to the "pearl withouten spot" as an allusion to the supposed illegitimacy of the child.[74]

But however sharply we may reject the fanciful speculations of some interpreters, we should not be blind, as others have been, to the essential truth of the personal interpretation. There cannot be any doubt that the poet is mourning the actual loss of a little child, who was not yet two years old when she died, so young and tender of age that she could not please God by good works nor pray to him, as she knew neither Pater nor Creed.[75] All purely allegorical interpretations break down completely at these passages. Nor can there be any doubt that the poet has fallen asleep on her grave, clearly pictured in the illustration to lines 57–64 and not in a monastery garden (Madeleva) or in a church (Garrett). The frequently repeated arguments of all allegorists that the child's behavior to the father is unchildlike is perfectly invalid as the whole supposition on which the poem proceeds is precisely a transformation of the two-year-old child into a wise, majestic inhabitant of the heavens, free from all earthly ignorance and affections. She, who was once so young and simple,[76] is now keen of wit and thoroughly knowing. This is entirely in accordance with the teaching of the church, for which the conferment of heavenly grace always meant a complete regeneration, a becoming similar to God, a state which implies heavenly beauty, heavenly wisdom and joyous freedom from earthly passions like envy, etc.[77] Besides, this transfiguration is nothing unusual in medieval literature: the Olympia of Boccaccio's Eclogue is similarly remote from Boccaccio's six-year-old daughter Violante, and the Beatrice of Dante's Paradise talks very differently from the earthly daughter of Folco Portinari.

Also the argument of those allegorists who grant these personal allusions, but explain them merely as a literary device for imparting a spiritual teaching is not convincing. It is, of course, true that the elegiacal purpose, the mourning of the child, is not the real purpose of the poem, as this is rather contained in the lesson which the beatified child is giving to the poet. The purely elegiac interpretation makes the poem an unartistic conglomerate, as it degrades the very center, the debate between the poet and the visionary girl, to a mere digression detrimental to its artistic unity. Nevertheless it is untrue to say that the personal loss clearly expressed in the poem is a mere device, a mere vehicle destined to convey the revelations in regard to divine grace and the heavenly rewards. All these lessons would, after all, scarcely interest the poet unless they would administer *personal* consolation and reassurement. The point of the poem is the conviction, which the poet carries away at the end of the poem, that the child is saved and that she even sees the face of God. In order to be convinced, the poet must entertain certain theological opinions which cannot therefore be considered an irrelevant digression. That these opinions are expanded by the figure of the girl should not blind us to the fact that they are the real opinions of the author, while the opinions put into the mouth of the dreaming poet are the opinions he is discarding—which he has overcome by the certainty of hope. The logical sequence of events is this: the death of the child, a period of doubt and despair, conviction arrived at by theological study or even confirmed by an actual dream that the child is saved, and lastly the composition of the poem, which embodies this spiritual progress. The essential contrast is that between the wretched will of the fretting mourner, his "del and gret daunger," the "strot" of his rebellious heart[78] and the joyful resignation of the verse towards the end of the poem:

Now al be to þat Prynceȝ paye.[79]

We may therefore very well call the dream and the vision a literary device—there is scarcely anybody who would imagine that it could have happened in this form—but we cannot call the existence of the child and the actuality of its loss a device, as without the reality of the loss the whole vision would manifestly lose any personal appeal to the poet and one could justly be astonished that the poet was at all interested in hearing that a two-year-old child can be saved and even incorporated among the followers of the Lamb. It is irrelevant whether the poet ever really dreamt such a dream: we shall never know it and if we knew that he did, we should still have to say that the poem is necessarily an elaboration, a concretization of a dream-reality and therefore more real and lasting than any dream could ever have been. Vision and theological lesson are closely intertwined: as a matter of fact the argument of the girl is nothing but a justification of the vision. The theological instruction is a ratiocination, which tries to defend the justness, possibility and likelihood of the vision, and on the other hand, the vision is also a device to give authority and weight to the theological opinions revealed by the girl. If we consider the question of the type or "genre" of the poem as at all important, we have to answer that the poem is a vision of the other world, in which the poet is administering consolation to himself for a personal loss. Inside of this vision we have a debate between the dreaming poet and the girl. In addition, the whole is permeated by the allegory of the Pearl.

The vision asserts that it is possible for a baptized child, who died before it was two years old and therefore had no opportunity to perform good works or to exercise Christian faith, to be saved and even to be received among the host which follows the Lamb of God. The debate merely reinforces the vision by arguments. Professor Brown has doubted the orthodoxy of this view advanced by the poet and has even made him out a sort of precursor of the Reformation. He quotes Bradwardine's testimony[80] to the fact that Pelagianism was widely accepted in fourteenth-century England. On grounds of Pelagianism, which, however, scarcely was ever held in this extreme form, there would be no possibility for a small child to acquire heavenly grace, as grace is entirely dependent on good works. But our author's rejection of this view is by no means heterodox. On the contrary, it is in perfect accordance with the views of the church, even though at the time of our poet doubt was still possible.

Let us examine the opinions of the church fathers on this point. The most important authority is, of course, St. Augustine, as he especially fought Pelagius in numerous writings and is very explicit on our question, as the grace of baptized children was a chief argument against Pelagius' exclusive stress on good works. The fundamental assumption is that God could not condemn an innocent, baptized child, as "all the ways of the Lord are mercy and truth."[81] The question is, rather, by what right a child, though devoid of any merits which it could not possibly earn, can nevertheless be granted eternal beatitude. The possibility is opened by a distinction between two titles to salvation: one the hereditary title which we have as God's children, the other the title by reward as God's laborers. The children have therefore a title to salvation merely as "filii Dei," which is a "titulus haereditatis," while grown-up persons either lose their title to grace, conferred by baptism, by committing sins or add to their title by good works (titulus mercedis). This means actually that there are two kinds of grace, which modern theology has come to distinguish as "gratia prima" and "gratia secunda." "Gratia prima" is completely free grace, "gratis data, donata, non reddita,"[82] while the second grace is additional and proportional to our merits. This first grace is

given by God as the remittance of original sin in baptism. All
the church fathers insist that the innocent children also have
inherited the sin of Adam and that they would be condemned
to eternal damnation if the death of Christ did not save them
in baptism.[83] In baptism, says Augustine, "parvulis infundi
occultissimam gratiam per quam ad Deum convertuntur."[84]
The efficacy of baptism is so great that it gives them also a
consciousness of the grace received[85] and a belief in the Son of
Man. "Inter credentes igitur baptizatos parvulos numerabis,
nec juidicare nullo modo aliter audebis, si non vis esse apertus
hereticus. Ergo ideo habent vitam aeternam, quia qui credit in
filium, habet vitam aeternam."[86] Exactly the same opinion is
also held by St. Chrysostomus and other fathers of the church,[87]
but apparently in the course of the Middle Ages the salvation
of baptized children does not seem to have been received quite
without question, though the prevalent view held to the kindly
theory of the fathers. This development can be illustrated by
the difference between two Popes. Pope Innocent III (1198 till
1216) simply thought that there are two opinions about the
question, but does not decide in favor of either: "Aliis asseren-
tibus per virtutem baptismi parvulis quidem culpam remitti,
sed gratiam non conferri; nonnullis vero dicentibus ed elimitti
peccatum et virtutes infundi habentibus illas quoad habitum
non quoad usum,"[88] that is, the child is not getting any assistance
for his actions, but a form of being, a state of existence. But already Pope Clement V (1305–1314) considers the majority of
opinions as inclining toward the second view favorable to the salvation of children. He declared at the council held at Vienne in
1311: "Quantum ad effectum baptismi in parvulis reperiuntur
doctores quidam theologi opiniones contrarias habuisse, quibus-
dam ex ipsis dicentibus, per virtutem baptismi parvulis quidem
culpam remitti, sed gratiam non conferri: aliis e contra asserenti-
bus quod et culpa eisdem in baptismo remittitur et virtutes ac
informans gratia infunduntur quoad habitum, etsi non pro illo

tempore quoad usum. Nos attendentes generalem efficaciam mortis Christi, quae per baptisma applicatur pariter omnibus baptizatis, opinionem secundam tamquam probaliorem et dictis sanctorum et modernorum theologorum magis consonam et conformem sacro approbante Concilio duximus eligendam."[89] Also St. Bernhard of Clairvaux defends the salvation of children and considers envy to be the cause of the doubts expressed against this view.[90] In the sixteenth century the Council of Trent codified this doctrine in so many words,[91] and also the founders of Jesuit neo-scholasticism of that time all accept the view expressed by Pope Clement V, e.g., Canisius, Vasquez and Suarez.[92] The quotations and references may be sufficient to show that our poet was completely in the line of orthodox teaching and that he lived at a time when doubt seemed still to be possible about this question. But a famous Pope decided in agreement with our poet and the ultimate decision of the Catholic Church lay with him. It is essentially a Christian doctrine to put such efficacy into the act of baptism. It not only remits original sin, but also infuses sanctifying grace. The point of view expressed in the *Pearl* is therefore precisely un-Protestant, as in the theory of sixteenth-century Protestantism, the justification of children by baptism remained unexplained. This is the reason why radical Protestant sects like the Anabaptists and the Menonites denied the possibility of efficient infant baptism. In this point certainly our poet is not a forerunner of Protestantism. He is absolutely at one with the opinions we have here expounded: he considers grace completely free, merely depending on God's liberality, it is the "heritage"[93] with which the bride is decorated. Baptism washes away the guilt of Adam:

> Þat wascheʒ away þe gylteʒ felle
> Þat Adam wyth in deth vus drounde.
> Now is þer noʒt in þe worlde rounde
> By-twene vus & blysse . . .[94]

The fact that the child did not know Pater or Creed is irrelevant, for the "grace of God is gret in-nogh."[95]

A question apart from the assertion of the possibility of salvation for the child is raised by her status in heaven. That she can be saved we have shown to be clearly orthodox, but there has been expressed doubt whether it is possible that she could be received among the followers of the Lamb. Professor Brown even suspected the poet of teaching a complete equality of heavenly rewards, in anticipation of Luther's famous sermon "De nativitate Mariae," where he says: "omnes Christiani aeque magni sumus, sicut mater Dei, et aeque sancti sicut ipsa." Our poet has been connected by Professor Brown with the Jovinian heresy asserting the same. It is not surprising that Professor Brown "had been unable to find a single orthodox theologian or poet, from the time of Jerome until the appearance of the Pearl, who asserts the equality of heavenly rewards."[96] We actually have in the poem passages which seem to assert that the poet is holding this view in order to promote the child, most clearly e.g. in the verses:

> "Of more & lasse in Godeʒ ryche,"
> Þat gentyl sayde, "lys no joparde,
> For þer is vch mon payed inlyche,
> Wheþer lyttel oþer much be hys rewarde."[97]

But with such an interpretation many other passages are in conflict, which implicitly recognize the established teaching of the church. The very idea that the girl is in the procession following the Lamb implies a distinction in heaven, and, even though the heavenly hierarchy is nowhere enumerated, the fact of its existence is clearly in the mind of our poet throughout the vision. He speaks not only of the hundred and forty-four thousand virgins of the procession, but also of the four beasts and especially of the "aldermen so sadde of chere" "ryʒt byfore Godeʒ chayere."[98] The aldermen occur once more coupled with "legyounes of aungeleȝ"[99] who cannot be imagined to be identical with the virgins in whose procession the girl is walking.

It is also not true that the poet would deny the importance of good works altogether. He says the opposite twice:

> Þe ryȝt-wys man schal se hys face

and

> Þe ryȝt-wys man also sertayn
> Aproche he schal þat proper pyle.[100]

Though the poet is no doubt not very definite about the hierarchy in heaven and though he makes no attempt to reconcile the assumption of the traditional distinctions with his assertion of the equality of the heavenly rewards, we must assume that he did not feel this contradiction and that he felt no qualms about the orthodoxy of his opinion. Actually his ideas are absolutely orthodox, only that the church felt more clearly the necessity of reconciling the parable of the vineyard and the denarius given to every laborer with the generally accepted ideas about a heavenly hierarchy. In our poet we have the parable stated and the traditional picture of heaven accepted side by side without a sense of contradiction. The church is merely conscious of the difficulty and solves it in a way satisfactory to religious thought. All the church fathers assert the inequality of the heavenly rewards, while dwelling on the perfect harmony and lack of envy in heaven. According to St. Augustine there is the same difference between the just as between the sinners.[101] As biblical support the passage about the many mansions in the house of the father[102] and the passage in the Corinthians which asserts that one star differs from the other in brightness[103] are constantly quoted. The Parable of the Vineyard is interpreted in such a way that the contradiction is solved rather ingeniously. John Chrysostomus, archbishop of Constantinople,[104] solves the question by suggesting that those who have come earlier in the parable of the vineyard were after all subject to the low passion of envy and jealousy in claiming a higher payment. The actual purpose of the parable is merely to give courage to those who became converted only in later years and to convince them that they are not worse off than others. St. Irenaeus, bishop of Lyons, does not seem to see the contradiction between the parable and the teaching about the inequality of heavenly rewards. Once[105] he elaborates the differences between those who are going to dwell in the heavens, those who will enjoy the joys of Paradise, and others who will own the splendid city. When he is explaining the parable of the vineyard,[106] he simply says that it means the same master of the house: some he has called immediately at the creation of the world, others in the middle of time and still others when the time had progressed and others again, when it was at an end, for there are many laborers, each one at his time, but only one father of the house, who calls them to work. There is only one vineyard, there is only one major domus, the Spirit of God, who arranges everything, and similarly only one reward, since all received the denarius with the picture and the inscription of the king, the knowledge of the Son of God, which is immortality. Only St. Augustine saw the difficulty and solved it thus: "Objectio de denario omnibus reddendo, contra diversitatem praemiorum. Quid sibi ergo vult, inquiunt, ille denarius, qui opera vineae terminato aequaliter omnibus redditur; sive iis qui ex prima hora, sive iis qui una hora operati sunt? Quid utique (Matth. XX, 9) nisi aliquid significat, quod omnes communiter habebunt, sicuti est ipsa vita aeterna, ipsum regnum coelorum, ubi erunt omnes quos Deus praedestinavit, vocavit, justificavit, glorificavit? Oportet enim corruptibile hoc induere incorruptionem, et mortale hoc induere immortalitatem: hic est ille denarius, merces omnium." Nevertheless it is true: "Stella tamen ab stella differt in gloria: sic et resurrectio mortuorum: haec sunt merita diversa sanctorum. Ita quia ipsa vita aeterna pariter erit omnibus sanctis, aequalis denarius omnibus attributus est; quia vero in ipsa vita aeterna distincte fulgebant lumina meritorum, multae mansiones sunt apud Patrem (Joan. XIV, 2): ac per hoc in denario quidem non impari, non vivit alius alio prolixius; in multis autem mansionibus honoratur alius alio clarius."[107] This theory was restated and simplified by the great codifier of dogma, Gregory the Great: "Ipse propter electos in Evangelio dicit: In domo patris mei mansiones multae sunt. Si enim dispar retributio in illa aeterna beatitudine non esset una potius mansio quam multae essent. Multae ergo mansiones sunt, in quibus et distincti bonorum ordines, et propter meritorum consortia communiter laetantur; et tamen unum denarium omnes laborantes accipiunt. Qui multis mansionibus distinguuntur: quia et una est beatitudo quam illic percipiunt, dispar retributionis qualitas, quam per opera diversa consequuntur."[108] Bonaventura[109] teaches a similar way out, asserting that though all will have the same blessedness, considered objectively, yet there will be a difference in the quantity of joy. The same point of view is succinctly phrased by St. Thomas: "Unitas denarii significat unitatem beatitudinis ex parte objecti; sed diversitas mansionum significat diversitatem beatitudinis secundum diversum gradum fruitionis."[110] Similar opinions can be found in Petrus Lombardus, Duns Scotus and Prosper.[111] The author of the *Pearl* might have been unacquainted with these solutions of the difficulty, since he stresses much more the obvious sense of the Parable without, however, drawing radical consequences which led Jovinian and Luther to quite different solutions. He is content to show that this parable justifies his belief that his child could be beatified, and not only beatified, but, thanks to God's unbounded grace, be received among the very followers of the Lamb.

That this particular elevation is quite possible was shown

conclusively by Miss Hart, who drew attention to a passage in Chaucer's *Prioress's Tale,* where a seven-year-old child is definitely associated with the hundred and forty-four thousand.[112] "Chaucer calls the little boy's mother 'his newe Rachel' (B 1817), alluding to Matthew 2, 18. This verse is the conclusion of the Gospel read in the Mass on the Feast of the Holy Innocents (Dec. 28); and the Epistle of that Feast is the very passage in which John describes the procession of the virgins. This is the only liturgical use of this particular passage from the Apocalypse and the association of the Holy Innocents with the procession must have been familiar enough in the Middle Ages. The fact that the liturgy describes such small children, 'a bimatu et infra' (Matthew 2, 16), as forming part of the procession of the centum quadraginta quatuor milia—this fact would seem amply to explain the poet's assigning a place therein to a little girl" of two years' age.[113] We may add in support of Miss Hart's thesis that in the All Saints' Day litany, in the third liturgical order the classes of saints are enumerated in the following order: "Maria—Angeli—Patriarchae et Prophetae —Apostoli et Evangelistae—Discipuli Domini—*Innocentes*— Martyres—Pontifices et Confessores—Doctores—Sacerdotes et Levitae—Monachi et Eremitae—*Virgines* et Viduae."[114] Occam finally gives a theological justification of this special position of the children by drawing a distinction between two kinds of predestination, one which he calls absolute and one which he calls hypothetic. To the hypothetic kind belong all ordinary people, as God has here to decide "post praevisa merita." To the privileged of the first class belong the Virgin Mary, the prophets and apostles, certain saints and all children dying in the grace of baptism.[115] The theology of the poem reveals itself then as entirely orthodox, consistent with the best teachings of the church and well informed on almost all points, though, of course, one cannot deny that it is used for purposes of special

pleading. The conclusion drawn from this that the poet must
have been an ecclesiastic is not entirely convincing, as we can
well imagine an educated layman, interested in these things
and well read in his Latin, to have acquired sufficient knowledge
in these matters, which touched so intimately the fate of a
beloved child or sister.

The third question raised by any study of the *Pearl* is the
question of the meaning of its allegory. Here again one must
grant to the defenders of the personal interpretation that it
would be quite possible to imagine the poem, i.e., the vision and
the teaching conveyed by the child without the allegory of the
Pearl. It is undoubtedly true that the poem has no allegorical
key to it: neither maidenhood (Schofield) nor the Eucharist
(Garrett) nor the own soul of the poet (Madeleva) will do.
There is no such solution of the allegory. On the other hand,
it is true that the allegory of the Pearl is the chief decoration
of the poem, one of the main devices of the poet to give it
artistic charm and unity. The title *Pearl,* which modern scholarship has given to the poem, is therefore perfectly justified, as
the whole poem from the beginning to the end is playing vari-
ations on the theme of the Pearl, even though the actual contents are a vision and a theological debate.

The Pearl represents several different things in the poem:
first of all the earthly child that went through the grass to the
ground—a use of the word, to which the visionary girl herself
objects, as she on earth could be rather compared to a flowering
and fading rose.[116] Then it means the visionary child in heaven,
which at the same time is richly decorated with pearls, especially with one "wonder perle, wythouten wemme" in the midst
of her breast, a Pearl which is also worn by all the other virgins
in the host following the Lamb.[117] This Pearl in the midst of
her breast is identical with the Pearl which the merchant in the
Parable bought with all his treasures and this is like the realm

of heaven's sphere,[118] i.e., it is nothing but eternal beatitude. The poet is then counseled by the maiden to forsake the mad world and to purchase this spotless Pearl.[119] When he will have purchased this Pearl, he will himself have become a Pearl, a precious pearl unto His pleasure, which is also the final aim and wish of all men on earth.[120]

The symbolism then is not simple and cannot be solved by a one-to-one identification with some abstract virtue, as maidenhood, cleanliness, or by identifying it with the Eucharist or the soul of the poet, but it is complex or rather double. First the Pearl is the girl before she is lost—here obviously Pearl is merely an ordinary symbol for the preciousness, uniqueness, beauty, purity, etc. of the dead girl. When she is found again in heaven, the Pearl is a symbol of an immaculate, pure blessed person in the hands of God. The poet and all men are aspiring to become such a one. Parallel with this symbolism which identifies Pearl with a person, runs the second symbolism, that of the Pearl which the girl is wearing on her breast and which the poet is counseled to purchase for himself. This is obviously the realm of heaven or the grace of God. The symbolism of the Pearl— while not exactly Protean—is shifting subtly, from the conventional and mere earthly meaning of preciousness to the heavenly symbol of grace and the realm of grace. This is really very simple and completely in agreement with traditional symbolism.

All allegorical use of the Pearl descends from the Parable, cited also by our poet, about the merchant who sold all his goods in order to win one precious pearl.[121] This Pearl is most frequently identified with Christ, e.g., as early as in Bishop Melito's *Clavis de Metallibus*, which is supposed to date back to the second century.[122] But very frequently indeed it means the blessed, the saints themselves, a symbolism which agrees with what we have considered the first meaning of the Pearl in our poem. We find this interpretation in Rupert of Deutz, in Hrabanus Maurus, the famous archbishop of Mayence, and in St. Bonaventura. The last says e.g.: "Bonae margaritae sunt omnes sancti; una vero pretiosa est Christus."[123] Even more frequent is the identification of the Pearl with the heavenly kingdom and heavenly grace or similar concepts as the word of God, the faith of the church. To Gregory the Great "margarita vero mystice significat evangelicam doctrinam sue dulcetudinem coelestis vitae,"[124] to Petrus Chrysologus it is identical with "vita aeterna,"[125] to Petrus Capuanus, a Parisian theologian at the end of the twelfth century, who gives a very elaborate symbolism of the Pearl, it means "Fides ecclesiae," "verbum dei" and the Apostles.[126] More confused is the symbolism of the Pearl in the "Testament of Love," a prose piece, which was first printed in Thynne's edition of Chaucer in 1532, but was probably written by one Thomas Usk about 1387. The allegory of the Pearl there returns again and again, but always in some connection with grace or mercy. At the end the writer says with extraordinary bluntness: "Margarite, a woman, betokeneth grace, lerning, or wisdom of god, or els holy church."[127] That this interpretation was a current one can be also shown from a fifteenth-century source, i.e., from Beati Alani (Redivivi Rupensis) Tractatus Mirabilis De Ortu atque Progressu Psalterii Christi et Mariae.[128] This curious book gives a whole synopsis of fifteen gems explaining or rather running parallel to the "Ave Maria, gratia plena." Gratia in the text of the Annunciation is identified with margarita, a symbol of Grace, while e.g. Ave is identified with Adamas, a symbol of Innocence, etc. The text gives a long and involved explanation, fortified by many authorities, why Mary can be represented by a Pearl, and why and how she is full of grace. Somebody who would make a closer search into allegorical literature might probably discover many more similar passages, which, however shifting the symbolism may seem, are perfectly consistent in the main point. We see the Pearl is even

here perfectly well set into the tradition of its time. The difficulties of the poem appear then largely as illusory, as many of
them were stirred up by scholarship which lost contact with the
actual text and indulged in mysterious interpretations or fanciful speculations.

All these debates, we feel, about dialect, authorship, elegy
versus allegory, theology, symbolism, etc., though they have been
almost the only occupation of scholarship, say very little about
the *Pearl* as a work of art. We may grant that a right conception
of the contents of the poem has cleared the way for an artistic
appreciation, but the actual study of the artistic value of the
poem is still in its beginnings. Even the obvious approach
through questions of meter and structure has not been much
utilized hitherto. Professor *Northup's* paper, "A Study of the
Metrical Structure of the Middle English Poem the Pearl"[129]
is rather a contribution to the history of final unstressed –*e* in
the West Midland than a metrical investigation proper. Also
Oakden's treatment of the meter is rather a statistical survey
of the alliteration and its use[130] than an attempt at artistic interpretation. In these questions much is still to be done by a
judicious use of modern methods, which, on the whole, could
come to many new results in Middle English scholarship.[131]

·•᠔[2]ᠥ•·

The Meaning of the Middle
English *Pearl*

MARIE PADGETT HAMILTON·

A solution to the mystery of *Pearl* must meet certain tests if it
is to answer the questions: What is typified by the jewel and the
jewel-maiden, and how are they related? What is the symbolic
import of the story? Specifically, as J. P. Oakden has indicated,
the gem must stand for something which the poet could represent as a pearl and at the same time as a maiden who had died
in infancy and had been redeemed by Christ. Further, says
Oakden, it must signify something that the poet (or his protagonist speaking in the first person) "lost, mourned, and could
recover through the grace of God, strengthened by partaking of
the Blessed Sacrament."[1]

What is more, the pearl found by the dreamer in his vision

Reprinted by permission of the Modern Language Association from
PMLA, LXX (1955), 805–24.
See also Ernst R. Curtius, *European Literature and the Latin Middle
Ages*, trans. Willard R. Trask (New York, 1963), 192–98; William J. Knight-
ley, *"Pearl:* The 'hyȝseysoun' " *MLN*, LXXVI (1961), 97–102; John Conley,
"Pearl and a Lost Tradition," *JEGP*, LIV (1955), 332–47; and Charles Moor-
man, "The Role of the Narrator in *Pearl*," *MP*, LIII (1955), 73–81.

must be the same as the one he had grieved for, except that it has been transformed by divine grace. The identity of the two jewels, notwithstanding the fact that it has been denied by more than one interpreter,[2] is everywhere implicit in the poem and is twice affirmed. The dreamer in the beginning of his dialogue with Pearl supposes her to be the gem that he had mourned for, and she confirms the assumption by rebuking him for having concluded that his pearl was "al awaye," when in reality it is now secure, as in a treasure-chest, in the gracious garden where he sees her (241–264). He then rejoices at finding the jewel that he had believed to be "don out of dawes," and is chided, not for identifying Pearl lost and Pearl found, but for trusting the testimony of his fallible senses that she is bodily present in the vale where he beholds her, and for his naive assumption that he may dwell with her there forthwith, without begging leave (277–300).

For clues to the nature of the treasure lost, then, we must look to the treasure found. It is twofold. Besides the maiden in her pearl-embroidered vesture and crown of orient pearl, there is the wondrous jewel at her breast, which she clearly identifies with the Pearl of Great Price and interprets as eternal felicity, "the blys that con not blynne."[3] This gem, which like the kingdom of God is common to all the righteous, was bestowed upon her, she says, as an earnest of the Atonement ("in token of pes") by the Lamb "that schede hys blode" (732–743). Clearly Pearl herself, as the "jeweler" (one "seeking goodly pearls") finds her in the enchanting garden, is a regenerate soul, restored by the sanctifying grace of baptism to the state of innocence and favor with God which mankind enjoyed before the Fall. No mere personification of purity, innocence, or any other abstract quality, she typifies the soul made pure by sacramental grace through the merit of Christ,* and as such speaks with authority for the

---

* Note her account of Christ's cleansing her garments before crowning her "in virginity" (766–768).

entire company of the blessed, whether living or dead, for God's kingdom, "Godes ryche." There is justice in Sister Mary V. Hillman's conception of her as "the Soul."[4]

Here, then, is the double treasure found in the vision. First there is Pearl, the maiden soul, who through baptismal regeneration and incorporation into the Mystical Body of Christ, the Church, has become "a perle of prys" (257–276). Secondly, there is the *pretiosa margarita* of Matthew XIII:45–46, the gem of eternal life and beatitude, which is the maiden's distinctive endowment and adornment as a bride of Christ, a soul in grace.

Both jewels, I take it, were lost in the primal bereavement announced in the first ringing stanza of the poem:

> Perle, plesaunte to prynces paye
> To clanly clos in golde so clere,
> Oute of oryent, I hardyly saye,
> Ne proued I neuer her precios pere.
> So rounde, so reken in vche araye,
> So smal, so smoþe her sydeȝ were,
> Quere-so-euer I jugged gemmeȝ gaye,
> I sette hyr sengeley in synglere.
> Allas! I leste hyr in on erbere;
> Þurȝ gresse to grounde hit fro me yot.
> I dewyne, fordolked of luf-daungere
> Of þat pryuy perle wythouten spot.[5]

"Alas! I lost her in a garden." If the Anglo-French *(h)erbere* here had been accurately rendered in modern English versions, the theme of the poem might have been sooner understood.[6] Competent fourteenth-century readers must have recognized the *erber(e)* as the Garden of Eden, where the maiden soul of man fell to earth and was lost, with her potential endowment of everlasting life and blessedness.

Not without reason Pearl's possessor had cherished her as unique among gems, "sette hyr sengeley in synglere." (St. Gregory Nazianzen, in a poem addressed to his soul, calls her "Of all bright things prized highest / Beneath the rolling sun.")[7]

Appropriately, too, the man bereft of Pearl speaks of her as meet
for a prince, for his pleasure, "to enclose in clear gold," gold
being a symbol of the divine kingdom,[8] to which man was to
have been transferred in time had he not sinned in Eden.[9] William Drummond of Hawthornden in *The Cypress Grove* employs the same metaphor in an address to his soul: "Think then
. . . that thou art a pearl, raised from thy mother, to be enchased
in gold, and that the death-day of thy body is thy birthday to
eternity."[10]

With equal propriety the disconsolate man speaks in the second stanza of *Pearl* of his distress at the thought of his once
spotless gem, now fallen and marred by earth, her delicate hues
shrouded in clay:

> To þenke hir color so clad in clot.
> O moul, þou marreʒ a myry iuele,
> My priuy perle wythouten spotte   (22–24).

Thus in a single metaphor the poet alludes to the bodily death
entailed in the decree "Unto dust shalt thou return," and to
the spiritual death and defilement by original sin which the soul
incurred in the Fall. The ancient figure of the clay-pent soul appears in similar idiom in Giles Fletcher's "Christs Victorie in
Heaven" (st. 17), wherein "wretched man" is described as
"Proude of the mire in which his soule is pend, / Clodded in
lumps of clay, his wearie life to end."[11] (Compare Honorius of
Autun, *Elucidarium,* Lib. III: "Cum homo peccat, anima moritur; quia a vita Deo deseritur, et in corpore quasi in sepulchro
sepelitur.")[12]

In like manner throughout *Pearl* the fitness of the metaphors
and allusions when applied to the soul is apparent. By a studied
ambiguity the poet carries out his design, with the result that
the reader, while responding to the moving story of a man's desolation at the death of a rare maiden, who was the wellspring of

his happiness, is at the same time made aware of the allegorical
and mystical intent of the poem by the vagueness and strange-
ness of the references to the girl's death and by the concurrent
motive of the jewel, fallen, sullied by earth, lost.

This contrapuntal technique also underscores the fact that
two gems were forfeited in the garden, both the soul and her
patrimony of sanctifying grace, which included the gifts of
blessedness and eternal life. The poet had the authority of tradition for making the pearl an emblem for each of these. The
Fathers often construe the parabolic Pearl of Price as everlasting life or beatitude; only the equation of the gem with Christ
rivaled this interpretation in popularity.[13] The undefiled human soul, or the soul redeemed in baptism, also was typified
by the pearl, and sometimes was identified with the *pretiosa
margarita*,[14] as apparently it is in *Pearl* 272. There the maiden
explains that the jewel which the dreamer had regarded as lost
has become "a perle of prys" by virtue of the chest that now
encloses it.

The poet also had ample precedent for making the two treasures and what they stand for appear at times as a single pearl,
involved in a single tragic loss. Compare the gem lamented by
Macbeth *(Macb.* III.i.69–70) as "mine eternal jewel, / Given
to the common enemy of man," sometimes construed as "his
eternal salvation," but more often as "his immortal soul." The
distinction, though convenient and even indispensable in ordinary parlance, is theologically more apparent than real. The
soul, St. Thomas Aquinas affirms, was the force which preserved
the human body from corruption; hence the loss of it and the
forfeiture of bodily immortality were one and the same.[15] The
soul in one sense was regarded not merely as man's hope of
eternal life; it *was* that life. As *anima* signifies both "soul" and
"life," so also in Early English "life" is often synonymous with
"soul"; thus it appears in the Wycliffite Bible and in *Pearl* 305

and 687. (In line 687 "lyf" translates the Vulgate *animam* of Psalm 23.4, rendered "soul" in the Douay and King James Bibles, as in some Middle English versions). In medieval allegory, therefore, the Lady Anima may appear as Dame Life, as she does in the Middle English poem "Life and Death," or as the Soul, "a lovelie lemmon lyk to [God] him-self," as she is called in *Piers Plowman;* and the identity between "life" and "soul" gave rise to finespun speculation and analysis.[16] In the language of the theologians, what was lost in the Garden of Eden was the supernatural life of man, or sanctifying grace, and that included the gift of life eternal or beatitude.[17]

Pearl is following this tradition when she castigates the dreamer for assuming that his jewel was "al awaye" (258), or "don out of dawes" (282), and thereby imputing a lie to God, who had "loyally promised" to raise his "life," though fortune in punishment of Adam's sin had caused his flesh to die:

> I halde þat iueler lyttle to prayse
> Þat loueȝ wel þat he seȝ wyth yȝe,*
> And much to blame and vncortayse
> Þat leueȝ oure Lorde wolde make a lyȝe,
> Þat lelly hyȝte your lyf to rayse,
> Þaȝ fortune dyd your flesch to dyȝe   (301–306).

(Cf. Heb. X.23, Titus III.7–8, and more especially, Titus I.2: "In hope of eternal life, which God, that cannot lie, promised before the world began.")

The soul, poetically conceived as feminine, time out of mind, was represented in medieval art as a child;[18] and the figure of the maiden soul of man, raised from her fallen state and espoused by Christ, is a commonplace of medieval mystical treatises, religious lyrics, and allegorical narratives, where not infrequently the legend is recast in terms of chivalric romance.[19]

---

* In this line (302) I reject the Oxford *leueȝ,* "believes," in favor of *loueȝ* (MS, Osgood), "praises" or "loves."

In one variation the allegory becomes a murder story. *The Goodman of Paris* describes the soul as the daughter of God, given
to each of us "without stain or blemish," but poisoned by
"draughts of mortal sin"; God will hold us accountable for her
death.[20] The *Pearl* poet's double metaphor for the soul as both
jewel and bride of Christ appears also in a lyrical poem by St.
Peter Damian: Christ, addresses the regenerate soul as "soror,
conjux, gemma splendissima."[21] Traditionally, too, the soul
as spouse (i.e., the soul in a state of grace) was depicted as
adorned, like Pearl, with precious stones, sometimes specified
as pearls, betokening virtues bestowed upon her by the Celestial
Bridegroom.[22]

So much for one of the questions with which this essay began:
What is typified by the jewel and the jewel-maiden, and how
are they related? The foregoing reply goes far toward answering
the related question, What is the import of the story? Pearl, at
the center of her defense of her rank as a queen in God's kingdom, gives a résumé of the Fall and the Redemption (637–660):
Mankind, created for perfect happiness, forfeited it through
Adam, and so was condemned to death and the pain of Hell;
but there came a remedy. Water and noble blood flowed on the
Rood. The blood delivered us from Hell and "the second
death"; the water is baptism, "that washes away the fell guilt
in which Adam drowned us." Consequently no barrier remains between us and bliss, and bliss itself is restored "in sely
stounde."

The whole of *Pearl* is a finely wrought elaboration of this
theme, the Biblical epic of the soul in delicate miniature, seen
in the epitome of one man's passionate experience. The hero is
not literally the poet, but "a type of the whole race of fallen
man, called to salvation," like Dante, the pilgrim of the *Commedia,* though less learned than Dante. What Francis Fergusson
says of the relationship between Dante as author of the *Com-

media and Dante as pilgrim might apply as well to the *Pearl* poet and the "I" of his narrative. "The distinction between Dante speaking as author, and Dante the Pilgrim, is fundamental to the whole structure," Mr. Fergusson reminds us. "The author knows the whole story in advance, the Pilgrim meets everything freshly for the first time. The two perspectives together produce a sort of stereoptical effect, that of an objective and partially mysterious reality. . . . The Pilgrim's awareness is always moving towards the author's."[23] In the English poem the dreamer's awareness is constantly moving towards Pearl's, as hers approaches the author's. Indeed, the dreamer is presented as one conveniently naive in theology, so as to call forth the inspired maiden's account of the plan of salvation, the plenitude of the divine grace, and the blessedness of souls wedded to Christ; for the poet's design, identical again with Dante's, is "to remove those living in this life from a state of wretchedness and lead them to the state of blessedness."

The Pearl-maiden, though typifying the soul of man, lost through "the fell guilt in which Adam drowned us," is the individual soul of the man who tells the story, his own "privy perle" (l. 24).[24] The universal historical bereavement was at the same time his immediate personal tragedy, shared by the reader, too, who also is expected to participate in the happy ending of the poem by heeding its lessons. The conception of an individual person or soul as epitomizing all persons or souls in like condition is too basic to medieval patterns of thought to need comment. It is implicit in the doctrine of the solidarity of the human race as springing from Adam, and of the corporate nature of the Church as the Mystical Body. "We are bidden everyone to the spiritual marriage at which the Bridegroom is Christ our Lord," writes St. Bernard. "Spouse indeed we are to him, if this seem not to you incredible; both all together one spouse, and every soul by itself a spouse singly."[25] As C. S. Baldwin, after quoting Bernard's words, warned, "Neglect of this mediaeval habit has hindered the interpretation of *Pearl*."[26]

Certainly the poet assumed his reader's acceptance of the doctrine set forth in Rom. V.12–19, that the will of all mankind rebelled in Adam when by disobedience he forfeited the gift of supernatural life. St. Augustine's "All men were that one man Adam,"[27] restated by Aquinas,[28] had found popular expression in the Middle English version of *The Castle of Love:* "Þorw Adam we sungedon furst uchon / And eeten þe appel wiþ him anon" (ll. 1381–82). The consequence of universal man's complicity in original sin is elsewhere stated in this rhymed allegory: "Alle heo beoþ I-brought to grounde / þat of his of-spring beoþ I-founde" (111–112).[29] The protagonist in *Pearl* apparently assumes responsibility for the loss of supernatural life when his soul was "brought to ground." He speaks in the first person: "I leste hyr in on erbere; / Þurʒ gresse to grounde hit fro me yot" (9–10). "Wilt thou," Donne asks in *A Hymme to God the Father,* "forgive that sinne where I begunne, / Which is my sin, though it were done before?"

As a type of the fallen race of man the dreamer in *Pearl* waited in longing* for that weal which had elevated his lot and his well-being (l. 16); and in a peaceful season was heartened by "never so sweet a song" (st. 2), heralding a brilliant harvest from his lost riches in decay. Spice-bearing plants, he is promised, will burgeon from that seed, the pearl without spot:

> Þat spot of spyseʒ mot nedeʒ sprede,
> Þer such rycheʒ to rot is runne;
> Blomeʒ blayke and blwe and rede
> Þer schyneʒ ful schyr agayn þe sunne.
> Flor and fryte may not be fede
> Þer hit doun drof in moldeʒ dunne;

---

* There is no textual warrant for the statement in modern renderings that the dreamer waited *on the spot* where the pearl fell to earth.

> *For vch gresse mot grow of grayneʒ dede;*
> *No whete were elleʒ to woneʒ wonne.*
> Of goud vche goude is ay bygonne;
> So semly a sede moʒt fayly not,
> Þat spryngande spyceʒ vp ne sponne
> Of þat precios perle wythouten spotte   (st. 3).

These lines (the substance of the song heard by the hero), phrased in the mystical language of spiritual renewal and fruition, echo Christ's pregnant metaphor for his own approaching death and resurrection, his allusion to the grain that must fall to earth and die ere it bring forth wheat (John XII.24; cf. I. Cor. XV.36–38). An utterance linking this allusion to the promise of a spice-garden of flowers and fruit that may not be "fede," "withered," together with a mention of the "precious pearl" (reminiscent of the *pretiosa margarita* of Matt. XIII.46), can hardly be anything short of a reference to the Incarnation and the Resurrection. The Biblical corn of wheat was so habitually associated with the Word made flesh, the Last Supper, and the Resurrection that only wheat flour might be used for the Eucharistic bread;[30] and the grainfield had become a familiar symbol of the Church. "The multitude of grain," Wyclif calls it, sprung from "Christ, the first corn," and derived its virtue from the divine seed.[31]

Appropriately, it was "when corn is cut by sickles keen" that the protagonist of *Pearl* entered the garden on the occasion of his vision. "In August in a high season," it probably was at the Feast of Our Lady in Harvest (the Assumption), a proper time for religious revelations[32] and particularly for this one, for the festival commemorates the restoration through Mary of what mankind forfeited through Eve. Lessons for the feast from Ecclesiasticus XXIV tell of flowers and fruits redolent of sweet odors, chosen as fitting metaphors for Mary, who in her Assumption was sometimes likened to a restored Eden,[33] and who in her virginity was typified by a garden, in allusion to the *hortus conclusus* of Canticles IV.12.[34] The familiar symbol had a special relevance when, as is the case in *Pearl*, the garden grew medicinal herbs, regarded as a token of the Virgin's healing powers.[35] Nevertheless, the medicine is Christ, the *flos campi* of Canticles II.1,[36] still heralded in Advent Masses through Isaiah's prayer: "Let the earth be opened up and bud forth a Saviour." The garden as a type of Mary was but a natural corollary of the ancient metaphor of the garden of Canticles as prefiguring Christ's human nature,[37] into which He descended, as the bridegroom descended into his garden; or as shadowing forth the Incarnation.[38] The garden also was said to signify Christ's Resurrection[39] and, above all, His spiritual body, the Church. In the 1914 issue of the Douay Bible the notes on the Song of Songs interpret the spice-garden as the Church, in keeping with a tradition at least as old as Origen, who regarded the Garden of Eden itself as an allegorical adumbration of the future Church.[40] The plants of the Terrestrial Paradise were sometimes described as medicinal;[41] and Honorius of Autun, identifying the garden of Canticles with the Church, notes that the Church likewise yields curative herbs for the wounds of sin.[42] The garden-symbol for the Church was, indeed, so generally a favorite with the Fathers and other theological writers[43] that it is not surprising to find the metaphor appearing and reappearing in Dante's *Commedia*[44] and occurring in the reported visions of other medieval mystics.[45]

The idea gained in sanction from the important rôle of gardens in the life of Jesus, as theologians with tireless ingenuity sought parallels between these and the Garden of Eden or the *hortus conclusus* of the Song of Songs, in their search for analogies between the Old and the New Adam, the Fall and the Atonement. Lapide, in his celebrated digest of Patristic and medieval exegesis, *Commentaria in Scripturas Sacras,* repeats the

familiar idea that the sepulchre of Christ was in a garden because Adam sinned and incurred the sentence of death in the
garden of Paradise. The Passion, he declares, also began in the
garden on Mt. Olivet, in order that Christ "might suffer and
expiate that sentence, and plant and institute that most delightful garden *(hortum amoenissimum)*, burgeoning with the flowers and fruits of every virtue, namely the Church."[46]

Such, I take it, is the "erber grene" where the dreamer of *Pearl*
falls asleep, an aromatic garden of healing spices, including
tropical ginger, which was alien to English gardens and the
graves of English babes:

> On huyle þer perle hit trendeled doun
> Schadowed þis worteȝ ful schyre and schene,
> Gilofre, gyngure and gromylyoun,
> And pyonys powdered ay bytwene.
> Ȝif hit watȝ semly on to sene,
> A fayr reflayr ȝet fro hit flot.
> Þer wonys þat worþyly, I wot and wene,
> My precious perle wythouten spot   (41–48).

Note that the plants are said to give forth shade *on* the hill
where the pearl had fallen. The illustration in the manuscript
of *Pearl* clearly pictures the dreamer asleep on the sloping crest
of a hill that is shadowed by trees and flowers,[47] and not as lying
on or beside a grave or clump of plants, as has been suggested.
Thrice in the poem "hill" *(huyle,* 41; *hylle,* 1172; *hyul* or *hyiil,*
1205) designates the place where the pearl fell to earth. In the
five other occurrences in *Pearl* the word invariably renders or
refers to *mons* in the Vulgate, and twice (976, 979) it stands for
the *montem magnum et altum* of Apocalypse XXI.10—evidence
hard to reconcile with Gollancz's contention that the "hill" of
the lost pearl and the sleeping dreamer is an infant's grave or a
clump of plants.[48]

Hills and mountains, perennial types of contemplation and

spiritual enlightenment, are frequently the scenes of religious visions.[49] In *Pearl*, however, a more precise meaning may be intended. The Terrestrial Paradise, where the pearl had "trendeled doun," was traditionally placed on a hill or mountain. Consequently it would seem logical to a medieval man for the restored Eden of the Church to have the same setting, and the more so since hill and mountain were recognized symbols of Christ and the Church,[50] and the metaphor of the Church as situated on a hill was also familiar.[51] Lapide suggests the idea in a commentary already cited above,[52] in speaking of the ecclesiastical garden planted by Christ in the Passion, which began in the Garden of Gethsemane on the Mount of Olives. The holy hill or sacred mountain of the Jews was interpreted in the light of the hill-settings of events in the drama of Redemption. Lapide, for example, identifies the mountain of myrrh in Canticles IV.6 with Mount Calvary, and the hill of frankincense in the same passage with "the lofty garden" *(hortus altus)* of Christ's entombment and resurrection.[53]

The habit of mind which linked the garden and hill settings of the Fall with those of the Redemption also associated the Cross with the Tree of Life, and sometimes with the Forbidden Tree, as every student of the Middle Ages knows. The convention is echoed in a proper Preface in the Ordinary of the Mass: "Who has appointed that the salvation of mankind should be wrought on the wood of the Cross: that whence death arose, thence life might rise again." The Latin Fathers generally credit the legend that Adam (or Adam's skull) was buried on Mount Calvary, in anticipation of his resurrection there through the life-giving blood destined to flow at the Crucifixion.[54]

The same tradition apparently is reflected in St. Ambrose's statement that the Crucifixion took place on Mount Calvary because "it was fitting that the first fruits of our life should be situated where death had its beginnings."[55] However, a legend that the Earthly Paradise was actually in Jerusalem gained enough currency to evoke denials from St. Athanasius and from Epiphanius,[56] and whatever its medieval fortunes were, a similar idea appears in Donne's "Hymn to God my God in My Sicknesse" (21–23):

> We thinke that Paradise and Calvarie,
> Christs Crosse and Adams tree, stood in one place.
> Look Lord and find both Adams met in me.

Donne may refer to the legend that the Cross was made of wood from the tree of the knowledge of good and evil.[57] He probably did not expect his bold juxtaposition of the scenes of Paradise lost and Paradise regained to be taken literally, any more than the ancient metaphor of the Adams meeting in him, or the identity of "West and East in all flat maps" (l. 14). He trusted the reader to recognize all three as arresting images of the paradoxical truth at the heart of his poem. *Pearl's* author, nurtured in the same religious tradition as Donne, also could count on his enlightened, and probably highly selected, readers to recognize the meeting place of the two Adams in the spot where the dreamer slept, as he could depend on them not to interpret the poem literally when it identifies the setting of the hilltop garden where the treasure was lost with that of the Church, where the reclaimed jewel has become a pearl of price.

The fragrance of the herb-garden also is noteworthy. The dreamer says that it produced the "sleeping-death" or trance whereby he was granted the vision:

> I felle vpon þat floury flaȝt,
> Suche odour to my herneȝ schot;
> I slode vpon a slepyng-slaȝte
> On þat precios perle wythouten spot   (57–60).

A perfume with special properties is a recurrent feature of saints' lives and visions, Grail legends, and accounts of mystical gardens, including the Earthly Paradise.[58] Sometimes the fragrance typifies the merit of Christ ("in whom the sweet odor of virtue dwells in its fullness and . . . flows out to others")[59] or of his saints; again it signifies divine grace, the infusion of the Holy Spirit.[60] Either or both of these allied meanings would be appropriate to the "fayr reflayr" described by the dreamer (46, 58), but the fact that it induces the salutary trance leading to his vision suggests the operation of the Holy Ghost, for it is "in Godeȝ grace" than the man's spirit is rapt in ecstasy (63–64).

After a somewhat detailed attention to the garden because of its importance in understanding the nature of *Pearl,* we may well review the evidence for its symbolic character. (1) The burgeoning of the garden is heralded by a song alluding to the Biblical corn of wheat, commonly identified with the incarnate and risen Christ, whence sprang the harvest of the Church. (2) As yielding spice plants, it is reminiscent of the garden of Canticles, traditionally interpreted as the Virgin, the Incarnation, the Church; so that a garden became a frequent emblem for each of these. (3) All of the plants of the garden that are named in *Pearl* are medicinal, in keeping with the healing function of the Church. (4) The flowers and fruit may not grow dull or wither ("be fede," l. 29). (5) Their remarkable fragrance, characteristic of mystical gardens, becomes a trance-inducing redolence, leading to a religious vision and a conversion. (6) The vision fittingly occurs during a high festival of the Church. (7) Like the Earthly Paradise, the garden is on a hill, symbol of contemplation and an appropriate setting for the garden of the Church, conceived as the recovered Eden. (8) In soil enriched by the decay of a unique pearl the garden has grown up from "that seemly seed," and now is the dwelling place of "that glorious one," the precious pearl without blemish.*

* The immaculate gem mentioned at the close of stanzas 3, 4 and 5 may be Christ Himself as the Pearl of Great Price in the setting of His Church, the Second Adam having replaced the first. Yet it may well be the dreamer's soul restored to innocence and thus identified with the ecclesiastical garden.

That the man who tells the story has become associated with the ecclesiastical garden, with access to its healing graces, is apparent from his presence there, especially at an important Church festival, "a high season," when concerned for the fate of his lost jewel, the soul, and apparently in an attitude of prayer (l. 49), he is granted the mystical slumber, which is both the sign and the herald of spiritual illumination. Already, he tells us, he had found consolation in the nature of Christ ("kynde of Kryst me comfort kenned," l. 55),[61] and Reason would have brought peace to his warring members (l. 52) had not his "wretched will" caused him to prolong his lament for the lost pearl (st. 5). Assailed by doubt and a perilous despondency, he needs direct and unmistakable testimony that his soul has indeed shared in the Atonement and the restored Paradise. This need is met in what Sister Madeleva aptly calls "his supernatural intercourse with his own soul."[62]

Their conversation is no medieval debate between Body and Soul. The man's body remains on the crest of the blossoming hill while his rapt "spyryt" soars past riven cliffs to the wondrous garden where the maiden Pearl upbraids and consoles him. It may be sheer coincidence that the compiler of the twelfth-century *Allegoriae in Sacram Scripturam,* under the caption "Anima," specifies contemplation as the proper function of *spiritus,* one among nine faculties of the soul in the broader sense.[63] However, some division of the non-material element in man into higher and lower faculties was assumed by every medieval thinker; and, strictly speaking, only the superior or rational soul was regarded as the image of God.[64] Contemplation as the Middle Ages understood it normally began in converse with one's own higher soul, reformed by grace to the divine likeness. "The soul," says Peter Lombard, "is a mirror in which in some way we know God."[65] St. Bonaventura teaches that "the spirit of man beholds itself immediately, and in this vision comes to a cognitive union with God."[66] The eye of contemplation was given us "to see God within ourselves," declares Hugh of St. Victor. "The way to ascend to God is to descend into oneself."[67] Richard of St. Victor, agreeing that "the ascent is through self above self," warns: "Let him who thirsts for God clean his mirror; let him make his own spirit bright."[68]

There is, then, nothing alien to Catholic mystical tradition in the situation of the dreamer's rapt spirit in communion with his superior soul, reformed to God's image, endowed with His life, and inspired by the spirit of wisdom and understanding, gifts of the Holy Ghost. Striking analogues to the interview appear in Hugh of St. Victor's colloquy of a man with his soul, entitled *The Soul's Betrothal Gift (De Arrha Animae)*,[69] except that here it is the man who rebukes his soul for her want of humility and gratitude for the transcendent beauty, splendor of jeweled attirings, and royal state bestowed upon her unworthy self in her betrothal to Christ. The contrasting abasement of our dreamer in the presence of Pearl, his "lyttel quene" (e.g., in 905–906), is matched by St. Gregory Nazianzen's humility in addressing his soul; for all her divine aspiration, he tells her, she while yoked to him is "as queen in butcher's clutches."[70] The tradition was still eloquently alive in seventeenth-century Protestant England; witness William Drummond's apostrophe to his soul in *The Cypress Grove*,[71] as he reminds her of her superlative beauty, wisdom, and power as a microcosmic Trinity, an image of God.

The colloquy with Pearl reveals her true state, as I hope to demonstrate in a later publication. Here a bare outline may suffice to indicate the relevance of the interview to the poet's central argument. The conversation falls into three parts. The maiden's teaching (241–360) is at first rather sternly disciplinary, as she corrects the dreamer's misconceptions regarding her and chides him for the pride and blindness of heart which have pro-

longed his grief and led him to set more store by his own opinion
and the testimony of his senses than by God's faithful promise
"to raise" his "life," though fortune (through Adam's fall) had
caused his flesh to die (301–306). The humbled and submissive
dreamer now expresses his longing for the unity with Pearl that
he had once enjoyed, and courteously implores her to tell him
of her life in her present high estate, which he declares to be
the highway of his own felicity (385–396).

Pearl's reply to this request constitutes the second phase of
the colloquy (397–768). First she describes her union with Christ
(409–420), of whose Mystical Body each Christian soul is a member, "a longande lym" (457–468). Then she explains how she
was raised to that eminence and, citing the Parable of the
Laborers in the Vineyard (493–564), gives an orthodox defense
of her rank, as justified by the innocence that was hers through
the grace of God and the merits of Christ, which were bestowed
upon her in baptism. Thus was she "brought into the Vineyard"
(cf. l. 628) and "made queen on the first day," even though she
at that time "had not lived two years in our country" and knew
neither Creed nor Paternoster (483–486).

Her plea for her right to be paid her wage in this manner,
though she was but a newcomer to God's kingdom, is in its
wider implications the Pauline argument for the New Law of
grace versus the Old Law of justification by works, the Law
being upheld by the dreamer until Pearl convinces him of his
error. In its immediate purpose, however, the debate is a defense of infant baptism, with the skeptical dreamer supplying
the usual arguments of its opponents, in order that his inspired
soul, bearing the image of the Divine Wisdom, may refute his
reasoning and thereby quiet his doubts concerning the efficacy
of his christening in infancy. This accomplished, the child of
grace, as though to clinch her argument, speaks of "the matchless
pearl" of everlasting bliss which "stode" (shone forth?) on her

breast when Christ placed it there "in token of peace"; and straightway counsels the dreamer to "forsake the mad world" and purchase his "pearl without blemish" (729–744).

The converted man, profoundly grateful, no longer argues, but asks eager questions, as the girl proceeds to the third division of her discourse (745–960). A rhapsody on the Lamb, as conceived in turn by Isaiah, John the Baptist, and St. John the Divine in the Apocalypse, here leads naturally to an account in Apocalyptic imagery of the jocund company to which Pearl belongs, the Lamb's own retinue, and thence to a description of their city, the New Jerusalem.

The revelation, in expository phase now complete, moves on to its climax in a visual demonstration of what Pearl has said about her place among the redeemed, when the dreamer is conducted (as St. John was) to a hill, and thence beholds the New Jerusalem and the maiden hosts of the Lamb in procession, the radiant Pearl amongst them (960–1150). The ecstatic man's awakening, after his impulsive attempt to join the throng by crossing the stream that separates him from his "little queen" (1151–1173), is a moving close to the adventure in contemplation, which had already reached his apex and served its purpose by convincing the dreamer that the Redemption had indeed taken place and that his soul has shared in it.

Early in his vision of Pearl, we may recall, he expressed delight at learning of her exalted rank and declared it to be the highway of his own joy:

> For I am ful fayn þat your astate
> Is worþen to worschyp and wele, iwysse;
> Of alle my joy þe hyȝe gate
> Hit is in grounde of alle my blysse   (393–396).

On awakening from his trance he acknowledges the same relationship between Pearl's fortunes and his own by concluding that all is well with him in "this dungeon of grief" if she does indeed go adorned with a "gay garland" (the crown of pearl) and is pleasing to the Prince:

> "O perle," quod I, "of rych renoun,
> So watȝ hit me dere þat þou con deme
> In þis veray avysyoun!
> If hit be ueray and soth sermoun
> Þat þou so stykeȝ in garlande gay.
> So wel is me in þys doel-doungoun
> Þat þou art to þat Prynseȝ paye" (1182–88).

The earthly prison-house has been transformed for him by his insight into the potential welfare of his soul, the avenue to his own blessedness. It remains, nevertheless, for the awakened dreamer to heed the girl's admonition to purchase his jewel: "I rede þe forsake þe worlde wode / And porchace þy perle maskelles" (743–744). At his baptism in infancy his soul had been endowed with the pearl of eternal life solely on the faith of the Church, after sponsors on his behalf had made the essential professions of faith and for him had renounced the prince of the power of this world and "all his works and all his pomps."[72] Now, as a responsible adult, the man must redeem his right to the jewel by an active personal faith and by renouncing worldly desires of his own volition.[73] To do so is to redeem the soul as well as the pearl of felicity. St. Augustine declares that we are not free to earn the "one precious margarite," for which the price is ourselves, until we have first liberated ourselves by despising the temporal possessions that have shackled us. To purchase the margarite, he explains, we must first reclaim and possess ourselves.[74] Further, if the dreamer is not in a state of grace, he must restore the innocence that was his after the guilt of original sin had been remitted in baptism; Pearl had specified that he must purchase his "pearl without blemish" ("maskelles"). For one already baptized "who sins anew," she had explained, the cleansing must be effected through the sacrament of penance (649–672). A sinful man may "shine" through shrift, we read in the companion-piece *Cleanness;* through penance he may "become a pearl," an undefiled soul.[75]

At all events we find the hero at the triumphant close of the story in a state of grace and friendship with God, as he quietly purchases the pearl, first of all by giving it up. Having learned, with St. Paul and Dante, that "His will is our peace" (1153–1200), the awakened dreamer commits his soul to God in terms of the Psalmist's prayer (Ps. XXXI.5), repeated by our Lord on the Cross ("In manus tuas commendo spiritum meum"):

> Ouer þis hyul þis lote I laȝte,
> For pyty of my perle enclyin,
> And syþen to God I hit bytaȝte   (1205–07).

Recited in the Daily Office, this prayer of Christ and David was also used commonly in the vernacular devotions of the laity, with *commendo* usually rendered by "bytake" or "byteche," and *spiritum* by "soule," "soule and lyf(f)," or "soule or lyf(f)."[76]

The passage in which the verses just quoted appear, the final stanza of *Pearl,* announces the triumphant culmination to which the poem has tended from its opening line ("Perle, plesaunte to pryntes paye"):

> To pay þe Prince oþer sete saȝte
> Hit is ful eþe to þe god Krystyin;
> For I haf founden hym, boþe day and naȝte,
> A God, a Lorde, a frende ful fyin.
> Ouer þis huyl þis lote I laȝte,
> For pyty of my perle enclyin,
> And syþen to God I hit bytaȝte.
> In Krysteȝ dere blessyng and myn,
> Þat in þe forme of bred and wyn
> Þe preste vus scheweȝ vch a daye,
> He gef vus to be his homly hyne
> Ande precious perleȝ vnto his pay   (1201–12).
>   Amen.   Amen.

The lines may be taken in more than one sense. According to
the traditional reading the speaker commended his jewel to God
in the Blessed Sacrament, and the last two verses constitute a
prayer that we may be servants in God's household and pearls
of price according to His pleasure. As I have punctuated the
stanza here, however, the last five lines simply affirm the privilege offered to mankind in the Eucharist, wherein the friendship
with God, just mentioned, finds its supreme sacramental expression. Thus construed, the final passage (1205–12), an epitome of
the story and its message, would read as follows: "This lot befell
me on this hill, bowed in sorrow for my pearl, and afterwards
I intrusted it to God. In the dear blessing and memorial of
Christ, whom the priest shows us daily in the form of bread and
wine, He granted us to be servants of His household and pearls
of price for His delight." The appended "Amen, Amen" then
becomes the usual closing prayer, a corroborating petition, "So
be it."

Fortunately, though, minor differences of interpretation
cannot obscure the central import of the closing stanza. A Catholic Paradise Lost and Regained, beginning with the death of
the soul and occupied at its center with the Atonement and the
grace of baptism, by which the soul is reborn to supernatural
life, would hardly close without some recognition of the prime
sacrament by which that life is sustained. "Baptism is the beginning of the spiritual life," writes St. Thomas, "and the door of
all the sacraments; whereas the Eucharist is, as it were, the con-
summation of the spiritual life, and the end of all the sacraments. . . . Baptism is the sacrament of Christ's death and Passion, according as a man is born anew in Christ in virtue of his
Passion; but the Eucharist is the sacrament of Christ's Passion,
according as a man is made perfect in union with Christ who
suffered."[77]

The dreamer's friendship with God is the continuation of his infant soul's espousal to Christ,[78] described and confirmed in his dream, a union which is both symbolized and actualized in the Eucharist. His part in the sacrament as a member of the Mystical Body also epitomizes his fellowship with Pearl's companions of the vision, the host of redeemed souls among the living and the dead, "the blessed company of all faithful people." Thus, within the limits of daily mundane life he sustains the relationships which in his trance were revealed ideally, under the aspect of eternity.

The tests for a consistent reading of the allegory which were specified at the outset of this essay have been met in the interpretation it proposes. The soul is something which the poet, with ample warrant, could represent as a pearl and at the same time as a maiden who had "died" in infancy and had been redeemed by Christ. The jewel of immortal life, with which the soul was identified and endowed, is something that the poet, and his hero, "lost, mourned, and could recover through the grace of God, strengthened by partaking of the Blessed Sacrament."

·ᵒ⟧ 3 ⟦ᵒ·

Pearl: Symbolism in a Garden Setting

C. A. LUTTRELL

In an attempt to contribute towards the understanding and appreciation of *Pearl,* a particular aspect of the opening—a section that employs a procedure no longer familiar to the reader—has been chosen for study within the context of the life and literature of the period. Two important and interlocking pieces in the mechanism that sets *Pearl* on its course are the *erber* and its *huyle,* on which the narrator came to lie and dream, and the aim of this inquiry is first to establish what they actually were like, and then to bring out their function and effect in the poem.

Much of the subject is traversed by R. W. V. Elliott, who, in "*Pearl* and the Medieval Garden: Convention or Originality?," *Les Langues Modernes,* XLV. 85 ff. (1951), sets out to determine the distinctive features of the medieval garden and the *erber,* and proceeds to relate his findings to the description of the sleeper's garden in *Pearl.* But the present writer disagrees both

Reprinted by permission of the author and the editors from *Neophilologus,* XLIX (1965), 160–76.

in details and fundamentally with Elliott's treatment, and by rebuttal intends to clear the way for different conclusions.

From illustrations, Elliott judges vines, arbors, and galleries to be common in medieval gardens, and asserts that *erber,* originally designating an herb-garden, gradually acquired the kind of sense we now associate with "arbor," being applied to an inner enclosure in the garden, turfed and planted with trees, in which more elaborate structures of laths with vine or roses trained thereon were in use from the thirteenth century. For its characteristics he cites Chaucer, *Legend of Good Women,* Prologue, G. 97 f., whose *erber* was *Ybenched newe with turves, fresshe ygrave,* and *Kingis Quair,* 211 ff., in which he finds "its agreeable cool shade suggested by" line 224, *The bewis spred the herber all about,* as well as *Flower and the Leaf,* 49 ff. where it is described as being like a pretty parlor, *roofe and all.* A similar conception of the *erber* is held by D. A. Pearsall, *The Floure and the Leafe* (1962), who believes that it was a shady bower tucked away in a corner of a garden, an arbor without which no fifteenth-century garden was complete. Yet in *Pearl,* explains Elliott, the pleasant features of the typical arbor are markedly absent, which leads to the following inference:

"The omission is undoubtedly a deliberate one, and instead of describing an arbor of the kind mentioned by Chaucer or King James, the *Pearl* poet uses the word as a convenient synonym for garden."

For much of his information Elliott leans heavily on Sir Frank Crisp's *Mediæval Gardens* (1924), going so far as to make use of his translation of a French report on the Latin text of Albertus Magnus, instead of the original, and he does not check the sense attached to *erber,* by a survey of contexts where the term appears, nor examine with any care the sleeper's garden portrayed on folio 37 of the manuscript of *Pearl* itself. The present account springs from consideration of these and other kinds of evidence; including Crisp's rich collection of pictures—which illustrate gardens of many types, and range from the fifteenth to the seventeenth centuries and from England to Persia—when the validity for the purpose is testified by correspondence with details found in texts.

The word is from OFr *erbier,* which means "greensward; herbage"; as well as *"kitchen-garden,"* a sense it shares with MedLat *herbarium.*[1] *Erber* is equated by the fifteenth-century *Promptorium Parvulorum* with *herbarium* (defined by *Hortus Vocabulorum* as "an erber, *ubi crescunt herbe, vel ubi habundant,* or a gardyn"), with *viridale* (compare *viretum,* in *Medulla Grammatice* explained as *"locus pascualis virens,* a gres-ʒerd, or an herber"), and with *viridarium,* a pleasure-garden, the same as Medieval French *vergier,* in which there was *erbier.*[2] Contexts confirm that *erber* ranged in application from "kitchen-garden" and "cottage-garden" to "grass-plot" and "pleasure-garden," and it seems that "orchard," one of the usages given by the *NED,* s.v. *arbour,* really should be "kitchen-garden, etc., with one or more fruit-trees." Eventually *erber* acquired the meaning "arbor," but it did not lose its former connotations for some time, and the co-existence of the two branches, the old and the new, sometimes led to an attempt to distinguish them, in the middle of the sixteenth century, by taking spelling variants such as *herboure* and *arboure* to represent different words, as in Levins, *Manipulus Verborum,* who defines them as respectively (i) *herbaretum, viretum,* and (ii) *arboretum.* Clearly, the sense-development that *erber* underwent could not be a gradual passage of the type A → B. It must be A → A + B → B, with the word in *Promptorium Parvulorum* showing no sign of the second stage, which it reached by the time of Levins. The rift A + B would be due to the use of *arbour* for something which, though grown out of its other applications, had so extended the arboreus quality that there arose semantic overload of the kind that produced pairs such as flower/flour, metal/mettle, and person/parson.

In contexts, there are instances of the *erber* right up to the sixteenth century, as will be seen below, which are identifiable with plesaunces in Crisp's pictures that are no more like arbors than are modern gardens with trees, and the first example of an *erber* resembling an arbor is that in *Flower and the Leaf.* In spite of the ascription of early citations by the *NED* to "espaliers, etc." and "a bower or shady retreat with sides and roof, etc.," none earlier than this poem, which Pearsall dates to the late fifteenth century, can be accepted as illustrating the B-branch of the word's meaning.

One kind of *erber* has a spring or fountain, by which people sit, and from which water flows to the rest of the garden, park, or chase. A man on horseback rides into such a place in Sir Gilbert Hay's *Buke of the Ordre of Knychthede* (1456), there is one in Metham(*fl.* 1448), *Amoryus and Cleopes,* 1612 ff., and Hawes, *Pastime of Pleasure* (1509), describes another, which is square, in the middle of a garden. This type of plesaunce is very familiar indeed. For instance, Machaut, *Rémède de Fortune,* in a park, and a *praiel* (Latin *pratellum* "little mead") of a *vergier* in his *Le Dit dou Lyon.* Such a part of a larger garden is treated romantically in the *Roman de la Rose,* whose *vergier* contains many springs from which water passes in conduits through velvet grass, where lovers can lie under trees forming a protective screen against the sun. A late fifteenth-century manuscript of the *Roman,* B. M. Harl. 4425, has a detailed and full-page illustration (in Crisp as fig. lxxv) on folio vi verso that shows a walled garden of which two parts, separated from each other by a lattice-work fence with a high gateway, occupy all but the background. In the center of the left-hand section, which is a square lawn with trees along one side only, the back, closed by a rose-

hedge grown on palings—the remaining two sides are the walls—
there is a fountain with people sitting near it and a runnel that
flows down a channel in the turf. From this type of garden is
descended that described in the sixteenth century by Estienne
and Liebault, *Maison Rustique,* in a passage whose *preau*
(= *praiel)* is rendered by *arbour* in the seventeenth-century
English version:

Il y a trois sortes de vergers, l'un que l'on appelle autrement
le preau, & ne contient autre cas qu'herbe verte, & la fontaine au
milieu.[3]

Where no spring with water-course is mentioned, as with the
praiel of a castle-garden in *Les Voeux du Paon,* 2682 ff., on
which carpets for sitting are spread under a branching tree, for
this *The Avowis of Alexander* (1438), 3687 ff. uses *erber.* Similarly in the English *La Belle Dame sans Mercy,* 191, for *preau* of
Chartier's line 164. People sit *on,* not in, the *erber* of a castle in
Sir Ferumbras, 1773, that is, on the grass-plot so characteristic
of the small *vergier,* and a typical description of one with plants
in the turf, giving the pattern of a flowery mead, is that in Lydgate's *Siege of Thebes,* 2279 ff., where a knight rides into the
grounds of a castle, finds an *erber* which is *Soote and fressh lich
a paradys, Verray heuenly of inspeccioun,* dismounts and lets
his horse loose to pasture on the grass, and lies down *Vpon the
herbes grene, whit and red.* A green *erber,* with a holly in it,
occupied the fireplace in summer,[4] imitating the plan, seen in
many contexts, and in Crisp's pictures, of a tree in the middle of
a lawn. There the juniper stands in *Kingis Quair,* whose noble
garden shows some familiar details. In each corner an *erber* was
with wandis long and small Railit about: a fenced-off and
grassed area, as often seen in Crisp. *All the place* was knit with
hedges and set about with trees that shaded the alleys, and those
walking past could hardly see within: the hedges and the trees
were related to each *erber* after the fashion illustrated in B. M.

Harl. 4425, so that it was screened from alleys running across
the garden. The juniper in the turf-plot, growing so well that,
as it semyt to a lyf without, its boughs extended all about the
erber, is of a slow-growing species with little spread, at best six
feet, hardly a shady tree, and the poet, who stresses flourishing
green growth throughout this passage, conveys that its head
looked impressive from the other side of the hedge.

A description which particularly recalls that of many a *vergier*
occurs in *Siege of Thebes,* 3024 ff., where Greeks scour a parched
land and come across an *erber:*

> With trees shadowed for the sonne shene,
> Ful of floures and of herbes grene,
> Wonder hoolsom both of syyt and ayr;
> Ther-inne a lady which passingly was fayr,
> Sittyng as tho vnder a laurer tre.

The flowers need not just spangle the turf, but, as in Froissart,
Le Paradys d'Amours, whose *praiel*—in a wood, like several instances of the *erber*—is enclosed by lilies and columbines, may
go round the grass as a border. For the layout of a small garden
of this type, we can refer to the prescription for a *viridarium*
that is found in Albertus Magnus, *De Vegetabilibus,* Lib. VII,
tract. I, c. xiv, and was imitated by Petrus de Crescentiis for a
chapter on the *viridarium herbarum parvum* in his *Opus Rura-
lium Commodorum,* Lib. VIII, c. i. There are borders about a
square lawn for all kinds of flowers and medicinal and aromatic
herbs, which not only please by the odor of their scent but, by
the variety of flower, refresh the sight. Elliott maintains that
plants were cultivated in medieval gardens primarily for utili-
tarian purposes, the element of pleasure being incidental
though beauty and aroma were not unappreciated, but Albertus
insists that it is considerations of usefulness which are secondary
here and must give way to those of delight: *delectatio enim*

quaeritur in viridario, et non fructus. In the turf, as a screen
against the sun, trees are to be planted, or alternatively vines
trained. The center of the lawn should be clear of trees, so that
pure air can play freely over the grassplot—superfluous shade
breeds impurities—and if possible there should be a spring flowing into a stone receptacle. A garden answering this description
appears in the early fifteenth-century picture given by Crisp in
fig. xlvi: it is square or rectangular, and by the planted border
illustrated there is a tree, and in the grass a spring-head in the
form of a trough.

The evidence shows that for the *erber* in *Pearl* we should expect to find a *praiel,* small *vergier,* or *viridarium parvum,* and
this is indeed what there is in the manuscript illustration, which
portrays, it will be observed, the kind of garden that has just
been described. Along the foreground, plants for one border;
two rows of plants and one or two trees marking off other borders, and converging towards the background from left and
right, to indicate, by their recession, the shape as a square or a
rectangle; a curve, by a form of perspective, defining the limits
of the *erber*—and beyond it trees in the distance.

The feature of this garden called a *huyle* is also spelt *hyul*
and *hylle,* the first two forms showing it is not "hill," for which a
West Midland type of spelling would be *hull(e),* while *uy* is
recognizable as the representative in this region of OE *ȳ* or
lengthened *y.* The proposed identification with Rochdale dialect *hile,* and some cases of *hylle* in *Catholicon Anglicum,* meaning "mound; clump of plants," must be accepted. This is a place-
name element in Lancashire and Cheshire, which form part of
the dialectal area to which the language of *Pearl* belongs. It may
go back to an OE *hygel "hillock," and such a sense need not
convey any idea of specific size, which allows Sister Mary Vincent Hillmann, a recent editor of *Pearl,* to take the *huyle* as
large enough to have the *erber* on it, and understand line 41,

On huyle per perle hit trendeled doun, to mean that the pearl was lost when it rolled away from its owner down the incline. Elliott also sees in the wording a suggestion that the ground sloped. Yet it may indicate no more than the revolving motion of a round object as it slipped and fell from someone's grasp, and down *purꝫ gresse to grounde* (line 10).

If one follows Hillmann's view, the poet becomes remarkably persistent in bringing before his readers the situation of the *erber.* There is the passage that has been quoted, then the narrator slept on a *balke,* which she says was the bank or slope of the hillside, woke up with his head lying on that *hylle* (line 1172), and refers to the dream as having taken place while he was prostrate *ouer þis hyul* (line 1205). After the pearl's loss what would be the point of emphasizing that the *erber* was on a hillock? To suggest actuality? But if the *huyle* was inside it, the position is quite different. The garden was nowhere in particular. Conversely, with the hillock carrying the *erber,* there is vagueness as to the exact spot within it where the pearl was lost. As Hillmann has it: "One day, on the hillock down which his pearl had rolled away from him, he sees a lovely growth of spice-blooms . . . [and] he falls prostrate upon the flower-grown hill." But the other way round there is some definite place in the garden where everything happened. One choice makes for intriguing topography of the *erber* and vague location of the loss; the other, a garden setting around a particular spot where the events took place. It will now be shown that the text, the manuscript illustration, and the set-out of this type of garden, all indicate that the *huyle* was inside the *erber,* and point to its identification with a feature to be expected there.

At the end of the lawn, between it and the plants, Albertus and Petrus prescribe a raised piece of turf, square, flowery and pleasant, and suitable as a seat, for mental refreshment and delightful repose:

Inter quas herbas et caespitem [planum] in extremitate
caespitis per quadrum elevatior sit caespis florens et amoenus et
quasi per medium *(or* modum) sedilium aptatus, cum quo re-
ficiendi sunt sensus, et homines insideant ad delectabiliter quies-
cendum.

For these turfed mounds, see Crisp, chapter xi. Several of his
illustrations have people sitting on them, and herbs and flowers
planted on the tops. A good example is portrayed in the picture
cited above for the *viridarium herbarum parvum,* fig. xlvi,
where it is square or rectangular, with high-standing flowers,
and at the end of the lawn. Crisp's volumes show that these
mounds came to have plank supports, or even brick sides, and
that continuous seating of this form, backed by a staked rose
hedge or a wall, could go along the borders of the lawn, and
so it does in the *praiel* of B. M. Harl. 4425; but the free-standing
mound still remained as an alternative. As late as the seventeenth century, the English version of *Maison Rustique* specifies
that some of the sweet herbs and flowers which are cited for nose-
gays should be set upon seats, and on these *The Country Housewifes Garden* puts daisies and violets, and herbs whose scent is
released by touch—pennyroyal and camomile.[5] In our own day
there may be no raised seat of this kind, but R. Genders, *Perfume in the Garden* (1955), p. 112, advises that a delightful addition would be a scented corner where:

> the refreshing fragrance of the plants will only be appreciated
> to the utmost if one has time to take out a cushion on which
> to rest one's head and then to lie flat over the carpet of fragrant
> herbs. Pennyroyal and the trailing evening primrose, camomile
> and semi-prostrate thyme, can all be used but like all herbs
> they are only richly fragrant if they are given a dry, sunny
> position where they can be warmed by the summer sun. Then
> let this warmth penetrate through one's clothes, so that upon
> arising you smell like a packet of fragrant herbs which will
> keep fresh and aromatic the whole day through.

The Middle English term for the turf-mound is *bench (MED,* sense 4), and on one, planted with camomile, the sleeper lay and dreamed in the fifteenth-century poem, *Why I can't be a Nun.*[6] A lady was torn by mental conflict, went into the *erber* section of a garden, prayed, and committed her cause to God. Upon her saying, *"Now do to me aftyr thy wylle"* (lines 111 ff.):

> At that worde for-feynte I fylle
> Among the herbes fresche and fyne;
> Vnto a benche of camomylle
> My wofulle hede I dyd inclyne.

Thus the turfed bench is a normal feature of an *erber,* and a seat on which one could lie, and dream. As in *Pearl,* 42 ff., on it there would be herbs casting their shadow in the summer sun, it would be seemly to look at, from it would float delicious scent, and as one lay across it the fragrance could be powerful. Planted as it would be with herbs and flowers, this would fittingly be called a *huyle.* In the manuscript illustration of *Pearl,* the curved sweep from the sleeper's legs to his side indicates its existence: his feet are on the ground, his trunk on the *huyle,* and he is leaning on his right arm. The head is outlined against the background half-way up a tree as well as far up the garden, and so is not lying on the mound, it is was when he woke up, but the posture is meant to show his visionary condition. Between him and the border plants in the foreground there are flowers, on a dark blue and sinuous patch, which will be the shadow cast by them in a strong sun, and dips down the side of the *huyle* to the ground. The situation is like that described in *Why I can't be a Nun,* and the sleeper looks as if he has fallen to lie on his side after sitting on the *huyle,* turned towards the flowers at this place where, *Syþen in þat spote hit fro me sprange, Ofte haf I wayted* (lines 13 f.), and, on this occasion, *Bifore þat spot* (line 49) clenched his hand.

He lay on a *balke* (line 62), the usual sense of which is an "unploughed ridge dividing furlongs," and between this and a turfed mound there were resemblances: both were pieces of raised ground with grass, plants, and flowers, across a lower surface. *Balke* never meant a hill, nor the bank or slope of a hill; it was a ridge or bank which ran across and divided or was an obstacle. So Hillmann's treatment of this word involves a slip from the latter to the former "bank," and *balke*, on her interpretation of *huyle*, can only give a disturbing complex of rises, a mound on a hillock.

It was þat *floury flaȝt* (line 57) on which he fell, to sleep, and *flaȝt*, so it is assumed, refers to a stretch of turf, the greensward. But this is not a usage known for the word, which normally means "a piece of turf cut from the ground," and sometimes "a snow-flake," in MScots "a flash." The basis is "a stripped-off piece, a detached fragment like a flake," the noun (probably an OE Angl. *flæht) being related to the verb flay. Taking *flaȝt* in its usual sense, the phrase will refer to a flowery slab of turf, and this is a suitable and imaginative appellation for a turfed bench, which looked like some gigantic cut sod, with flowers, dropped on the lawn. Elliott's identification of the *floury flaȝt* with a flowery mead is therefore rejected.

But he also sees reference to a flowery mead elsewhere, and even a possible suggestion of fruit on trees. This is in the third stanza, which is read:

> Þat spot of spyseȝ mot nedeȝ sprede,
> Þer such rycheȝ to rot is runne;
> Blomeȝ blayke and blwe and rede
> Þer *schyneȝ* ful schyr agayn þe sunne.
> Flor and fryte may not be fede
> Þer hit doun drof in moldeȝ dunne;
> For vch gresse mot grow of grayneȝ dede;
> No whete were elleȝ to woneȝ wonne.
> Of goud vche goude is ay bygonne;

So semly a sede moʒt fayly not,
Þat spryngande spyceʒ vp ne sponne
Of þat precios perle wythouten spotte.

Yet if *schyneʒ* were *schyne,* infinitive, dependent like *sprede* on *mot,* and a comma, instead of a semi-colon, supplied after the second line, the stanza would be argument from beginning to end, with the narrator saying that spices, flowers, and fruit *ought* to spring from the pearl. It is in the following lines that he mentions the occasion when he entered the *erber* and found spices flowering at the site of the loss. With this simple emendation there comes a unity to the whole stanza—no longer does he suddenly shunt to a description of the *erber* and back again to the main track of his thoughts—a balance between the first two pairs of lines, and a smooth operation of the foursome, as a complete piece in the pattern, that carries its own conviction. Now we have only an expectancy of spices and their blooms and ripening seeds somewhere sunny in the *erber,* and in the ensuing stanza this idea can only be connected with the *huyle,* that *floury flaʒt,* and its herbs. There is no suggestion of trees with fruit, and Elliott's flowery mead is completely dispelled, so that, apart from the turf-bench and its plants, the only detail given about the *erber* is that it was green.

Elliott comments on the comparative absence of description of the garden, and his observation is even truer now that the discussion has denuded the *erber* of some features he sees there. Instead it has been found that to all intents and purposes the poet gives nothing in it except a feature that is not apparent to Elliott, and this by itself leads to results that differ from his, to begin with, on the question of convention or originality.

The details of the garden given by the author of *Pearl* are strictly conventional, Elliott says, because "the poet adorns his garden with the customary flowers and fragrant herbs whose powerful aroma pervades the scene," and the ground is "decked with flowers: the familiar pattern of the flowery mead." But this is not so. The plants are not, in the usual manner, vaguely arrayed about the *erber,* but only on the *huyle,* the sole source of that powerful aroma. And yet, on the other hand, "convention gives place to a deliberate and truly admirable artistic originality" because "plants and flowers grow, not in neat raised beds or pots, but in apparently indiscriminate profusion," without the conventional touch of "severe uniformity." But to think so is to confuse the pictorial and literary arts, for any English or French poem of Chaucer's day speaking of flowers and plants in neat raised beds or pots would be refreshing, and, if the author of *Pearl* had his plants in indiscriminate profusion about the *erber,* no reader of the literature of this period, in which, with garden after garden, writers do just this, would find any artistic originality. Thus, in having the herbs so definitely located, on a turfed mound, the poet is unconventional, and draws on reality.

Then Elliott argues that, as a garden was a playground of joy and happiness, "clearly no suitable setting for sorrow," somehow in *Pearl* it had to be reconciled with the mood, and so the poet is careful to omit those features felt to be most expressive of joy and delight. Therefore, since it would conflict with the elegiac and mournful effect that the author intends, spring is avoided, in deliberate rejection of an accepted poetic tradition, since customarily the medieval plesaunce is almost instinctively associated with this season. Claiming that the poet practices, in a manner reminiscent of the Anglo-Saxons, the art of making Nature share a person's mood, Elliott extends himself on the topic of the natural background in the garden being "one with the heart of man, while it rejects the thoughts and passions that agitate the latter." But how and why this is so, it will emerge, differs from what he supposes, and, as will now be shown, his arguments have no foundation.

The effect of melancholy is anything but spoilt by a contrast between an unhappy person's condition and the blissfulness of Nature, and in fact it is used by medieval poets as a conventional method of emphasizing mournfulness. In *Why I can't be a Nun* the writer goes into joyous detail of the *erber,* and has birds singing away merrily on every spray:

> But my longyng and my dolowrys
> For alle thys sport wolde not away.

Which is typical. As for *Pearl's* choice of season, first of all why should August, which is *a seson mery & glad,* according to Lydgate, *Debate of the Hors,* 134, and the time of harvest, so joyous in the seasonal headpiece of *King Alisaunder,* 5745 ff., make a garden suit sadness? More fitting would be a setting somewhat later, in the fall, as in *The Assembly of Ladies,* Hoccleve's *Complaint,* and various French poems. Second, is there such a seasonal contrast between the garden scenery of *Pearl* and that of other medieval literature, when in half of the poems set in a plesaunce by Machaut, the most influential poet of this period, there is no mention of spring, but an impression given of only a summerish part of the year, and our author does not show an August in the *erber* at all? There it is just a time when spices flower. The season of harvest and ripe fruit is not in the garden, but the atmosphere, harmonizing the date of the dream with the subject which is to be treated, an example of a technique of which illustrations are readily available both in English and in French medieval poetry. There is a harvest-time and August opening in the dream-vision poem of *La Panthere d'Amors,* and from R. Tuve's *Seasons and Months: Studies in a Tradition of Middle English Poetry* (1933) one can conclude that in using the seasonal motif of the kind found in *Pearl,* 40, *Quen corne is coruen wyth crokeȝ kene,* the poet adopts a convention.[7] Chaucer drew on both the Middle English tradition and the French model of a plesaunce. Clearly, in placing the dream in August, and shunning a picture of the garden in the manner of French literature, the author of *Pearl* is not rejecting any poetic tradition, but taking only what is to his purpose. And this is not to avoid description because it would not go with elegiac impression, nor, blending external setting with thought and inward sentiment as the Anglo-Saxons did, to make the *erber* reflect the narrator's mood, for mournful associations are not conveyed by it as a garden. Beautiful flowers are not sad things, though flowers connected with sad things are.

To lay the foundation for an understanding of the *Pearl* poet's use of the garden it has to be related to the practices of his period. He was on the same cultural level as Chaucer, and, as with the one it has been found useful to scan contemporary French literature, so it would seem likely that light can be thrown on the work of the other from there, too, and especially by the prime fourteenth-century exponent of such scenes in gardens, that is, Machaut. In a characteristic poem of his, *Le Dit dou Vergier,* the narrator goes into a garden which appears to be virtually a terrestrial paradise as he looks around it, savoring its delights. In this setting he has throes of conflicting thoughts concerning a lady, until a visionary state supervenes that settles his heart. The same type of situation occurs in *Rémède de Fortune,* and also *Le Dit de l'Alerion,* where there is no vision proper, but the narrator has a transport of rapture, the mental change setting in after realization of the *vergier's* fragrance and beauty. Particularly from the last it can be seen that, while in medieval poems a forest is often a place in which an alteration of mood is associated with a change of scenery, with the garden is implied rest till the therapy of the surroundings, by sight and smell, exerts its effect. For a modern reader the impression which a medieval garden made is lost chiefly with respect to the perfume, which, right up to much later times, is repeatedly said to comfort and revive the spirits. The location of a mental conflict there, one gathers, suggests that there will be a cure.

Unlike Machaut, the poet of *Pearl* does not mention trees, flowers in profusion on the ground, birds singing, etc., but the same implication is stamped on the *erber,* because of its aromatic herbs of strong impact:

> On huyle þer perle hit trendeled doun
> Schadowed þis worteʒ ful schyre and schene,
> Gilofre, gyngure and gromylyoun,
> And pyonys powdered ay bytwene.
> ʒif hit watʒ semly on to sene,
> A fayr reflayr ʒet fro hit flot.

Yet one must inquire why all attention is concentrated on no other feature of the garden but a *huyle,* and no other source of delight but spices on it—and of strange nature. The peony should not, in August, cause odor to float from it, its month being May. If *gilofre* were the clove-pink, as is assumed, then this is a July flower, but is it necessary to consider the native plant when there is ginger here, and in *Wars of Alexander,* 5426, strange snakes of the East browse on ginger and *gyloffre* the clove-spice? The collection is divorced from season and geography, and has no place in physical dimensions, even if gromwell does flower at this time of the year. With the effect of a mosaic the plants were disposed as they would be in decorative art, like a charge on a field of green—*powdered* was a heraldic term. Or, to place beside other contexts with *bytwene* "here and there," like an ornamental pattern, as on embroidered stuff, upon which in *Sir Gawain,* 611, appear *papiayeʒ paynted pernyng bitwene;* or on the apparelled and painted walls of a hall, which have *dyamountis full dantely dentit betwene* in *Rauf Coilʒear,* 665.[8] And *gyngyure* alliterates with *gylofre,* in the same context as *gromyl,* along with nutmeg, cinnamon, etc., in a stanza of

Annot and John (B. M. Harl. 2253) which employs them in an extended metaphor of the curative powers of a lady. To the same sphere belonged peony seeds. The mound in the *erber* bore plants that appear to be really dried spices, springing from the pearl, and flowering, with neither their medicinal nor spicing qualities brought out by the poem, but beauty and aroma, which if not synaesthetic, as if the narrator was seeing and smelling things by his sense of taste, are metaphoric, of healing properties. The mention of a tropical plant such as ginger, according to Elliott, here exemplifies the conventional element in medieval plant lists, and "its inclusion may simply be an alliterative device or a straight borrowing from the *gingere* of the English *Romaunt.*" Against this prosaic view of a piece of imaginative poetry can be cited the *Roman de la Rose* itself, in which the presence of ginger, there with *clowe-gelofre* and other spices *To eten whan men rise fro table (Romaunt,* 1372), is bound up with the nature of the dream-garden. The plants in the *erber* must correspond in some way to the pearl, from which the previous stanza has led one to expect the rise of appropriate spices, and they put the *huyle* on the level of the contents of the garden of the *Roman de la Rose*—imagery.

This is not the only occasion when an *erber* in late fourteenth-century poetry contains a symbol. The Tree that bears the fruit of Charity in *Piers Plowman,* B. xvi. 4 ff., grows from the root of Mercy in the *erber* of Man's Heart. The figure of being rooted in the heart is a common one, illustrated, for instance, by the Medieval French usage, with *cuer,* of the verb *enter* "to implant," or in Augustine's writings, as when he speaks of *duae radices, charitas et cupiditas,* each of which might be planted in the heart. A homily by Hugh of St. Victor, like *Piers Plowman,* has an allegorical Tree in the *cordis hortus.* The conception of a parallel between inmost processes and those of horticulture is imbedded in Christian writing, and derived from such New Testament passages as the sowing parables, and John XV. 1,

Pater agricola est. We also have the idea of the *mentis hortus,* therefore, as in a lyric by Philip the Chancellor; the heart being the seat of what goes on in the *animus,* the soul as thinking, feeling, willing, a relation exists between it and the mind. Because there is many a metaphor resting on the response of Man to Nature—such as Hugh of St. Victor's interpretation of *flores apparuerunt in terra nostra,* in which the flowers are *aeterna gaudia,* and the land *intus, in nobis*[9]—and the private garden was a place where one often stayed in reflection, or even prayer, as contexts often show, such a locality is a fitting symbol for the heart, or the mind, on which its workings are projected. If the garden well renders these, so is suitable, for an occasion when within them a process takes place, the going into it. In the allegory of a lyric, by the fifteenth-century poet Charles d'Orleans, one enters alone, with the heart, into a garden of Thought:

> Dedans mon jardin de Pensée
> Avecques mon cueur, seul entray.[10]

Imagery of this nature is also to be found in Machaut. A simple type is used in the lyric that treats a lady as truly like the spring, clothing the heart with verdure by turning misery into delightful thought:

> Tout resjoit, tout ranature
> Cuer secrement en verdure,
> Et fait de tristece obscure
>   Joieuse pensée.[11]

And, for a case of full deployment, expressing the conception of the garden setting illustrated from Charles d'Orleans, we return to *Le Dit de l'Alerion,* which proves to be a poem of importance for our purpose.

It is an allegory drawn from hawking, and tells of hunting-birds that passed through the narrator's hands, in representation of a series of love-affairs. The break-up of the last relationship left him very unhappy. He wandered till he entered a garden, sat down, and was tossed between pleasurable and grievous thoughts, until his heart prayed to Amours for deliverance, and he emerged from his brown study to smell the delicious fragrance, see the verdure and the colorful flowers, and to realize what a beautiful spot he was in, a veritable paradise. He was led to have a *dous souvenir* of the *alerion,* a hunting-bird of his past, and then it appeared and perched on his wrist, and he was enraptured. When true lovers part, he explains, they should preserve the memory of their love through thick and thin and any further affairs, and in times of depression have recourse to Amours, who will send them to the *vergier amoureus,* that is, call their hearts to sweet remembrance of love; and where they will find fragrant plants—sweet thoughts—which give hearts peace. And so on. This garden is interpreted in a passage that begins in lines 4691 ff.:

> Cils vergiers dont je ci raconte,
> Par quoy je ne faille a mon compte,
> C'est Amours especiaument
> Qui cuers rapelle doucement . . .
> Après, les herbes odorans,
> Qui tient cuers en pais demourans,
> Ce sont les trés douces pensées
> Selonc l'art d'Amours apensées.

That the symbolism of *les herbes odorans* is not coined by Machaut for the occasion can be seen from his *Le Lay Mortel,* 191 ff., where perfume surpassing that of scented plants comes through thought of a lady:

> Rose, lis, mente, cerfueil
> Tant douce oudeur à mon vueil
> N'ont com celle que je cueil,
> Quant parfondement
> Pense bien à son acueil.

Romaunt, 1025 ff., has the conception not only that sweet thoughts have perfume, but also that it is perceived in the heart, as with the scent of symbolic roses in lines 1661 ff.

In *Le Dit de l'Alerion,* then, we have an allegory which at first is related to events which are physical, of people coming together and going apart. But in its further development, the scene in the garden, it is taken to refer to an occasion, no matter where, when these experiences are thought over. The allegory now pertains to the mental. Seeing the garden with fresh eyes, and appreciating its fragrance and beauty, is coming to remembrance of affection and attachment, having Sweet Thought that, in the *Roman de la Rose:*

> makith lovers to have remembraunce
> Of comfort, and of high plesaunce . . .
> For Thought anoon thanne shall bygynne,
> As fer, God wat, as he can fynde,
> To make a myrrour of his mynde.

And the arrival of the *alerion* stands for this calling to mind of the loved lady. When the bird remains for ever after with the narrator, it is because a picture of the beloved is kept in the heart:

> de ceste douce figure
> Que Douce Pensée en toy figure,
> S'en dois en ton cuer une ymage
> Faire.[12]

That is, to apply the phraseology of a lyric by Machaut—and come full circle—in the place where she had planted memories and thoughts like a gardener's slips:

> elle ente
> Un dous penser et souvenir parfait
> Dedens mon cuer.[13]

As in *Le Dit de l'Alerion* the narrator of *Pearl* entered a garden, from nowhere. How the *erber* reflects thought and inward sentiment bears no relation to practices in Anglo-Saxon, but can be understood against the background of French literature of the poet's day. The marvelous Fountain of the dream-garden of the *Roman de la Rose* appears in garden settings for persons who fall asleep and dream, for example in Machaut's *La Fonteinne Amoureuse;* so in the *erber* there was an expressive object, a *huyle* that is more than a blend of *les herbes odorans,* in *Le Dit de l'Alerion,* and, in the same author's *Le Lay de Plour,* 17 ff., the surviving root of a tree torn out of the ground—a dead lover—producing green growth, flower, and fruit, which are *souvenir.* When the mournfulness of the flourishing root's symbolism it lay within a setting often used by Machaut for a scene of mental turmoil, while its fragrant and beautiful spice-plants hold his other image's promise of relief, and also point to significance. And in *Pearl* as in *Le Dit de l'Alerion* the scene is a further development of an initial allegory about a past that was responsible for what happened in the garden. One can interpret the narrator's entry into the allegorical garden as his thinking deeply, and the plants on the *huyle* as memories and thoughts concerning what lay in it, and (lines 15 f.):

> Þat wont watȝ whyle deuoyde my wrange
> And heuen my happe and al my hele.

There were lovely and richly scented herbs on the *huyle,* i.e. he thought of what it stood for, and memories crowded upon him; he remained grief-stricken before the spot where the *worteȝ* were, i.e. these thoughts caused an onset of great sorrow: grief and reason strove in his confused mind, till the odor of the herbs shot to his brain and overcame him, i.e. he had a mental crisis; and he slid into sleep on the *huyle* and its plants, and his spirit left the *erber,* i.e. he was rapt out of his senses while in-

tent on nothing but the matter represented by the *huyle* that
so stirred him because there he had lost the pearl:

> I felle vpon þat floury flaȝt,
> Such odour to my herneȝ schot;
> I slode vpon a slepyng-slaȝte
> On þat precios perle wythouten spot.

Because *Pearl* shares here basic structural elements with *Le
Dit de l'Alerion,* there is cogency in the use of the *Dit,* not only
to shed light on the methods of the English poem, but also to
throw into relief the distinctive handling of fundamental in-
gredients in its opening. The *Pearl* poet takes the conventional
garden setting for a dreamer and makes it the foundation of an
initial allegory. The scene before the dream is further antici-
pated both by the preliminary visits to the site and by a stanza
of argument using a metaphor, to do with its nature as a place
of herbs and flowers, that prepares one to find them growing
where the pearl was lost. As with the *Dit,* a change in level is not
explicit, and, in the passage from one to the other, allegory per-
taining to the physical melts into what relates to the mental.
So much so in *Pearl,* because the integration of the initial allegory and the scene in the garden telescopes the former into the
latter, that the preparatory visits can figure either going to a
place or thinking about a loss. Since this structure of super-
position limits the narrator's concern to what is within the
erber, and makes him react for its own sake, and not in relation
to any thing, matter, or event outside, physical action is com-
patible with self-withdrawal, whereas in Machaut portrayal of a
pensive is also that of a non-active condition. In the garden, as
the Frenchman makes parts of it into symbols, so the author of
Pearl turns for an image, and an unconventional one, to a normal characteristic of an *erber,* the *caespis elevatior, florens et
amoenus et quasi per medium sedilium aptatus.* With this

choice the poet achieves great economy and fulfils many unities, for at one stroke he acquires the essential symbol and a feature which can be, on the one hand, the location of thought and act, at the very place where one would expect a person, engaged in reflection, to be in an *erber,* and, on the other, the dreamer's couch, not, as usual, devoid of implication, but charged with it —and he strips the garden of everything but this and the verdure.

Pearl differs from the *Dit,* obviously, for instance in the poet's restriction of both parts of the structure of the opening to a brief compass—his aim is to develop instead the dream—and in the lack of interpretation, which is replaced by an overt symbolism in the presence of those spices. But also, subtly, in the reliance on ambiguity. Machaut makes some use of simultaneous verbal reference to the literal and the allegorical, but he has nothing like the delicate play with connotations that the *Pearl* poet displays when describing the garden and what it contains. At first, the *erber* is a *praiel* or *viretum,* a place with a plot of turf. The pearl was lost in the grass. Later, in the *erber,* the features of a *viridarium herbarum parvum* are implied. Yet it is no more definitely a garden than the pearl is a pearl:

> So rounde, so reken in vche araye,
> So smal, so smoþe her sydeʒ . . .

Erber, supposed by Elliott to be merely a convenient symbol for "garden" in *Pearl,* proves to be so convenient that it is used three times and any alternative appellation is excluded. The usage is not only proper and precise, but deliberate, the *erber* remaining both a grass-plot and a garden, and the poet exploiting this range of meaning, on the one hand to strengthen the application of the allegory, and to give, on the other, scope for garden imagery to follow. And the *huyle* that appears to be such a natural part of an *erber*—were it not for those herbs—is never called a *benche,* nor is it explicitly a seat, but only a mound with plants, a transverse piece of raised ground overgrown with herbage, and a flowery sod.

But when the loss of the pearl is told, the narrator's attitude towards this is less in terms of a pearl than of what it signifies, as also during the distressing visits to the *erber,* so that it becomes a grass-stretch with a particular implication. This is carried into the scene at the site of the loss, which now comes fully into focus. There he acted a little one-man play, clenching his hand before the place of the herbs, and performing his part as if concerned, in thought, more with a mound on turf in a locality of another kind than with a feature of a garden. A certain significance, to do with that other sort of grassy plot, is thus attached to the *huyle,* and yet, given what it would be in a garden, its purpose was to be sat on, and for him to lie there and dream, as in *Why I can't be a Nun,* was natural. But, if it were not for the transcendent whole of which part is the conception of this situation as a scene in a garden, he might as well have been anywhere, completely absorbed in thought, even lying where he grieved for Pearl, *Regretted by myn one on nyȝte* (line 243), that is, in bed, with head on pillow.

On one level, therefore, he was in a garden and on a turfed mound; on another, the mound was on the *erber* of the initial allegory; on a third, he was in a Garden of Remembrance. The aspects of the *erber* and the *huyle* are so related that if they stand, in terms of the initial allegory, for graveyard and grave, there is a shift to Garden of Remembrance and thoughts about one who has died. Between a grave and a turf-bench, even if both were planted with herbs, there were indeed differences in use and appearance, but they did not exceed those between a graveyard and a pleasure-garden, and the symbolic power of the *erber* and the *huyle* is made to rest partly on the symbolic power of language. Also, the narrator lay in a garden on a turfed seat, not on what it means except as a topic that engrossed him, for there is no free-for-all among the dimensions, and the bones of the structure are articulated thus:

An Initial Allegory (about a sad Event), made up of the same kind of material as its further development, a Garden Scene [before a Dream], which functions as a Critical Occasion (somewhere) of Reflection and Remembrance (about the Event) that to a mind in torment brought repose [after the Dream].

No side of the *erber* and the *huyle* works by itself, and one can only arrive at a proper idea of the organism by synthesis. In addition, rather than definite and clearly defined interpretations leaping at one from the text, suggestions of their nature are apprehended, as with the comparable fantasies of Machaut and his disciple Froissart, in which the literal level exists very much in its own right, as a story shimmering with significance. This is even so when explanations are provided by the author, for in *Le Dit de l'Alerion* the garden stands not simply, but *especiaument,* for what it is taken to mean, and the *alerion* is not just one's lady, but *Ce puet estre sa douce dame* (line 4723). So, too, in *Pearl,* as one begins to read, it should be felt that the garden and the turfed mound, in the context of the loss, *could* be a graveyard and a grave, and, on that dramatic occasion before the dream, they *could* be the mirror of thought and the thought about.

Also, the appeal, in image-making scenes of the French poems, is first not to the understanding but the imagination, and expressiveness lies in evocation by what in itself is already poetically evocative. Their luxuriance may be lacking in the treatment of this *erber,* but there is richness in the shifting symbolism, when the garden of the allegory becomes a garden of the heart, and here again evocation not only suggestive of meaning is the poet's procedure. Primarily, his *huyle* impinges as a feature which fully partakes of an *erber's* attributes of

beauty and perfume, and specially promotes the deep reflection
and mental refreshment associated with it, a penetrating rich
fragrance, enveloping and soothing, in the drowsy sunshine
being exhaled from plants no less efficacious than the pepper-
mint that is "valuable for fatigue as everyone knows who has
gone off to sleep on a bank" of it (Genders, p. 109). And, dreamlike in the spices it bears and the grief directed upon it, the
huyle where the pearl was dropped recalls a certain mound on
its turf in a way that presents it as if preserved, without account
of place or time, within a garden of the kind that was delightful, like a little paradise, and pleasantly green—the poet refers
to this quality—a place of rest among the fresh and unwithered.
So the dynamic flow of effect begins from the potential in the
form, and the reader is led towards a dream in whose Paradise
the narrator was made to understand wherein, for him who had
lost such a Pearl, lay comfort and peace of mind.

·∘⟨ 4 ⟩∘·

Precious Metal and Gem
Symbolism in *Pearl*

ROBERT J. BLANCH

The author of *Pearl* employs precious metal and gem symbolism in order to suggest facets of the complete virtue whereby
the poet-dreamer may attain spiritual peace. Gem symbolism in
Pearl, rooted in the lapidary tradition, is identified with the
ideals to which the poet must aspire and frequently points to the
imperfections of his earthly existence. With the exception of the
first stanza, which establishes the author's dependence upon
lapidary material, this paper will deal solely with precious metal
and non-pearl gem symbolism in the poem.

In the opening stanza of *Pearl,* the author employs the phraseology and formulae of medieval lapidaries in order to emphasize
the pearl's connection with earthly values: "Perle, plesaunte to
prynces paye / To clanly clos in golde so clere."[1] Conventionally, "each set of verses in the lapidary should have as its first
word the name of the precious stone that was to be discussed."[2]
The gem is usually described as being a valuable possession of

Reprinted by permission of the editor from *The Lock Haven Review,*
No. 7 (1965), 1–12.

a worldly prince or king. Likewise, the lapidary often alludes to a suitable setting for the gem; in most instances, gold becomes the ideal setting, for it is the most costly metal. In the Middle Ages, gold symbolized the divine kingdom,[3] perhaps adumbrating in *Pearl* the poet's evolution from worldliness to spirituality.

After his initial description of the pearl and its subsequent loss, the poet soon falls asleep and assumes the form of the dreamer. His trance is precipitated by the fragrance exuding from the "floury flaȝt," a recurrent motif in the religious visions and in the terrestrial paradise. Although the dreamer's body remains rooted to earth, his "spyryt" soars to a paradisiacal jewel-garden—a garden somewhat reminiscent of Guillaume de Lorris's Garden of Love in the *Roman de la Rose*.[4] Like de Lorris's garden, an earthly paradise, this jewel-garden contains "frech flauoreȝ of fryteȝ" (II, 87) and "fowleȝ . . . / Of flaumbande hweȝ, boþe smale and grete" (II, 89–90), which "songen wyth a swete asent" (II, 94). Unlike de Lorris's garden, however, natural phenomena in the jewel-garden are bathed in supernal radiance. Everything is effulgent and shimmering (II, 73–80).

In this passage, the dreamer alludes to crystal and silver, two elements in medieval descriptions of the earthly paradise. Crystal, a clear ice-like stone, "haþe pale greynes þer-of schinyng toward þe coleur of gold."[5] Silver, on the other hand, is conventionally symbolic of purity[6] and is second only to gold in purity, value, and radiance. Since crystal and silver are inferior reflections of the brilliance of gold, symbolic of the divine kingdom, it is appropriate that these worldly treasures be found in an Edenic setting, thereby underscoring the difference between the earthly and heavenly regions.

Finally, the dreamer approaches a river, the banks of which are compared to "fyldor fyn" (II, 106). This river barrier evokes memories of the Latin visions of the other world,[7] an observation which is substantiated by the inclusion of fine gold thread, with its heavenly associations, in the description. Furthermore, the stream "which separates the narrator from heaven is a traditional death-and-rebirth water symbol,"[8] one of the mystical and conventional lines of demarcation between the earthly and celestial spheres.

Significantly, the stream is paved with glistening jewels—jewels which suggest the Garden of Eden.[9] Only three precious stones are specifically mentioned in the dreamer's description (II, 109–14 and 117–20).

Beryl, the first of the precious stones, "is a stone þat is a colour like to water when þe sonne shyneth."[10] "An emblem of the entrance into heaven of the sum of all virtue,"[11] beryl signifies "þe holy age of þe Resurrection,"[12] the rebirth into a new and purer life. Furthermore, the "bonkeʒ bene of beryl bryʒt" (II, 110) are like "fyldor fyn" (II, 106), thereby symbolizing the resurgence of life in the celestial state. In order to cross the river of eternal life and thus attain heaven, the maiden in the vision subsequently discloses, each man must pass "þurʒ drwry deth" (VI, 323).

Emerald, the second gem, "is greene & cometh from the Streame of Paradis."[13] It signifies the "grennes of gud fayth, for ye gud patriarkes and ye gud profettes wer so fynly gretly grennhed, yerfor yai have ye gret Ioy of heuen."[14] Prior to his vision, the poet was besieged by doubts and "deuely dele"; his "wreched wylle" questioned the will of God. Due to a lack of faith in God, accompanied by "hyʒe pryde," the poet experienced spiritual agony. In seems clear, therefore, that the poet needs faith in order to attain the spiritual peace and joy of heaven.

Emerald also suggests chastity, another prerequisite for eternal glory:

> . . . he þat bereth emeraude aboute hym,
> þe more he shal loue his body in

clennesse, & þe lesse wille to seye
vilanies & þe more loue to thenke
on his solle, & to be of better
berynge & to loue gode werkys, for
god to this stone yave suche vertues.[15]

Sapphire, the third jewel, has the color of heaven. Since
sapphire is imbued with a celestial nature and hue, this gem is
identified with spiritual qualities, truth and wisdom. Through
the contemplation of sapphire, men's souls may be raised to the
contemplation of the heavenly kingdom.[16] In this context,
sapphire suggests the hope of salvation through the source of
eternal life, Jesus Christ:

> . . . þat [sapphire] signifieth þat gode
> hope þat a gode man is touched with
> þe sonne þat is Ihesu Xrist; & the
> more strongely he secheth the kyngdome
> of heuen right as þe sighte maketh
> vs to knowe þe syghte of heuen,
> right to þe vnderstandyng maketh vs
> to vnderstande þe blisful blysse
> of heuen.[17]

All three jewels in the stream—beryl, emerald, and sapphire—
point to the prerequisites for heavenly existence. Simultane-
ously, these gems underscore the essential difference between
heaven and earth. The dreamer unwittingly substantiates this
interpretation when he likens the gems to "stremande sterneȝ,
quen stroþe-men slepe, / Staren in welkyn in wynter nyȝt" (II,
115–16). The radiance and height of the stars contrasts sharply
with the dark, low earth of the "stroþe-men."

After alluding to the jewels in the stream, the dreamer wan-
ders farther along the shore. His sorrow dispelled, his joy builds
to a resounding crescendo. He desires to intensify this euphoria,
to enter into greater beauty and brightness (III, 145–48).

Imagistically, the superior realm on the far side of the stream is linked with pure light, an aesthetic concept, and with royalty:[18]

> I seȝ byȝonde þat myry mere
> A crystal clyffe ful relusaunt;
> Mony ryal ray con fro hit rere   (III, 158–160).

Since the "crystal clyffe" is associated with pure light, the effusion of God,[19] and with royalty, a quality commonly assigned to celestial inhabitants and objects in *Pearl,* crystal suggests the purity of the heavenly kingdom. In *The Peterborough Lapidary,* crystal is clearly identified with purity, for this gem "kepeþ a man chaste, & makeþ a man myche worchipid."[20] At the foot of the crystal cliff sits a resplendent maiden who wears a "blysnande whyt" mantle and has a "vysayge whyt as playn yuore" (III, 178), white being conventionally associated with purity. Her supernal brightness is likened to "glysnande golde þat man con schere" (III, 165). Even the maiden's hair shines "as schorne golde schyr" (IV, 213).

In both instances, gold signifies the purity, glory, and brightness of the heavenly state and of the beatified maiden. Furthermore, gold is a scriptural symbol of "faith triumphant . . . , while its brightness and value make it equally appropriate as a symbol of majesty and honour."[21] When fused with her crown, traditionally a sign of heavenly reward and a proof of victory,[22] and with her "araye ryalle" (IV, 191), the maiden's gold-like radiance and hair suggest the divine kingdom.

Following the initial description of the maiden's "araye ryalle," the debate between the dreamer and the maiden begins, wherein they discuss the nature of divine grace and of heavenly rewards. The maiden subsequently affirms that she is included among the brides of the Lamb in the New Jerusalem—as recounted in St. John's Apocalypse. When the dreamer receives his vision of the New Jerusalem, a heavenly city of purity and spotlessness, he notes that "Þe borʒ watʒ al of brende golde bryʒt" (XVII, 989). This reference to the celestial purity of gold is reinforced by the comparison of the gold city to "glemande glas burnist broun" (XVII, 990)—shining glass somewhat reminiscent of the relucent "crystal clyffe" in line 159.

Employing many explicit references to St. John and the Apocalypse, based upon the conventional lapidary treatment of the apocalyptic stones, the dreamer then enumerates the twelve foundation stones of the New Jerusalem *(Rev.* XXI, 19–20) (XVII, 997–1016).

Jasper, the first of the foundation stones, is "Þat stone Þat is cleped feith, . . . & he Þat grene Iaspe beholdeth ayeins day, of Þe feith of Ihesu Xrist he shulde haue mynde."[23] Furthermore, since the walls of the New Jerusalem are strengthened by jasper, this gem is identified with strength and fortitude—qualities needed to subject falsehood to truth.[24] In her discourse with the dreamer, the maiden emphasizes the need for faith and moral strength. Since the dreamer views the maiden's celestial life as a kind of marvelous extension of her earthly life, the maiden upbraids him for his pride and spiritual blindness, for his reliance upon sense knowledge rather than upon faith in God, "Þat lelly hyʒte your lyf to rayse, / Þaʒ fortune dyd your flesch to dyʒe" (VI, 305–306). The maiden also attempts to relieve the dreamer's anguish over the loss of the dead girl by claiming that God created man for perfect happiness. Through the grace of God the two-year-old girl has been transformed into a perceptive heavenly creature—one who is divested of the shackles of worldly ignorance and affections.

Sapphire, the second foundation stone, signifies "Þe seconde vertue Þat is hope . . . & who Þat saphire beholdeth he shulde be in memoire of Þe blisse of heuen, & in gode memoire of hymselfe."[25] Prior to his vision of the New Jerusalem, the dreamer despairs because he is unable to join the maiden across the stream. The maiden then exhorts him to "Stynt of þy strot and fyne to flyte, / And sech hys blyþe ful swefte and swyþe" (VI, 353–54). She also alludes to the future salvation of the dreamer (VII, 403–406).

Chalcedony, the third jewel, is "a stone of a troubles whitnes, & is of þe Eest."[26] It suggests "þe gode men þat drawen þe synful men blisfully to her gode werkys."[27] In order to attain spiritual peace, the maiden reveals, the dreamer must divorce himself from "Maysterful mod and hyȝe pryde" (VII, 401) and cling to the godlike quality of meekness.

Emerald, the fourth apocalyptic gem, symbolizes the faith of the four Evangelists.[28] Emerald also "voydeth lechery, for God gaue it such vertue; / And to a man that kepeth it, his body and members should be euer cleane and without euell."[29] In *Pearl,* the dreamer's need for chastity is underscored by the frequent allusions to the pure nature of the visionary maiden and to Mary, "Þat ber a barne of vyrgyn flour" (VIII, 426).

Sardonyx, the fifth precious stone, signifies the repentance of men, "hem þat suffren grete peines . . . for þe loue of our lord god & dispisen her flesche as þei were synful men."[30] In the vision of *Pearl,* the maiden contends that through the instruments of "Ryche blod" and "wynne water," the redemptive sacrifice and baptism, man was regenerated and freed from the bondage of "deth secounde" and "glyteȝ felle." However, if man sinned anew, he could still attain heavenly bliss if he were truly penitent—a thought which should prove to be somewhat consolatory to the doubting, rebellious dreamer. Since "þe grace of God is gret innogh" (XI, 660), even the sinner would not be barred from heaven (XII, 661–64).

Ruby, the sixth foundation stone, presents special difficulty because sardius, not ruby, was the sixth apocalyptic gem in the Vulgate text *(Rev.* XXI, 20)[31]—a principal source for the material of *Pearl*. Sardius, the color of clear blood, symbolizes "þe blode of Ihesu Criste þat was shadde for man on þe sixte day, þat was at þat tyme."³² In *Pearl*, the maiden alludes frequently to the redemptive sacrifice of Christ, of Him "on rode þat blody dyed, / Delfully þurʒ hondeʒ þryʒt" (XII, 705–706). The maiden notes especially Christ's "Ryche blod [which] ran on rode so roghe" (XI, 646) and His "blod [which] vus boʒt fro bale of helle" (XI, 651).

Although the text of *Pearl* clearly supports the symbolic meaning attributed to sardius, an explanation of the confusion of sardius and ruby may prove necessary. In his edition of *Pearl*, E. V. Gordon claims that the poet of *Pearl*, not a scribe, included ruby in his description of the New Jerusalem:

> The man who wrote *rybé*, however, must have made some investigation into the names of the gems, and the poet is more likely to have gone to this trouble than a copyist. Moreover, the phrase *as her byrþ-whateʒ* in 1041 . . . shows that the poet had connected the description of the Heavenly City with the details of the high-priest's ephod and breast-plate, given in Exod. xxviii, the very passage which is the source of the tradition that the *sardius* was a ruby. Hence there can be little doubt that *rybé* was the poet's own word.³³

Ruby, a red stone like sardius, is also linked with Christ, for "al thei þat þe rubie & the veray bryghtnes of þe rubie beholden shulde beholde þe veray lighte of Ihesu Xrist."³⁴ In her discourse with the dreamer, the maiden notes that no man may enter heaven "Bot he com þyder ryʒt as a chylde" (XIII, 723). One must be "Harmleʒ, trwe, and vndefylde, / Wythouten mote oþer mascle of sulpande synne" (XIII, 725–26); one must attain childlike innocence and purity before entering the presence of Christ.

Chrysolite, the seventh apocalyptic gem, suggests "þe holy predicacions & miracles of Ihesu Xrist."³⁵ In *Pearl*, the maiden focuses her attention on the prophecies and miracles of Christ's redemptive sacrifice:

> In Jerusalem watȝ my lemman slayn
> And rent on rode wyth boyeȝ bolde.
> Al oure baleȝ to bere ful bayn,
> He toke on hymself oure careȝ colde.
> Wyth boffeteȝ watȝ hys face flayn
> Þat watȝ so fayr on to byholde.
> For synne he set hymself in vayn,
> Þat neuer hade non hymself to wolde.
> For vus he lette hym flyȝe and folde
> And brede vpon a bostwys bem;
> As meke as lomp þat no playnt tolde
> For vus he swalt in Jerusalem.
>
> In Jerusalem, Jordan, and Galalye,
> Þer as baptysed þe goude Saynt Jon,
> His wordeȝ accorded to Ysaye.
> When Jesus con to hym warde gon,
> He sayde of hym þys professye:
> "Lo, Godeȝ Lombe as trwe as ston,
> Þat dotȝ away þe synneȝ dryȝe
> Þat alle þys worlde hatȝ wroȝt vpon.
> Hymself ne wroȝt neuer ȝet non;
> Wheþer on hymself he con al clem.
> Hys generacyoun quo recen con,
> Þat dyȝed for vus in Jerusalem?"   (XIV, 805–28).

Beryl, the eighth jewel, connotes "þe holy age of þe Resurrection."[36] In *Pearl*, the maiden claims that those souls who live in unblemished purity will becomes brides of Christ in heaven for "þay arn boȝt fro þe vrþe aloynte / As newe fryt to God ful due, / And to þe gentyl Lombe hit arn anioynt, / As lyk to hymself of lote and hwe" (XV, 893–96). Likewise, the maiden alludes to the resurrection of the body in the phrase, "Of on dethe ful oure hope is drest" (XV, 860). "In so far as *hope* implies 'hope' it must mean of the resurrection of the body: we have died the ordinary

death of corruption, but from Christ's death, which alone is in-
corrupt, our *full* [editor's italics] hope proceeds."[37]

Topaz, the ninth foundation stone, symbolizes the "nyne
ordres of angeles þat lyven in þat joye þat noon hath enuye of
othre, þat is þe life corouned, in þe which shal noon entre but he
be kyng corouned or quene, for all be corouned be name."[38]
Although *Pearl* contains no specific references to the nine orders
of angels, except for the allusion to the "Vertues of heuen"
(XIX, 1126), the crown is mentioned frequently as a symbol of
heavenly reward. The maiden, for example, is crowned queen by
the Lamb "in blysse to brede / In lenghe of dayeȝ þat euer schal
wage" (VII, 415–16). Furthermore, the maiden states that every
inhabitant of heaven is crowned queen or king (VIII, 445–52).

Chrysoprase, the tenth gem, signifies the travail of earthly
men.[39] In *Pearl*, the maiden employs the parable of the Vineyard (Matt. XX, 1–16) in order to prove to the dreamer that
God's grace, not individual merit, is the *sine qua non* for eternal
glory. Although the first laborers in the Vineyard "bygonne to
pleny / And sayden þat þay hade trauayled sore" (X, 549–50),
the maiden demonstrates that it is God's prerogative to reward
"with the penny of heavenly beatitude those who have labored
but one hour, quite as He does those who have labored the
whole day."[40] Once the dreamer views the New Jerusalem, however, he is released from the bodily sensations of rest and weariness—sensations common to earthly men who aspire to the
heavenly state:

> I stod as stylle as dased quayle
> For ferly of þat frelich fygure,
> Þat felde I nawþer reste ne trauayle,
> So watȝ I rauyste wyth glymme pure   (XVIII, 1085–88).

Jacinth, the eleventh apocalyptic stone, suggests "wyse clerkes
& maistres þe whech preched & speke to men after þat thei were

. . . & chaunged hem."⁴¹ Jacinth also "shal put fro man idel
thoughtes & sorow."⁴² While the dreamer gazes upon the New
Jerusalem, his earthly sorrow melts into celestial rapture, for
"So watȝ I rauyste wyth glymme pure . . . / Hade bodyly burne
abiden þat bone, / Paȝ alle clerkeȝ hym hade in cure, / His lyf
were loste an-vnder mone" (XVIII, 1088 and 1090–92). Furthermore, when the dreamer views the procession of virgins before
the throne of the Lamb, he notes that all the beatified souls experience ineffable "delyt." In the presence of the Lamb, "glory
and gle watȝ nwe abroched; / Al songe to loue þat gay iuelle"
(XIX, 1123–24).

Amethyst, the twelfth and last foundation stone, is "of purpure colour & draweth to colour of blode newe shedde."⁴³ It
signifies "þe clothynge of purpure þat god was clothed inne atte
his deethe, where-inne þe Iewys clothed hym in scornyng, & the
lordeshippe of / angeles & þe deethe of martyres."⁴⁴ Although
Pearl contains no explicit reference to Christ's purple garments,
the dreamer suggests purple, the color of newly shed blood, in
his depiction of the Lamb. While the Lamb wears white garments, symbolic of celestial purity, a wound "ful wyde and weete
con wyse / Anende hys hert, þurȝ hyde torente; / Of his quyte
syde his blod outsprent" (XIX, 1135–37). This reference to
blood, shed by the Lamb when He assumed the earthly form of
Christ and died on the Cross, is echoed ultimately in the "wyn"
(blood) of the Eucharist. All men must partake of Christ's re-
deeming blood, in the form of Eucharistic wine, in order to
attain salvation.⁴⁵

After the dreamer enumerates the twelve foundation stones
of the New Jerusalem, he alludes to the "streteȝ of golde as
glasse al bare" (XVII, 1025) and the "golden gateȝ þat glent
as glasse" (XIX, 1106). Since "bare," in the first reference, signifies unobscured by dust,⁴⁶ the comparison of the streets of
gold to the radiance and clarity of glass underscores the differ-

ence between heaven and earth. Heaven, a sphere of purity and spotlessness, is clearly divorced from the "mokke and mul" of earth.

Finally, the dreamer depicts the Lamb "Wyth horneʒ seuen of red golde cler" (XIX, 1111). Red suggests the blood gushing forth from the wound in the Lamb's white side. Gold, on the other hand, signifies the celestial purity of the Lamb. Through the juxtaposition of red and gold, the author of *Pearl* emphasizes the double nature of the Lamb—the human nature of the Lamb as Christ and the divine nature of the Lamb as God the Son. Furthermore, since the Lamb has "seuen" horns, this number may be identified with the seven sacraments, the graces of which flow from the redemptive sacrifice of the Lamb as Christ.

Through his artistic manipulation of precious metal and gem symbolism, the author of *Pearl* emphasizes the essential difference between the earthly and celestial spheres and elucidates the prerequisites for the dreamer's spiritual peace, including the need for Christ's saving blood.

·⋅❧[5]❧·⋅

Symbolic and Dramatic
Development in *Pearl*

A. C. SPEARING

Both before and since the beginnings of the current controversy about the application of patristic exegesis to the study of
medieval literature, the poem *Pearl* has been subjected to allegorical interpretations of various kinds, and these have naturally been chiefly concerned with the poem's central symbol,
the pearl itself. Some commentators have claimed that the pearl
stands for the soul of the poem's narrator;[1] others, among them
one of the leading proponents of the exegetical approach in general, have asserted that it is to be understood according to the
standard "four levels" of scriptural exegesis;[2] and there have
been many other interpretations.[3] Although such attempts to
find some hidden layer of meaning in the poem seem to me mis-
conceived, it is not my purpose here either to enter into the
theoretical controversy about exegesis (to which so distinguished
a contribution has recently been made in this journal by Pro-

fessor Bloomfield[4]) or to offer any detailed criticism of the various existing interpretations of *Pearl*. I hope simply, by outlining an adequate non-allegorical reading of the pearl symbolism, to show that whether or not allegorical explication is desirable it is at least not necessary. I think, certainly, that one strong argument against supposing that the poem's readers need make some effort of allegorical interpretation is the fact that the poet seems to make the pearl-Maiden herself provide exegesis wherever exegesis is necessary. Thus, after the parable of the vineyard has been recounted, the Maiden does not rely on the Dreamer, and the poet does not rely on his reader, to interpret it out of his own knowledge of current exegesis. An explicit and careful interpretation is supplied in the poem:

> Bot innoghe of grace hatʒ innocent.
> As sone as þay arn borne, by lyne
> In þe water of babtem þay dyssente:
> Þen arne þay boroʒt into þe vyne.
> Anon þe day, wyth derk endente,
> Þe niyʒt of deth dotʒ to enclyne:
> Þat wroʒt neuer wrang er þenne þay wente,
> Þe gentyle Lorde þenne payeʒ hys hyne   (ll. 625–32).[5]

The intended meaning of each element in the parable is expounded, in the manner of a medieval sermon—that is to say, of a work which *uses* allegorical exegesis, but is not itself allegorical. Again, after nine stanzas have been devoted to a description of Jerusalem, with constant references to John's vision in the Apocalypse—references which, if some effort of interpretation were expected, one would think sufficient to incite the audience to apply their knowledge of exegesis—the pearl-Maiden goes on to make at some length the elementary distinction between the Old Jerusalem, the city of God, and the New, the vision of peace.[6] Cases such as these seem to me to make it unlikely, on the ground of simple probability, that the poem or its

central symbol has any *concealed* allegorical meaning.[7] But to
say this is not to deny that the pearl symbol as it is presented in
the poem is extremely rich in meaning, and rich in a way which,
if like many scholars we are unfamiliar with the richness of
meaning that belongs to poetry, we may be tempted to call allegorical rather than literal. And it seems likely enough that for
an educated fourteenth-century reader the pearl concept would
have been felt to be pregnant with symbolism per se, quite apart
from the poem *Pearl.*[8] These two facts are certainly connected:
the particular kind of success which the *Pearl* poet has achieved
would hardly have been possible if he had not shared with his
audience a common pre-existing symbolism. But this must not
lead us to suppose that there is no difference between the pearl
symbol as it existed in the fourteenth-century consciousness and
the pearl symbol as it exists in *Pearl,* so that in order to discover
the meaning of the latter we have only to look up lapidaries,
biblical commentaries, and so forth for evidence about the former. The *Pearl* poet is a poet; he *uses* the symbol provided for
him by his age; and if we wish to understand his poem as a poem
we must surely begin not by superimposing on it some system of
allegorical significance drawn from external sources, but by
examining carefully those symbolical meanings which are indicated by what the poet actually says. Within the religious verse
of the Middle Ages, many short pieces, such as lyrics, and also
the less successful of the longer works, tend to be parasitic upon
the symbolic consciousness of their age: they depend upon it for
what power they possess, and give nothing in return. To understand the appeal of such works, we have to try to reconstruct
artificially the world of symbolism which lies behind them. But
there are certain long poems which are successful as poems,
which reconstruct current symbols within themselves, and in
doing so give them a permanent and unique validity. The out-
standing examples in Middle English are *Pearl* and *Piers Plow-*

man, and the way in which these poems reconstruct symbols is
to incorporate them in an extended dramatic narrative, so that
we do not have to apprehend their significance instantaneously,
but can feel it being built up piece by piece over a period of
time. In some ways it may be that we can better take *Pearl* as a
guide to medieval symbolism than medieval symbolism as a
guide to *Pearl.* If only for this reason, it seems worth while to
attempt a detailed study of the treatment of the poem's central
symbol. If this is done, it will be found that, as Schofield wrote
over fifty years ago, "The author's plan is to let the symbolism
of his poem disclose itself slowly."[9] The pearl symbol is not static
but dynamic: it develops in meaning as the poem extends itself
in time, and this development in meaning is coordinated with
the developing human drama of the relationship between the
Dreamer and the Maiden.[10] The whole force and poignancy of
the poem derives from its basic structure as an encounter involving human relationship; and it is through the synthesis of
symbol with drama that the writer of *Pearl* conveys his meaning, and not, I believe, through any concealed layers of allegory.

The pearl symbol appears in the first word of the first line
of the poem, and the similarity between this line—"Perle,
plesaunte to prynces paye"—and the last—"Ande precious perleȝ
vnto his pay"—has not escaped notice. The "his" of the last line
refers to a prince, but to the Prince of Heaven, and this fact has
led even so moderate a modern interpreter of the poem as Gordon to follow the earlier commentators cited by Schofield[11] and
claim that the prince of the first line means "literally a prince of
this world and symbolically Christ."[12] It is true of course that
the parallel between the first and last lines is quite deliberate,
and that on a second and subsequent readings of the poem the
first line will recall the last. But this is not to say that it will
mean the last, even symbolically; and we can hardly agree that
it does mean the last without denying the nature of the poem as

an object which, for its reader, is extended in time, and is therefore capable of discursive or dramatic development. And in this
case we may miss the whole point of the first section of the poem.
If we read the poem's first four lines:

> Perle, plesaunte to prynces paye
> To clanly clos in golde so clere,
> Oute of oryent, I hardyly saye,
> Ne proued I neuer her precios pere

we shall see that, taken by themselves, they refer to the pearl as
a lapidary might, as a literal precious stone, valued by literal
earthly princes. This is the primary meaning of *perle* throughout the first group of five stanzas, but not the only meaning.
For the symbol *is* being used in a secondary sense here— a sense
which might be called "allegorical"—but this secondary sense is
not one which is concealed now and only disclosed later in the
poem, but one which is glanced at in the first stanza. In line 4,
quoted above, the pearl is referred to as feminine, and the gen-
der might be either natural or merely grammatical; but the next
two lines develop the hint of natural femininity:

> So rounde, so reken in vche araye,
> So smal, so smoþe her sydeȝ were   (ll. 5–6).

The first of these lines is appropriate mainly to a precious stone,
but the second both to a precious stone and to a girl (with *sydeȝ*
meaning "flanks"). We are therefore to understand, though the
equation is not explicit, that the narrator is using the image of
the loss of a precious stone to express the loss, presumably
through death, of a girl. The vagueness here—the fact that the
suggestiveness of the phrasing is not pinned down by any explicit statement—no doubt belongs to poetry rather than theology; but it is made clearer by the use of the language of courtly
love in the last two lines of the first stanza:

I dewyne, fordolked of luf-daungere
Of þat pryuy perle wythouten spot   (ll. 11–12).

If the poem went no further, its implied allegorical structure would be similar to that of the *Roman de la Rose*. After the first stanza, which gives us the necessary hint of his human reference, the narrator reverts to his metaphor, and speaks of his loss as that of a "myry iuele" (l. 23), which "trendeled doun" on a "huyle" (l. 41). This continuing use of jewel terminology is important. It is clear that what the narrator has lost is something intrinsically precious and precious to him, but he is seeing its preciousness as that of a beautiful and valuable stone—he thinks it appropriate to speak of the girl's death as involving an irrevocable and total loss of her preciousness. To this loss he reacts with an attitude of elegiac melancholy, somewhat reminiscent of that of the "man in blak" in *The Book of the Duchess*. In *Pearl,* even more than in Chaucer's poem, this melancholy is made attractive, framed as it is in a scene which delights the senses with strange music and with the brightness and fragrance of flowers and herbs. But our response to the melancholy should not be one simply of surrender. The *locus amoenus* of the *Pearl* garden is presented not on the conventional May morning but in August, harvest-time, "Quen corne is coruen wyth crokeȝ kene" (l. 40); and this unusual season may have symbolic associations of one sort or another,[13] but it also has an inescapable poetic effect, an effect in harmony with the landscape's noticeable lack of one essential feature of the traditional *locus amoenus,* namely the stream or river.[14] The landscape provides an objective correlative to the emotions of the narrator: about both there is a hint of the overripe, the unrefreshed, and, indeed, perhaps of the merely passive—the corn awaiting the scythe, the narrator surrendering to his luxuriant emotion. He does not see things with May-morning clarity; though he feels the pearl to be precious, by relying merely on feeling he undervalues its preciousness, seeing it *not,* as at the end of the poem, as precious to the Prince of Heaven, but as precious only to earthly princes. That we are intended to adopt a critical attitude toward the narrator, even while feeling fully the pathos of his situation, is suggested by his reference to the flowers growing on the spot where his pearl was lost:

> Blomeʒ blayke and blwe and rede
> Þer schyneʒ ful schyr agayn þe sunne.
> Flor and fryte may not be fede
> Þer hit doun drof in moldeʒ dunne;
> For vch gresse mot grow of grayneʒ dede;
> No whete were elleʒ to woneʒ wonne   (ll. 27–32).

The last two lines embody an allusion to John 12:24: "Verily, verily, I say unto you, Except a corn of wheat fall into the ground and die, it abideth alone, but if it die, it bringeth forth much fruit." But it is clear that the narrator has misunderstood the scriptural text to which he alludes: he has taken the fruit which grows from the dead grain to be material, like the flowers on the grave, but it is in fact, as the next verse in John makes clear, the spiritual fruit of eternal life. By forgetting that the girl's soul is immortal, even though her body dies, the Dreamer has underestimated her absolute value. The nature of his underestimation is partially hinted at in the last stanza of the poem's first section, where the earliest explicit Christian reference occurs:

> A deuely dele in my hert denned,
> Þaʒ resoun sette myseluen saʒt.
> I playned my perle þat þer watʒ spenned
> Wyth fyrce skylleʒ þat faste faʒt;
> Þaʒ kynde of Kryst me comfort kenned,
> My wreched wylle in wo ay wraʒte   (ll. 51–56).

But this suggestion of a conflict between the narrator's actual feeling about his loss and an as yet undefined rational and Christian attitude toward it is not developed here, for at this point the narrator falls alseep and becomes the Dreamer.

His body remains in the garden, but his spirit is transported to a new landscape, once again a version of the traditional *locus amoenus,* but this time a different version, shining with brilliant light and hard with metal and precious stones. It is towards the end of a description emphasizing these qualities of the dream landscape that the pearl symbol is next introduced:

> Dubbed wern alle þo downeȝ sydeȝ
> Wyth crystal klyffeȝ so cler of kynde.
> Holtewodeȝ bryȝt aboute hem bydeȝ
> Of bolleȝ as blwe as ble of Ynde;
> As bornyst syluer þe lef on slydeȝ,
> Þat þike con trylle on vch a tynde.
> Quen glem of glodeȝ agaynȝ hem glydeȝ,
> Wyth schymeryng schene ful schrylle þay schynde.
> Þe grauayl þat on grounde con grynde
> Wern precious perleȝ of oryente   (ll. 73–82).

This particular context draws out two further aspects of the meaning latent in the symbol: the brilliance of the pearl and its hard permanence. Light, the effusion of God Himself, is the favorite medieval expression of beauty, and here the more human, though idealized, beauty which the pearl had at first in the narrator's memory—"So smal, so smoþe her sydeȝ were"—has begun, through emphasis on new aspects of the same symbol, to merge into a heavenly beauty, to become part of a landscape dazzling, overpowering in its brightness:

> For vrþely herte myȝt not suffyse
> To þe tenþe dole of þo gladneȝ glade   (ll. 135–36).

And the preciousness which was capable of death has in the same way begun to turn into a more permanent but harder preciousness. Thus although the pearl symbol has for the moment reverted to its original sense of a precious stone, it has done so

only in order to develop in other directions. We shall find that
none of its separate senses is abandoned, but that any may
momentarily become primary for the sake of a further development of associations.

This is the only mention of pearls in the second or third sections of the poem; but in the third section the Maiden appears
for the first time. She is not at once identified with the lost pearl;
by making use of the slow perception of his Dreamer, the poet
is able to unfold his symbolism gradually, to hint before he
states. And so at first the Dreamer sees in the Maiden only the
whiteness and brilliance of the pearl:

> A mayden of menske, ful debonere;
> Blysnande whyt watȝ hyr bleaunt.
> I knew hyr wel, I hade sen hyr ere   (ll. 162–64).
>
> On lenghe I loked to hyr þere;
> Þe lenger, I knew hyr more and more   (ll. 167–68).

In this slow process of recognition, the development of the symbolism is communicated to us in human terms: the growth of
meaning is possible only through a growth in understanding on
the Dreamer's part, and this is accompanied by a reluctant intellectual exertion which is sometimes comic in effect:

> Wyth yȝen open and mouth ful clos
> I stod as hende as hawk in halle   (ll. 183–84).

As a sign that the recognition is complete, I think we may take
the following lines, with their reminiscences of the poem's
opening stanza:

> Þat gracios gay wythouten galle,
> So smoþe, so smal, so seme slyȝt,
> Ryseȝ vp in hir araye ryalle,
> A precios pyece in perleȝ pyȝt   (ll. 189–92).

"So smoþe, so smal" recalls line 6 ("So smal, so smoþe her sydeȝ were"); "hir araye ryalle" recalls the royal associations of line 1. In the stanzas which follow, the Maiden's "pearl" qualities are intensified by the normal medieval descriptive method, that of accumulation rather than selection of detail. Her garments are described one by one; each is covered with pearls, and we remember that in the fourteenth-century pearls were highly prized as ornaments by the fashionable,[15] so that it is now apparent that the courtliness suggested by the earlier use of the language of courtly love has not been abandoned with the development of a Christian significance. This fact is emphasized by a recurrence of the ideas of royalty:

> Perleȝ pyȝte of ryal prys
> Þere moȝt mon by grace haf sene   (ll. 193–94).
>
> Her semblaunt sade for doc oþer erle   (l. 211).

The culmination of this description of the Maiden's garments is reached with the single pearl on her breast:

> Bot a wonder perle wythouten wemme
> Inmyddeȝ hyr breste watȝ sette so sure;
> A manneȝ dom moȝt dryȝly demme,
> Er mynde moȝt malte in hit mesure.
> I hope no tong moȝt endure
> No sauerly saghe say of þat syȝt,
> So watȝ hit clene and cler and pure,
> Þat precios perle þer hit watȝ pyȝt   (ll. 221–28).

To attempt to distinguish this one pearl in symbolic significance from the pearl-Maiden herself is, I believe, to misunderstand the poet's methods. Certainly, this pearl seems to have special associations with purity or virginity, in such phrases as "wythouten wemme," but these only recall and develop an idea which had been present from the first stanza group, with its use of "wythouten spot" as the refrain phrase. The order in which the poem's symbolism is unfolded is, as I am arguing, significant, but it is a single symbol, with a single though complex meaning, which is being evolved, and any attempt at such minute allegorical distinctions will only obscure the central achievement of the poem.

We may note that in the last passage quoted the idea of overpoweringness, hitherto applied generally to the whole landscape of the dream is transferred to the Maiden's pearl:

> A manneʒ dom moʒt dryʒly demme,
> Er mynde moʒt malte in hit mesure.

There is a dramatic significance in the fact that the Dreamer should see this quality in the Maiden's chief decoration, for he sees that her appearance "exceeds our organs," but does not take the hint that her teaching too may now be beyond his earthly understanding. This give a certain pathos to his earlier "So smoþe, so smal, so seme slyʒt," and to his first speech to her in the next section; and perhaps a similar intention, dramatic rather than doctrinal, may help to explain the controversial line, "Ho watʒ me nerre þen aunte or nece" (l. 233). The poet leaves the Dreamer's relationship with the Maiden undefined so as to be able to draw at once on the emotions of romantic love and of fatherly affection; and he makes the Dreamer use the phrase "aunte or nece"—slightly comic, slightly pathetic—in order to indicate that he is continuing to think of the relationship in naively familial terms, comically and pathetically unaware of their inadequacy for the visionary situation in which he is now placed. Similarly, in a line quoted above—"Her semblaunt sade for doc oþer erle"—he expresses a naively earthly conception of the Maiden's regal qualities.

In the fifth section, after the Dreamer's touching speech of rec-

ognition has been met with an austere rebuke from the Maiden
—"Sir, ȝe haf your tale mysetente" (l. 257)—she does her best to
make him understand that the situation is not as he has been
seeing it, by explaining that what he has lost was not a pearl
at all, but a rose "Þat flowred and fayled as kynde hyt gef"
(l. 270): it belonged to the merely natural world of *amour courtois* represented by the garden and the elegiac tone of the beginning. And this rose has now become a "perle of prys" (l. 272). It
must be observed that the courtly rose, subject to "kynde," is not
the same as the pearl, nor is it something totally different, which
must be rejected and replaced: it has "proved to be" the pearl,
which is to say that, from the Dreamer's point of view, it has
been *transformed* into the pearl:

> . . . þurȝ kynde of þe kyste þat hyt con close
> To a perle of prys hit is put in pref.   (ll. 271–72)

Between the earthly and heavenly worlds there exist at once
difference and continuity, and this complex relationship is
easily misunderstood: it is misunderstood by the Dreamer, who
sees only continuity, and expects the heavenly Maiden to be
the same as the earthly pearl he lost, and it is misunderstood by
those modern commentators such as Hoffman, who see only
difference,[16] and wish to make a total distinction between the
earthly and heavenly pearls. But the combination of continuity
and difference is figured forth in the fact that the "erber grene"
and the brilliant dream landscape are different versions of the
same traditional *locus amoenus,* and it appears centrally in the
developing conception of the nature of the pearl's preciousness.
This is accompanied by the gradual disclosure of a Christian
courtliness including and transcending the worldly courtliness
which is limited by transience. The language of *amour courtois*
recurs throughout the poem from the beginning, where we have

already seen it applied to the earthly pearl, to the climactic point
at which the Dreamer sees the heavenly pearl among the Brides
of the Lamb and exclaims that

> Þat syȝt me gart to þenk to wade
> For luf-longyng in gret delyt   (ll. 1151–52).

It is also applied, as in many devotional lyrics, to the relationship between Christ and the individual soul:

> In Jerusalem watȝ my lemman slayn
> And rent on rode wyth boyeȝ bolde   (ll. 805–6).

A continuity is thus established in *Pearl* between earthly and
heavenly love, and this is a familiar motive in medieval literature, both secular and religious. It is for instance a fundamental
idea of Chaucer's *Troilus and Criseyde,* where earthly love is
first celebrated in religious terminology and then finally gives
way to the love of Christ; while in *The Wooing of Our Lord* (to
take a well-known example of devotional writing, and one
which was still being read in the fourteenth century as part of
A Talking of the Love of God) Christ, the heavenly lover, is
shown successively to possess in the highest degree all those qualities which win love in the world. Thus the continuity found in
Pearl between earthly and heavenly values, which makes possible a movement from the one to the other, is nothing new in
medieval literature. But, as I have said, along with continuity
we also find difference, and in this way the *Pearl* poet offers a
considerable refinement of the attitudes displayed in *The Wooing* and in many other medieval devotional texts—works in
which we often feel that by the use of erotic imagery heavenly
love has simply been reduced to the level of earthly love. In
Pearl earthly feelings and relationships are themselves conceived
with a finer courtliness than other religious texts usually have
to offer, and although these feelings and relationships have

analogies in the heavenly world of the dream, it is precisely the inability of the Dreamer to realize the disparity between the two, the transcendent relation of the one to the other, which provides the poem's human and emotional interest.

To return to the text: the "perle of prys" in line 272, suggests, of course, the pearl of great price of Matt. 13:45–46, to purchase which the merchant sold all he had. This allusion, for which we have perhaps been prepared by the repeated references in the refrain line to the Dreamer as a *juelere,* is reinforced by the following two lines, which continue the language of trade, of profit / and loss:

> And þou hatȝ called þy wyrde a þef,
> Þat oȝt of noȝt hatȝ mad þe cler   (ll. 273–74).[17]

But these allusions are lost on the Dreamer. He has totally failed to understand the situation, and, seeing the Maiden's heavenly life simply as a kind of miraculous prolongation of her earthly life (seeing, that is, continuity but not difference), he assumes that he will now be free to join her, and that they will "live happily ever after"—

> I trawed my perle don out of daweȝ.
> Now haf I fonde hyt, I schal ma feste,
> And wony wyth hyt in schyr wod-schaweȝ,
> And loue my Lorde and al his laweȝ
> Þat hatȝ me broȝt þys blys ner   (ll. 282–86).

This misunderstanding draws an even more stinging rebuke from the Maiden and a devastatingly complete analysis of his error. With this, the fifth section closes, and a complete change comes over the poem. By his failure to understand the Maiden's image of the transformation of the rose into a pearl, the Dreamer has shown himself unable to make any further progress through the development of symbolism. He is impossibly literal-minded and the method of symbolic development is therefore abandoned in favor of simpler, more explicit forms of exposition. For more than four hundred lines the pearl symbol undergoes no further development, and indeed the very word *perle* occurs only four times: twice in Section VI as a name—"My precios perle dotʒ me gret pyne" (l. 330) and "When I am partleʒ of perle myne" (l. 335)—and twice in Section VII in the form of references to what has already occurred when the poem begins:

> Fro þou watʒ wroken fro vch a woþe,
> I wyste neuer quere my perle watʒ gon (ll. 375–76).

> Þow wost wel when þy perle con schede
> I watʒ ful ʒong and tender of age (ll. 411–12).

In Sections VIII to XII the word *perle* does not occur at all. The Maiden's second rebuke has the effect intended: the Dreamer is startled out of his fool's paradise and is made to recognize that submission is the only attitude appropriate to his position:

> For þoʒ þou daunce as any do,
> Braundysch and bray þy braþeʒ breme,
> When þou no fyrre may, to ne fro,
> Þou moste abyde þat he schal deme (ll. 345–48).

He apologizes for his mistakes and displays a new humility:

> Þaʒ cortaysly ʒe carp con,
> I am bot mol and manereʒ mysse (ll. 381–82).

The Maiden expresses her approval of this change:

> "Now blysse, burne, mot þe bytyde,"
> Þen sayde þat lufsoum of lyth and lere,
> "And welcum here to walk and byde,
> For now þy speche is to me dere" (ll. 397–400).

The emotional readjustment makes possible further intellectual progress, and now direct doctrinal exposition replaces symbolic development as the mode in which meaning is communicated.

The Maiden speaks discursively, making plain her position as a royal Bride of the Lamb, and employing the parable of the vineyard to explain the *cortaysye* of God by which she is granted this position. Against her the Dreamer quotes the authority of the Psalter (ll. 593ff.). She replies with a further theological explanation of grace and merit, plentifully supported with other scriptural confirmations and concluding, in the last lines of Section XII, with a reference to Matt. 19:14:

> Do way, let chylder vnto me tyʒt.
> To suche is heuenryche arayed   (ll. 718–19).

Since my chief concern is with the development of the pearl symbol, I shall not discuss any further this part of *Pearl* in which the symbolism is in abeyance and more straightforward homiletic methods of instruction are used,[18] except to mention that it contains further references to the ideas of royalty previously associated with the pearl—references which show to what extent the Dreamer remains confined by earthly notions. Thus he protests against the Maiden's claim to be a queen in heaven, saying:

> Of countes, damysel, par ma fay,
> Wer fayr in heuen to halde asstate,
> Oþer elleʒ a lady of lasse aray;
> Bot a quene! Hit is to dere a date   (ll. 489–92),

and we are reminded of his earlier attempt to express her dignity: "Her semblaunt sade for doc oþer erle" (l. 211). A countess is the wife of an earl: he is unable to conceive of hierarchy in any other than these familiar terms.

The way in which the pearl symbolism is taken up again after this long gap is of particular interest. The idea of "the kingdom of heaven," introduced by the reference to Matt. 19:14 with which Section XII concludes, is used by the Maiden as a transition to Matt. 13:45–46, in which "the kingdom of heaven" is likened to a pearl of great price:

Þer is þe blys þat con not blynne
Þat þe jueler soȝte þurȝ perré pres,
And solde alle hys goud, boþe wolen and lynne,
To bye hym a perle watȝ mascelleȝ   (ll. 729-32).

But the pearl of great price was an association with which the
symbol was given in line 272, immediately before the long homiletic interlude, and thus the pearl symbolism is taken up again
in Section XIII at precisely the point in its development at
which it was abandoned in Section V. The *jueler* of lines 252 to
301, who was then the Dreamer, is reintroduced in line 730 as
Matthew's merchant, and the scriptural reference which was
before only implicit is now made explicit. We could hardly ask
for a more striking indication that the meaning of the pearl
symbol is developed step by step along with the poem's human
drama, and that it is intended to be apprehended in this way
rather than as totally present in allegorical simultaneity from
the beginning. In the stanza which follows, the new extension of
the pearl symbolism which associates it with the kingdom of
heaven is further emphasized, and there seems to be an attempt
to gather together some of the other associations previously
accumulated by the symbol:

This makelleȝ perle, þat boȝt is dere,
Þe joueler gef fore alle hys god,
Is lyke þe reme of heuenesse clere:
So sayde þe Fader of folde and flode;
For hit is wemleȝ, clene, and clere,
And endeleȝ rounde, and blyþe of mode,
And commune to alle þat ryȝtwys were.
Lo, euen inmyddeȝ my breste hit stode.
My Lorde þe Lombe, þat schede hys blode,
He pyȝt hit þere in token of pes.
I rede þe forsake þe worlde wode
And porchace þy perle maskelles   (ll. 733-44).

"Wemleʒ, clene, and clere" reminds us of such previous phrases as "wythouten wemme" and "wythouten spot," and our attention is now again focused on the single pearl on the Maiden's breast, as it were the symbol of the symbol. But, once again, there would surely be no profit in trying to distinguish separate layers of meaning in the pearl, and to differentiate between the pearl as the Maiden and the pearl as the kingdom of heaven. These figurative senses are inextricably entangled, and any attempt to schematize them is only too likely to result in an impoverished perception of the richness of the symbolic whole.[19] The fusion of the various senses is recognized by the Dreamer in the very phrasing of the lines in which "he sums up the complex symbolism of the passage"[20] we have been discussing:

> "O maskeleʒ perle in perleʒ pure,
> Þat bereʒ," quod I, "þe perle of prys . . ."   (ll. 745–46).

There is now a return to a question discussed previously: the Dreamer again asks how the Maiden can be a Bride of the Lamb to the exclusion of all others. But he has now become more reverent and patient in his enquiry than he was before:

> Why, maskelleʒ bryd þat bryʒt con flambe,
> Þat reiateʒ hatʒ so ryche and ryf,
> Quat kyn þyng may be þat Lambe
> Þat þe wolde wedde vnto hys vyf?   (ll. 769–72).

> "Neuer þe les let be my þonc,"
> Quod I, "My perle, þaʒ I appose;
> I schulde not tempte þy wyt so wlonc,
> To Krysteʒ chambre þat art ichose"   (ll. 901–4).

This time, enlightenment is his reward. The Maiden, with frequent *confirmationes* from the Apocalypse, explains to him about the 144,000 Brides, expounds the doctrine of Christ as the sacrificial Lamb of God, and goes on to describe the New Jeru-salem. This last description includes a list of precious stones taken directly from John (Rev. 21:19–20), but there is no evi-dence that these are to be understood in any allegorical sense. It may be, of course, that the type of audience for which *Pearl* was written would be sufficiently familiar with lapidaries and scriptural commentaries for the mere naming of the stones to evoke allegorical significances. Certainly, if we wish to recapture a fourteenth-century reading of the poem, we shall do well to find out what these significances were. But it must be remem-bered that the poem itself does not indicate any particular set of significances, so that as many interpretations would be pos-sible as could be found in commentaries on the Apocalypse. This fact surely makes it clear that no such allegorical sense could be more than peripheral to the poem's meaning. The chief function of the catalog of stones is decorative, which is to say, not that it is a meaningless ornament, but that it has a *poetic* func-tion, to evoke by the normal medieval accumulative method the color and brightness of the New Jerusalem. Still following John, the Maiden adds that each of the city's twelve gates was made of "a margyrye, / A parfyt perle þat neuer fateȝ" (ll. 1037–38). And here, we may be sure, the pearl has precisely the value as a symbol which it has acquired in the poem so far.

During this long passage based on the Apocalypse there has been occurring a further, and final, development of the pearl symbol. In answering the Dreamer's question, "Quat kyn þyng may be þat Lambe?" the Maiden has referred to Christ as "My Lombe, my Lorde, my dere juelle" (l. 795); *juelle* is a term which has previously been applied to the Maiden herself—"That juel þenne in gemmeȝ gente" (l. 253)—in the section where the Dreamer is called a *jueler*. From this point onward there is a gradual movement toward the association of Christ himself with the pearl symbol. Thus as the Lamb of God he is given the pearl's whiteness and its spotlessness:

> Thys Jerusalem Lombe hade neuer pechche
> Of oþer huee bot quyt jolyf
> Þat mot ne masklle moȝt on streche,
> For wolle quyte so ronk and ryf   (ll. 841–44).

And when the Dreamer achieves his vision of the New Jerusalem, he sees the Brides of the Lamb, his own pearl among them—

> Depaynt in perleȝ and wedeȝ qwyte;
> In vchoneȝ brest watȝ bounden boun
> Þe blysful perle wyth gret delyt   (ll. 1102–4)

—and at their head the Lamb himself:

> Wyth horneȝ seuen of red golde cler;
> As praysed perleȝ his wedeȝ wasse   (ll. 1111–12).

The association of the pearl with the Lamb goes no further than this: there is never any identification of the two, and this inconclusiveness seems to me an essential element in the poem's doctrine and drama. The Dreamer has been brought to see an increasingly deeper meaning in the symbol which at the beginning of the poem appeared as a literal pearl. Its preciousness, at first thought to be transitory, has gradually been shown to transcend the merely human; but to see in the precious stone the ground of its own preciousness—to achieve the genuinely mystical experience of seeing God in a point—is denied to the Dreamer by the failure of his own patience. *Pearl* has connections with the great efflorescence of English devotional writing in the fourteenth century as much as with the tradition of secular dream poetry which goes back to the *Roman de la Rose,* but the experience of the poem does not represent a completed mystical experience. As the Dreamer rashly tries to cross the river and join the Maiden, he awakes from his dream, and his awakening returns him to the garden and pearl of the poem's opening:

> Þen wakned I in þat erber wlonk;
> My hede vpon þat hylle watȝ layde
> Þer as my perle to grounde strayd   (ll. 1171–73).

He at once laments his lack of patience and its unfortunate results:

> To þat Prynceȝ paye hade I ay bente,
> And ȝerned no more þen watȝ me gyuen,
> And halden me þer in trwe entent,
> As þe perle me prayed þat watȝ so þryuen,
> As helde, drawen to Goddeȝ present,
> To mo of his mysterys I hade ben dryuen   (ll. 1189–94).

The *mysterys* which he has failed to attain are no doubt adumbrated in the incomplete movement toward an identification of the pearl and the Lamb. However, despite its incompleteness, the Dreamer's visionary experience has a significant effect on his life in the waking world. His loss of patience in the dream situation has deprived him of a deeper insight into God's *mysterys,* but his recognition of this fact brings to him a gain of patience in his real-life situation: submitting to God's will, he now accepts positively the loss of his pearl, as he was unable to do at the beginning of the poem. "Lorde," he exclaims, "mad hit arn þat agayn þe stryuen" (l. 1199), and he goes on, summing up his experience:

> Ouer þis hyul þis lote I laȝte,
> For pyty of my perle enclyin,
> And syþen to God I hit bytaȝte
> In Krysteȝ dere blessyng and myn   (ll. 1205–8).

Though the Dreamer's visionary experience is incomplete, the dramatic possibilities of his initial situation have been brought to a satisfying conclusion. The body of the poem has taken the form of a dramatic process in which symbolic development has gone along with human development, and which we are able to act out imaginatively for ourselves as often as we read it. It is this process, and not merely the doctrine embodied in it, which gives *Pearl*—the poem and the symbol—its lasting value.

Sir Gawain

Cotton MS. Nero A. x., folio 90b

··✲[6]✲··

The Two Confession Scenes in
Sir Gawain and the Green Knight

JOHN BURROW

On the last of the three days of hunting and temptation which
occupy the third fit of *Sir Gawain and the Green Knight*,
Gawain, having accepted the gift of the lady's girdle, rises and
goes to the castle chapel. On the two preceding days, like Bertilak, he has gone to Mass. This time, however, while Bertilak
again attends hunter's Mass, Gawain goes instead to confession:

> Syþen cheuely to þe chapel choses he þe waye,
> Preuely aproched to a prest, and prayed hym þere
> Þat he wolde lyfte his lyf and lern hym better
> How his sawle schulde be saued when he schuld seye heþen.
> Þere he schrof hym schyrly and schewed his mysdedez
> Of þe more and þe mynne, and merci besechez,

Reprinted by permission of the author and The University of Chicago
Press from *Modern Philology*, LVII (1959), 73–79. Copyright © 1959 by The
University of Chicago Press.
    For other studies of moral theology in *Gawain*, see David Farley Hills,
"Gawain's Fault in *Sir Gawain and the Green Knight*," *RES*, XIV (1963),
124–31; George J. Engelhardt, "The Predicament of Gawain," *MLQ*, XVI
(1955), 218–25; and G. V. Smithers, "What *Sir Gawain and the Green Knight*
Is About," *Medium Ævum*, XXXII (1963), 171–89.

And of absolucioun he on þe segge calles;
And he asoyled hym surely and sette hym so clene
As domeȝday schulde haf ben diȝt on þe morn   (ll. 1876–84).[1]

In comparison with the earlier temptation scenes, this scene is brief and unobtrusive; but it is significant because it serves to introduce a theme which is to play an important part in the rest of the poem—the theme of *penance.*

This theme has, it is true, already made its appearance, before the scene of Gawain's confession, in a passing reference to "crabbed lentoun þat fraysteȝ flesch wyth þe fysche and fode more symple," and in the account of the entertainment of Gawain at Bertilak's castle on the fast day of Christmas Eve; but in these passages "penance" is presented as no more than a traditional public observance which good wine and cooking can mitigate:

"Þis penaunce now ȝe take,
And eft hit schal amende."
Þat mon much merþe con make
For wyn in his hed þat wende   (ll. 897–900).

So, in the dinner scene from which these lines come, there is more of "merþe" than of "penaunce" (Gawain even calls the meal a "feast"); and it is in keeping with the festal character of the scenes at the courts of Arthur and Bertilak that this should be so.

The confession scene between Gawain and the priest is different, for here we are introduced to a kind of "penaunce," the sacrament of penance, which is not gregarious or festive; and this, unlike the observance of public fasts, represents something new and important in the poem. The introduction of this scene at this point marks, in fact, the beginning of a shift in balance which is to carry the poem out of the public world of mirth into the private world of penance. Its function is proleptic, inasmuch as it anticipates the main penitential theme of the fourth fit.

At the same time it is very far from giving a full statement of that theme, though, to see exactly how this is, one must look at the scene rather closely. On first reading it seems simple and straightforward enough—Gawain confesses his sins "schyrly" (completely, without omission) and receives from the priest complete absolution:

> he asoyled hym surely and sette hym so clene
> As domezday schulde haf ben dizt on þe morn.

Yet the modern reader, reading these lines, may notice an irony behind this, seemingly hypothetical, reference to a doomsday "on þe morn" (that is, of New Year's Day, when Gawain is to suffer the "dome of my wyrdes" [l. 1968]); and a medieval reader, more certainly, would have seen the general implication which this irony reflects. To such a reader it would have been clear, I think, that Gawain was not "clene" and that the priest's absolution was invalid.

W. A. Pantin has observed that "the correct use of the sacrament of penance is a theme which dominates or underlies most of the religious literature of the thirteenth and fourteenth centuries."[2] As a result of the proliferation of such writings (Chaucer's *Parson's Tale* is a well-known example), any audience in this period was certain to be familiar with at least something of the theory of the sacrament, either directly from the treatises themselves or, more commonly, through sermons. A fourteenth-century layman would know that a "right shrift" depended on a number of necessary conditions (what Robert Mannyng calls "poynts of shryfte"), without which the priest's absolution was invalid. He would also know that one of the fundamental "points" was that effective absolution depended as much on the penitent's "disposition" as on the correct observance of external forms. So the *Pupilla oculi*, a representative treatise of the 1380's:

Non enim sacerdos efficaciter absoluit, nisi reus sit in se debito modo dispositus ut sit capax absolutionis; quia sacramentum exterius est signum interioris absolutionis que nullo modo communicatur sine vera dispositione in mente interius absoluendi.[3]

In another fourteenth-century work, Bromyard's *Summa predicantium,* we find this necessary inner disposition conveniently analyzed. The author describes the "modus seu dispositio requisita ex parte confitentis" as follows:

Haec autem dispositio debet esse quod doleat commissa . . .; secundo quod restituat ablata; tertio quod promittat cessare, et ut de hoc pleniorem faciat fidem quod fugiat peccati occasiones . . . In tam necessario opere [he comments] nisi bene disponatur, maximum imminet periculum.[4]

These contemporary quotations are, I think, sufficient to suggest how Gawain's confession is to be interpreted. We are meant to see that Gawain takes part in the "sacramentum exterius"—the verbal forms of confession and absolution—without being "capax absolutionis." He goes to confession, rather than to Mass, because he realizes that he has sinned in agreeing to conceal the gift of the girdle from Bertilak, against his promise; but, though, presumably, he confesses this, he neither makes restitution ("restituat ablata") by returning the girdle nor resolves to sin no more ("promittat cessare"). It is, on the contrary, clear from what follows that his intention to conceal the girdle from the host is never in doubt—he has no intention either of returning it to the lady or of giving it up, according to his promise, to the host. This fact is quite enough to invalidate a confession, according to all contemporary writers on the subject:

Non dimittitur peccatum nisi restituatur ablatum, si restitui potest. . . . Oportet ergo ut de omnibus rebus iniuriose acquisitis fiat restitutio. Vel ad minus quam habeat firmum propositum restituendi si quid ab alio iniuriose ablatum est, antequam valeat satisfactio sacramentalis.[5]

This reading of the confession scene is supported in several ways by what follows. First, the failure of Gawain's confession to "lerne hym better" appears immediately in the following scene of the New Year's Eve festivities, with which the third fit ends. Gawain, believing his life to be saved by the lady's girdle, and his soul by the priest's absolution, "mace hym as mery among þe fre ladyes . . . As neuer he did bot þat daye"; but the presence of a feeling of guilt behind this gaiety is clearly, though obliquely, suggested in the scene of the exchange of winnings. Whereas on the first two days the host has called Gawain into the hall (from a chamber where he has been sitting with the ladies, as it can be inferred) and offered his winnings first, this time he finds Gawain already waiting for him in the hall, "fire upon flet, þe freke þer byside," and it is Gawain, meeting Bertilak "inmyddeȝ þe flore," who offers his winnings first. The suggestion of bad conscience in this, though faint, is confirmed in the following conversation, where Gawain for the first time shies away from the host's pleasantries and hastily changes the subject:

> "Inoȝ," quoþ Sir Gawayn,
> "I þonk yow, bi þe rodc"   (ll. 1948–49).[6]

Again, it is an assumption in the action of the fourth fit that Gawain is not "clene" and that his absolution, like the green girdle itself, is of no power to save him, though it is implied that a true act of penance (which would have involved the yielding-up of the girdle, as we have seen), like a real magic belt, *would* have saved him. It is because his act of penance was imperfect that "maximum imminet periculum."

Last, the interpretation given above of the scene between Gawain and the priest is confirmed by the occurrence at a crucial point in the action of the fourth fit of a second confession scene which complements and, as it were, completes the first at exactly that point at which we have seen it to be deficient. I refer to the

scene between Gawain and the Green Knight after the delivery
of the three blows—or, more precisely, to the exchanges between
them which immediately follow the Green Knight's revelation
that he was Gawain's host at the castle (ll. 2369–94). This scene
follows, clearly though informally, the pattern of the confessional, with Gawain again the penitent and the Green Knight
playing the part of confessor. It is easy to detect the sequence
of the three "acts" of the penitent (contrition, confession, and
satisfaction) when Gawain 's contrition ("schome") leads him to
confess (ll. 2379–86) and to offer satisfaction (l. 2387);[7] and the
point is put beyond doubt by the Green Knight's reply, in which
he uses the two terms "confess" and "penance":

> I halde hit hardily hole, þe harme þat I hade;
> Þou art confessed so clene, beknowen of þy mysses,
> And hatȝ þe penaunce apert of þe poynt of myn egge,
> I halde þe polysed of þat plyȝt and pured as clene
> As þou hadeȝ neuer forfeted syþen þou watȝ fyrst borne
>   (ll. 2390–4).[8]

It will be noticed that the last two lines of this passage, in
which the Green Knight "absolves" Gawain, resemble in their
structure the lines used earlier to describe the priest's absolution:

> he asoyled hym surely and sette hym so clene
> As domeȝday schulde haf ben diȝt on þe morn.

The echo may well be unconscious, but it suggests that the two
confession scenes were in some way connected with each other in
the poet's mind, and this view is confirmed if one reads the
passages side by side. What emerges from such a reading, in fact,
is the conviction that the two scenes are intended to form a
contrasting pair. Each has what the other lacks. In the scene
with the Green Knight the emphasis lies on Gawain's "vera
dispositio," as Bromyard defined this phrase—on his contrition

("doleat commissa"), his desire to make restitution to the Green Knight ("restituat ablata"), and his resolve to sin no more ("efte I schal be ware"—"promittat cessare")—and it is exactly that which is missing in the earlier scene. There it was the "sacramentum exterius" which held the stage, and the scene passed without any suggestion of the intensely felt sense of personal guilt and responsibility which Gawain displays in the fourth fit. Conversely, the external conditions of the sacrament are not satisfied in the second scene as they are in the first. The Green Knight is not a priest, and so is not able to absolve Gawain, though he can forgive him.

At this point, however, theological terms are no longer appropriate, for the Green Knight is a figure from the world not of theology but of poetic myth. Like the Minos of Dante's *Inferno,* he is a "conoscitor delle peccata"[9] ("Now know I wel þy cosses and þy costes als"), and, like Minos, he lacks clear theological credentials because his origin is non-Christian. It is partly for this reason that it would be wrong to look for any dogmatic or polemical intention in the contrast which we have noted between the two confession scenes. It is true that the fourteenth century saw much controversy on the subject of the sacrament of penance—on the relative significance of the external forms and the inner "disposition," the conditions under which confession to a layman was valid, etc.—and the poem probably reflects this controversy; but it is certainly not intended as a contribution to it. Here *Piers Plowman* provides a point of contrast. In the *Visio of* Langland's poem, as Miss Hort has pointed out, there are, again, two confession scenes—Lady Mede's "shameless" confession to the friar (III, 36–54) and the confession of the Seven Deadly Sins to Repentance (V, 61 ff.)—and they are related to each other by contrast in a way which recalls *Gawain.* But Langland's presentation of the issues *is* polemical. His handling of the "sacramentum exterius" in the scene between Lady

Mede and the corrupt friar, for example, leaves no doubt of his intentions; and there is no difficulty in seeing, with Miss Hort, that he "took the subjective, ethical view of the sacrament of penance rather than the objective, forensic view." The *Gawain* poet would probably have accepted Langland's emphasis on "sorow of synne" as "savacioun of soules"; but I do not think it possible, or necessary, to define his position in the contemporary penitential controversy, as Miss Hort defines Langland's, because his poem is not directed toward a polemical conclusion.[10]

Nevertheless, it does reach a kind of "conclusion," though not a polemical one, in its handling of penance; and this we may now consider.

We have spoken so far as though the last part of the poem were concerned only with Gawain's private contrition; but this is clearly not the case. It is true that, if we compare this part of the poem with what has gone before (as we have been comparing Gawain's second with his first confession), it is Gawain's intensely conveyed private sense of guilt which stands out, because it is that which is distinctive of the closing scenes. Gawain, however, is not alone in these scenes. He shares the knowledge of his guilt, first, with the Green Knight, as we have seen, and then, finally, with Arthur and his court; and he does *public* penance for it. The effect of this is curious. In one way it strengthens the penitential theme; for it was one of the most powerful commonplaces of penitential writings that sins unrepented or unconfessed on earth would be revealed to all on the Day of Judgment—"Men sholden eek remembren hem of the shame that is to come at the day of doom to hem that been nat penitent and shryven in this present lyf. For alle the creatures in hevene, in erthe, and in helle shullen seen apertly al that they hyden in this world"[11]—and it seems probable that the circumstances under which Gawain discovers that "non may hyden his harme" would have evoked this idea in the mind of a contemporary reader.

At the same time, by basing the closing scenes of his poem on this penitential commonplace, the poet achieves another, quite different, effect. Gawain's fault, by being known to others, is thrown open to their judgment; and it is noticeable that this judgment does not agree with Gawain's. He sees his sin as grievous:

> Now I am fawty and false, and ferde haf ben euer
> Of trecherye and untrawþe . . .   (ll. 2382–83);

but the Green Knight praises him as "on þe fautlest freke þat euer on fote ʒede," minimizes his fault (ll. 2366–68), and even laughs (l. 2389) at the end of his passionate confession; and the same attitude is to be found in Arthur and his court:

> Þe kyng comfortez þe knyʒt, and alle þe court als
> Laʒen loude þerat . . .   (ll. 2513–14).

The laughter of the Green Knight and of Arthur's court is unexpected, like many things in the poem; but its effect is, I think, carefully calculated and delicate. It serves to modify the penitential tone of the ending by reintroducing something of the "mirth" of the earlier fits and so to establish a kind of emotional equilibrium. It is this equilibrium which is delicate. Both Bertilak and the knights of Arthur's court, of course, accept the Christian and courtly values for which Gawain stands and admire him as an exemplary representative of these values. Their attitude to him is not meant to be taken as either frivolous or satirical. Nevertheless, it is hard to read these last scenes without feeling that the mirth does, in some sense, reflect on Gawain and that it is there because it furnishes some sort of corrective to an extravagance in him.

Speaking: in attacking women Gawain is rejecting cortaysye.. the whole courtly system ~~bass~~ of behaviour based on devot to women. He knows from experience how fragile a defence Xnity adulterated by cortaysye provdes ... when he returns to Camelot, however, he finds out those who have not shared his experience do not understand it. the courtiers take the girdle, not as a bridge of shame, but as a badge of honour. By the end of the poem, Gawain is both wiser & sadder, & the gaiety of Camelot has come to seem rather shallow.

That this was the author's intention is suggested by a small but significant feature of the fourth fit which may be noticed here. At the beginning of the fit, in the account of Gawain's arming on the morning of New Year's Day, the following curious passage occurs (Gawain has just put the girdle around his waist):

> Bot wered not þis ilk wyȝe for wele þis gordel,
> For pryde of þe pendaunteȝ, þaȝ polyst þay were,
> And þaȝ þe glyterande golde glent vpon endeȝ,
> Bot for to sauen hymself . . .   (ll. 2037–40).

This passage is oddly gratuitous; there seems no reason why the author should go out of his way to exclude a motive which the reader is hardly likely to have thought of ascribing to Gawain under the circumstances. One might be tempted to dismiss the lines as an aberration, if it were not that the same point is twice repeated, first by the Green Knight in his "judgment" of Gawain:

> . . . here yow lakked a lyttel, sir, and lewte yow wonted;
> Bot þat watȝ for no wylyde werke, ne wowyng nauþer,
> Bot for ȝe lufed your lyf . . .   (ll. 2366–68),[12]

and a second time by Gawain himself when, a little later, he accepts the gift of the girdle from the Green Knight:

> "Bot your gordel" quoþ Gawayn "God yow forȝelde!
> Þat wyl I welde wyth guod wylle, not for þe wynne golde,
> Ne þe saynt, ne þe sylk, ne þe syde pendaundes,
> For wele ne for worchyp, ne for þe wlonk werkkeȝ,
> Bot in syngne of my surfet . . ."   (ll. 2429–33).

The clue to the intention behind these passages is, I believe, to be found in Gawain's confession to the Green Knight. Here, in a semi-allegorical style which recalls the didactic literature

of the period, he formally confesses to three faults—"cowardyse,"
"couetyse," and "untrawþe" (or "trecherye"):

> For care of þy knokke cowardyse me taȝt
> To acorde me with couetyse, my kynde to forsake
> Þat is larges and lewte þat longeȝ to knyȝteȝ.
> Now I am fawty and falce, and ferde haf ben euer
> Of trecherye and untrawþe . . .   (ll. 2379–83).

The point is that Gawain here—and twice elsewhere in the closing scenes[13]—confesses to covetousness (and correspondingly dis-
avows it in accepting Bertilak's gift a little later); whereas the
poet and Bertilak, in his role of "conoscitor delle peccata," both
explicitly rule it out, as we have seen. That is, he confesses three
times to a sin which the poem twice authoritatively asserts that
he did not commit. The fact would hardly have escaped contemporary readers, who were accustomed, both from sermons
and from the literature and practice of the confessional, to the
exact analysis of moral behavior. They must have seen that it
was Bertilak's rather than Gawain's version which was the right
one and that Gawain's remorse was, to that extent, extravagant.
[But see pp. 135–6 of my *Reading of Sir Gawain and the Green
Knight* (London, 1965).—J. B.]

That this should be so gives a kind of sanction to the laughter
of Bertilak and Arthur's knights; for they are right—Gawain is
"on þe fautlest freke þat euer on fote ȝede." But, exactly because
Gawain is a hero, the violence of his remorse is itself heroic; and
so the poem ends, not in a victory of Good Sense over Enthusi-
asm, or—in its own terms—of Mirth over Penance, but rather
in a graceful blending of the two, through the symbolism of the
girdle, worn both by the knights as an emblem of their brotherhood and by Gawain as an emblem of his guilt. In this way the
penitential theme, with which I have been concerned in this
essay, is worked back into the traditional Arthurian setting,

without being lost in it. The girdle may be meant to suggest the Garter; but, as the "bende of blame," it also forms part of the traditional iconography of penance:

> About þy nekke hanggeþ a wyþþe
> Þat haþ þe departed fro Goddys gryþþe.
> Þy self beryst þan on þy bak
> Þy vyle synne þat makeþ þe blak.
> May none fro þat dome þe borrowe
> But ȝyf hyt be with byttyr sorowe.[14]

··❧[7]❧··

Morgan le Fay in *Sir Gawain and the Green Knight*

ALBERT B. FRIEDMAN

"Le joyau de la littérature anglaise du moyen âge," as Gaston Paris called *Sir Gawain and the Green Knight*,[1] is obviously flawed in one crucial passage. When the giant has brought his ax down for the third time and cut a token gash in Gawain's neck, the hero bounds away from the block, and, after his temper has cooled, hears in astonished relief the Green Knight's explanation of why he had come to court to challenge Arthur's knights. The ancient lady of the castle, now revealed to be Morgan le Fay, was behind the whole adventure. She it was who had sent the Green Knight (in human guise, Bercilak the Hautdesert) to Arthur's court, her purpose being to test the renown of the Round Table and to frighten Guinevere to death. "Every reader," says Kittredge, "finds [the object assigned for Bercilak's visit to court] unsatisfactory. It is the one weak spot in the

Reprinted by permission of the author and The Mediaeval Academy of America from *Speculum*, XXXV (1960), 260–74.

See also T. McAlindon, "Magic, Fate, and Providence in Medieval Narrative and *Sir Gawain and the Green Knight*," *RES*, XVI (1965), 121–39.

superb English romance."[2] For so elaborate an adventure, the initiating motive does indeed seem surprisingly slight and vague. In the result, Guinevere was not fatally shocked and Morgan did not succeed in humiliating Arthur by proving that his leading knight lacked the virtues of knighthood. Though Morgan's evil plans were defeated, her discomfiture is neither dramatized nor even made explicit. Once the reader has entered into the spirit of the fairy tale machinery and accepted with credulity the monstrous challenger who demonstrates his supernatural powers by speaking from his severed head, the remaining events follow conventionally. Kittredge calls Morgan "the moving cause . . . of the entire plot,"[3] but here he is deferring tentatively to the Green Knight's statement. After considering her role more closely, Kittredge describes her rather as an intrusion, an attempt by the English poet to draw his story more solidly into the Arthurian tradition. Hulbert, whose analysis of the sources of the legend differs so widely from Kittredge's, also holds that Morgan is a substitution and excrescent.[4]

Recently the question of Morgan le Fay's function in the poem has been revived by Professor Denver E. Baughan, who argues that her role has been completely misunderstood.[5] The Green Knight's explanation of the dynamics of the adventure is altogether valid. According to Professor Baughan, Morgan's plan to humiliate the Round Table and frighten Guinevere does in fact succeed. A high purpose of hers has been realized in Gawain's lapse from strict virtue. Indeed, she had foreseen the outcome. More important: Morgan's presence in the poem, far from being unnecessary or imperfectly worked into the narrative fabric, as Kittredge and many of the older commentators believed, is actually an ingenious device for giving thematic integrity to the poem. In support of these views, Professor Baughan has shown dangerous unfamiliarity with romance conventions in general and Arthurian romance in particular and has badly misinterpreted the poem. In this essay I shall combat his reading of *Sir Gawain* and his analysis of Morgan's part in it and then proceed to sketch what seems to me a far more tenable explanation for the poet's introduction of Morgan.

I

Arthur's humiliation, for Baughan, occurs in the first episode of the poem, the New Year's banquet at Camelot. Upon this splendid scene bursts the monstrous Green Knight and asks for the ruler of the company, all the while scanning the banqueters to see "quo walt þer most renoun."[6] The intent of this examination, says Baughan, is to embarrass Arthur, "for while the knights were turning their eyes toward" the king, "Bercilak's eyes were turning everywhere except toward Arthur" (p. 244). "Powerless to resist Bercilak's insults to the king, the knights become more and more afraid" (p. 244). The poet, however, less sensitive about Arthur's honor, does not feel that insults have been passed. He attributes the court's speechless fright to their absorption in the appearance of the monster; furthermore he excuses the knights' silence by saying it was not entirely fear that kept them silent but politeness somewhat: protocol demanded that only the king answer. Arthur welcomes the Green Knight, introduces himself, and hearing that the visitor wants to indulge in some game, assures him that he will not be disappointed if he craves battle. To Baughan Arthur's proposal is petulantly bellicose and inept: "Since the knights had been wondering how any man could survive the blows of such a giant and why he had not equipped himself for battle, the poet seems to have intended the beheading episode as an antidote to the follies of knight-errantry" (p. 245). To imply that our poet, for all his moral earnestness, could find anything foolish in the casual challenges and joustings, which are among the chief hap-

penings in romances, is to foist upon him an Ariosto-like attitude that would have disqualified him from writing this poem.
In a later passage, when Gawain is setting out from Camelot for
the Green Chapel, the poet shows us courtiers of little faith
lamenting the hopelessness of Gawain's undertaking by way of
dramatizing its perils and Gawain's bravery, and it is clear that
he regards such low-minded folk with disdain.

The Green Knight now divulges his peaceful Yule sport: he
offers to allow any one of the knights present—not specifically
Arthur—to chop off his head with the ax he carries, providing
the knight will contract to seek him out a year hence to receive
the same blow in return. The assemblage after hearing this proposal is depressed into even deeper gloom than before. The
silence is broken by the Green Knight's taunts:

> "What, is þis Arþureȝ hous," quoþ þe haþel þenne,
> "Þat al þe rous rennes of þurȝ ryalmes so mony?
> Where is now your sourquydrye and your conquestes,
> Your gryndellayk and your greme, and your grete wordes?
> Now is þe reuel and þe renoun of þe Rounde Table
> Ouerwalt wyth a worde of on wyȝes speche,
> For al dares for drede withoute dynt schewed!"   (ll. 309 ff.).

These words fire the king with shame and anger, but it is not
the helpless shame he might feel if he were conceding the truth
of the Green Knight's remarks, but rather angry shame that the
court's momentary fright could discredit its long-standing reputation. Here called "dauntless by nature" and earlier "never
afraid" (l. 251), Arthur steps from the dais and takes up the ax.
His opponent has meanwhile alighted.

> Now hatȝ Arthure his axe, and þe halme grypeȝ,
> And sturnely stureȝ hit aboute, þat stryke wyth hit þoȝt.
> Þe stif mon hym bifore stod vpon hyȝt.
> Herre þen ani in þe hous by þe hede and more.
> Wyth sturne schere þer he stod he stoked his berde,

And wyth a countenaunce dryȝe he droȝ doun his cote,
No more mate ne dismayd for hys mayn dinteȝ
Þen any burne vpon bench hade broȝt hym to drynk of wyne
(ll. 330 ff.).

According to Baughan's understanding of this passage, Arthur actually strikes the Green Knight two or more "great blows," though they fail to make an impression on the giant. Gawain interrupts the proceedings to beg that the contest may be his, a request to which Arthur, with the advice of his nobles, consents. Gawain's blow of course severs the Green Knight's head from his trunk and sends it rolling along the floor.

The crux of the passage is whether Arthur in fact struck the blows. Baughan insists that he did:

> In order to make assurance doubly sure regarding the second half of Morgan le Fay's plan, Arthur had to strike. Yet, through respect for the divinity that hedges a king, even a debased one (as Arthur was at this time), the poet gave to the account something of Morgan's magic so that it seems almost as if Arthur did not strike. Thus because of the deceptive wording (particularly *þat stryke wyth hit poȝt*), Tolkien and Gordon, Hulbert and Kittredge undoubtedly read *mayn dinteȝ* as "threats" or "threatened blows." On the other hand, G. H. Gerould and B. J. Whiting both read the two words in question according to the definitions set down in [the dictionaries] and (curiously enough) Tolkien and Gordon's gloss, i.e., as "great blows" or the equivalent (p. 246).

Citing the Green Knight's comment on Morgan's power late in the poem, he asks:

> What would have been the point then of having Arthur merely prepare to strike? To achieve her purpose not only did the so-called greatest of all the knights have to strike with great strokes, but his great strokes had to avail him nothing. On the other hand, his nephew's one stroke had to do the task with what seems perfect justice (p. 247).

But Arthur did not strike.

For the meaning of *mayn dinteȝ,* one need not ransack the dictionaries: the phrase means simply "great blows." The authorities read "threats" or "threatened blows" because they are, with sound instinct, carrying forward the hypothetical overtones which reverberate from the poet's earlier *þat stryke wyth hit poȝt.* Gollancz's edition suggests that the *mayn dinteȝ* were blows that Arthur was "about to give."[7] If Baughan thinks that Gerould or Whiting stand with him, he is deceived. Gerould renders *mayn dinteȝ* as "strokes," and his phrasing has the force of qualifying the *dinteȝ* into feints;[8] and Whiting, who translates "great blows," to be sure,[9] has told me that if he had thought anyone could possibly have squeezed the meaning from his translation that Baughan has, he would have forestalled the error with an emphatic note.

Clearly—but apparently not so—the poet is saying that Arthur brandished the ax, making several test blows with it in the air to get the "feel" of the massive weapon. There are, further, overwhelming dramatic and semantic reasons for ruling out Baughan's interpretations. For one thing *dinteȝ* is plural: the contract called for a single blow. Would Arthur cheat? And in the presence of the whole court? Secondly, if one reads the lines carefully, he will observe that the Green Knight started pulling down his coat to receive the proffered blow *after* Arthur had made the troublesome *mayn dinteȝ.* Moreover, to have Arthur literally strike the Green Knight is dramatically impossible. Arthur's unavailing blow would have thrown the banqueters into another fit of amazement, which does not occur; and surely if the poet had intended to contrast the impotence of the physical Arthur with the efficacy of the spiritual Gawain, he would have spared at least a few lines (remembering the eighty lines on the Green Knight and his equipage) to point up the contrast and not fumble it away in a phrase. One must add that Arthur's granting the contest to Gawain is not to be taken as a sign of surrender or cowardice. He has demonstrated his bravery by his willingness to undertake the adventure; kings in romances were expected as a matter of course to delegate such tasks to their henchmen. Indeed, in one of the earliest analogues of this story, the king is expressly excepted from those allowed to take up the challenge.[10]

Another part of Morgan's plan was to "frighten Guinevere to death." Guinevere does not die, but perhaps Bercilak is being hyperbolic. Did the monster even frighten Guinevere in any significant way? Baughan takes strong exception to Kittredge's observation that "there is no indication, in our author's own description of the scene at court, that Guinevere showed any particular alarm."[11] True, Arthur turns to comfort his queen once the Green Knight has withdrawn, gory head in hand, but he takes the time to frame his words elegantly, and from the cheerful style he adopts, it is plain that he is not dealing with a woman in a state of shock. In the *Vulgate Lancelot* there is a scene roughly similar to the beheading episode. A damsel sent by Morgan falsely announces Lancelot's death and says that he confessed before dying to adulterous relations with the queen. As a token of her veracity, the damsel tosses in Guinevere's lap Lancelot's ring—*"cest anel par cui vous donastes a lui vostre cuer & vostre amour"*—at which the queen shows great distress, swoons away, and is only with difficulty recalled to her senses.[12] Our passage has nothing comparable, though Morgan supposedly intended Guinevere's fright to be fatal.

"Arthur's attempt to console Guinevere in her fear and his attempt and failure to behead Bercilak" impress Baughan as "two important pieces of internal evidence" that Morgan's plans for the beheading episode were successful (p. 248). I trust I have demonstrated that both these items of evidence are based on misreading of the text.

II

We now come to Baughan's major proposition: that Morgan's plan and its alleged success contribute vitally to the thematic integrity of *Sir Gawain*. If her plan, he insists, is to be "artistically successful," that virtue which allows Gawain to succeed in beheading the Green Knight after Arthur failed must be the same as that he exhibits in the Temptation scenes. The unifying virtue, therefore, is chastity, and to accept chastity as the theme of romance, opens the way to understanding its moral content and the role of Morgan le Fay:

> In a court where even the king himself, as portrayed in the secular romances, was guilty of moral looseness, the opportunity for the poet to capitalize on Gawain's essential goodness in this virtue, even at the expense of the king's humiliation, was without parallel. . . . In connection with [Morgan], this "only begetter" of the entire plot, as Kittredge calls her, it is inconceivable that the poet should have viewed her as a cheap enchantress. Except for her enmity toward Guinevere her plan and her fame as a healer are in the best traditions of the theurgic art as opposed to the goetic practices of that time. As Arthur would one day "fare to Avalun, to the fairest of all maidens, to Argante [Morgan] the queen, an elf most fair . . ." who would make his wounds all sound, so here that same Morgan would send Bercilak to purge and heal the court of its moral corruptness. . . . Thus through Morgan le Fay's plan the beheading episode is no less an apotheosization of chastity than are the other parts of the romance (p. 251).

A number of wonderful assertions are embedded in this statement. For convenience, I shall divide Baughan's remarks into two major sets of ideas and discuss each set separately. The first may be fairly summarized as follows: In the beheading episode Gawain succeeded where Arthur failed because Gawain represents the knight of chastity, but Arthur was guilty of moral looseness, specifically adultery. Arthur's failure was personally humiliating and shameful to his court.

Our analysis of the beheading episode revealed that the contest between Arthur and Gawain staged there by Baughan did not take place. There was no test for Arthur to fail and consequently no shame in his non-failure. But for purposes of argument, let us put this objection aside and also temporarily go along with the notion that the *Gawain* poet—like Spenser for each book of *The Faerie Queene*—intended the adventure he was narrating to illustrate the practical and moral force of a particular knightly virtue—chastity. How well actually does the Gollancz epithet "knight of chastity" apply to Sir Gawain?

For Tennyson, whose Gawain is a "light-of-love," the faithless libertine who betrayed Pelleas, it would not do at all, and Tennyson's portrait is not far out of line with Malory's Gawain and completely in accord with the thirteenth-century French romances of the Round Table, especially the interminable Vulgate prose versions. In certain of them, as Whiting has fully shown, our hero is "painstakingly vilified," and not least for suave amorousness.[13] He is in and out of bed with so many complaisant damsels – not to mention his fairy mistresses—that it is surprising that more of his bastards, among whom are the hero of *Wigalois* and Gingelein of *Libeaus Desconsus,* do not turn up. One good mark in Gawain's favor is that, unlike Lancelot and Tristram, he does not participate in sustained adulterous connections, though Whiting finds it hazardous to say that he was never guilty of adultery "in view of the number of women with whom Gawain is intimate" (p. 203). That Gawain may well have had a reputation as a lecher in fourteenth-century England is suggested by the Wife of Bath's Tale, for pieces like the analogous romance of the *Weddynge of Sir Gawain and Dame Ragnell* and the ballad of "The Marriage of Sir Gawain" (Child No. 31) imply that the "lusty bacheler" of Arthur's court who took the maiden "by

verray force" was probably the degenerate Gawain, although
Chaucer of course does not name him.

But whether or not Gawain's reputation was already be-
smirched in English romance or in popular story when the *Sir
Gawain* poet wrote, he could not have been unacquainted with
the Gawain of the French romances. Kittredge indeed assures us
that he was thoroughly familiar with the "ins and outs" of the
Arthurian saga (p. 132). It would be foolish of course to assert
that the poet was required to reproduce the portrait of Gawain
which tradition gave him, but it would be equally foolish of
course to deny that the poet's invention was to some extent inhibited by the associations with which he knew his readers'
minds to be furnished. Obviously the Gawain in our poem is not
a "light-of-love," yet it is still hard to see him as the champion
of chastity. And surely it would have been perverse of our poet
to select as his "knight of chastity" that one of the principal
knights of Arthur's who was notoriously the least chaste!

If chastity is important anywhere in the poem, it is in the
Temptation scenes, and it is extremely doubtful that chastity
is being tested even there. Thanks to the poet's skill in reporting
during the bedroom conversations not only the speeches of
Gawain and the lady but also his thoughts and dreams, we come
to know Gawain's processes of mind intimately, and for that
reason can decide definitely what is at stake in the Temptation.
The preservation of his chastity is clearly only a secondary concern to Gawain, if present in his mind at all. Hardly for a moment does he feel himself drawn toward his temptress in a
passionate way. He kisses her with no greater fervor than he
renders up the kisses to her husband in the evening. Under pres-
sure he has acquiesced in becoming the lady's courtly servant,
but it is only after the lady has appealed to his duty as her
newly contracted knight and to his reputation as a past master
of courtesy that he can be prevailed upon to bestow even per-

functory kisses. And though compelled to dally, he is scarcely in the mood for dalliance. As we are reminded at crucial points by the poet, Gawain's anxiety as to the outcome of the ordeal he must shortly undergo deprives him of all pleasure in the lady's flirtatious banter:

> "Þaȝ I were burde bryȝtest," þe burde in mynde hade,
> "Þe lasse luf in his lode"—for lur þat hc soȝt
> > boute hone,
> Þe dunte þat schulde hym deue,
> And nedeȝ hit most be done   (ll. 1283 ff.).

And as if Gawain's tension were not already sufficiently acute to prevent the lady's teasing from arousing an answering ardor in him, there is the additional inhibition of the bond Gawain has contracted with the host to yield up each evening his earnings of the day. Even supposing that Gawain entertained no fears about the appointment at the Green Chapel and had found himself susceptible to the erotic wiles of his temptress, he would still have been severely inhibited by his loyalty to his bond and his sense of honor from taking his hostess. If a test of chastity was the poet's purpose, he has certainly managed to drain it of any challenge, for Gawain's temptation is accompanied by circumstances which make it singularly untempting.

The girdle or lovelace the lady forces Gawain to accept at their last session would seem on the surface the key prop in a chastity drama, but one must remember that Gawain accepts it only because of its alleged magical properties and to be quit of the nagging importunities of his hostess. But though Gawain wants the girdle as an amulet, it is not simply because it is an amulet that he cannot yield it up to his host as their bond requires. The girdle is also, of course, a sexual trophy; the lord would surely draw damaging inferences (so Gawain would naturally think) from Gawain's possessing it. Thus it could be argued that the poet wanted us to understand that Gawain failed to carry out his pledge not only out of fear but also in order to spare his host unnecessary hurt and to protect the lady's reputation, which as her knight and a man of honor he had promised to do. In this conflict of duties, chastity has no part.*

Mr. Baughan's second body of contentions is even more curious. Morgan le Fay, he claims, is no "cheap enchantress"—she is a goddess doing the holy work of healing. She sends the Green Knight to Camelot not out of petty envy for the renown of the Round Table but to "purge and heal the court of its moral corruptness."

Sycorax and Prospero, goetic and theurgic magic, have been strangely confounded in this interpretation. It is true that the chroniclers, who were most concerned with the twilight of British rule, with Arthur's battles, mysterious demise and afterlife, picture Morgan waiting to heal her brother when he is finally wafted to Avalon. Such is her role in the *Vita Merlini,* her first appearance in literature. But "in all other episodes of the romances in which she is associated with [Arthur] . . . except in late sources, she is the perpetrator of some malign scheme against him."[14] As Malory puts it, extending Morgan's persistent hatred of Arthur, the "ruling motive of her career," to Arthur's knights, "And ever as she myght she made warre on kynge Arthure, and all daungerous knyghtes she wytholdyth with her for to dystroy all those knyghtes that kynge Arthure lovyth."[15] That the *Gawain* poet sees Morgan in the same light should be sufficiently evident from his references to her envy of Arthur's court and her hatred of Guinevere. By speaking of her as a goddess, the poet deepens the sinister gloom about her: a pagan goddess becomes automatically a Christian demon. One also notes that Morgan was instructed in magic by Merlin during a love affair between them. Here the poet associates Morgan with Niniane/

---

* Note also that chastity is not specifically mentioned in the long passage (ll. 619–699) which discusses the symbolism of the pentangle.

Viviane, the mistress who wheedled Merlin's secrets out of him and then used them wickedly against her instructor.[16] Further evidence that the poet intends Morgan to be fixed in our minds as an evil enchantress is his stress on the ancient dame's ugliness, cruelly particularized in the passage which ends with the ironical exclamation

> A mensk lady on molde mon may hir calle,
> For Gode! (ll. 964–5).

Reminiscences of Morgan's earlier role as a beautiful fay skilled in the art of healing linger in the romances, for the romance writers cannot forget the part she is destined to play in the final act of Arthur's earthly career. Her beauty, however, is usually a guileful enticement to lust, and she uses her skill in medicine to drug inimical or unwilling knights or so to enflame the wounds of those she agrees to heal that they surrender to her to be spared further torment.[17] Still the romance writers were troubled by the conflicting portraits of Morgan handed down by tradition: the beautiful healer, the beautiful witch, the ugly witch. The author of the *Huth Merlin* hit upon one explanation. When Morgan was a healing nurse she was beautiful, but as her knowledge of the wicked arts of sorcery grew, she became progressively uglier.[18] From this we may reasonably infer that Morgan's ugliness in *Sir Gawain* is to be taken as an indication of her evil nature and sinful purposes.[19]

Granting for the moment that Arthur's court is sexually immoral or otherwise corrupt and in need of reform, is Morgan the proper agent for such a task? By nature fays are sexually insatiable, and Morgan is perhaps the most promiscuous lady, mortal or immortal, in all Arthurian romance. She is dimly identifiable in the deep backward of mythology as the fairy mistress of Arthur himself, which perhaps accounts for her unrelenting hatred of Guinevere, her supplanter in Arthur's affection.[20] Another explanation of the feud between these ladies has it that Morgan was frustrated by the new queen in her love affair with Guiamor (Guigamor in Chrétien's *Erec*), a cousin of Guinevere's.[21] If Miss Paton and Loomis are correct in equating Benoit de Ste-Maure's Orva with Morgan, in the second literary reference to her she figured as the spurned mistress of Hector.[22] She was also flouted by the unnamed lover, perhaps Guiamor, who became the initial bespelled inhabitant of the *Val des Faux Amants (Val sanz Retor)*, and when Lancelot finally broke the spell of this valley, over which Morgan presided from "vn lit moult bel & moult rice de fust," it was a numerous company of lovers that was released from disenchantment.[23] A liaison with Julius Caesar, chronicled in *Huon de Bordeaux*, produced Auberon; by Renoart of *Bataille Loquifer* Morgan has a son Corbon ("un vif diable, qui ne fist se mal non"); a son also resulted from her escapade with Guiamor.[24]

Married to Urien, Morgan nonetheless carries on a passionate affair with Accalon de Gaul in the *Huth Merlin* that leads her to attempt the life of her husband.[25] Morgan's revenge pursues the hero through the pages of the prose *Tristan* for having slain her lover Huneson.[26] To Floriant of *Floriant et Florete* she is a benevolent fairy mistress; Ogier the Dane, cited as Morgan's lover in *Brun de la Montaigne*, spent 200 years under her amorous protection; in *Les Prophécies de Merlin* Morgan is the mundane mistress of the worst of knights, Bréhus (Brun, Breunys, Breuz) sanz Pitié.[27] At several points in the *Vulgate Lancelot* Morgan throws herself shamelessly at the hero, but she is no more successful in her attacks on him than she is in her pursuit of that minor Lancelot, Alisandre l'Orphelin, who protests that he would rather die than embrace the lustful harridan.[28] Our own poet's mention of Morgan's illicit "dalt drwry" (l. 2449) with Merlin shows us that his Morgan is just as remote from Geoffrey of Monmouth's *regia virgo* as that of his fellow romancers. How Baughan can cast a lady with this unsavory reputation as the reformer of sexual immorality at Arthur's court is baffling.

And where has the poet said or suggested that Camelot is in need of reform? Baughan's charge of "moral corruptness" seems to be based on nothing more substantial than the fact that some unspecified romance fathers a bastard (Mordred?) upon Arthur. One must grant that in the course of romance literature, Arthur becomes progressively a weaker and less dignified person, but there is nothing in our poem to warrant the belief that the poet is picturing for us a morally degenerate Arthur or that his praises of the Round Table are perfunctory or grudging.

If the poet had wished to suggest general or specific immorality at Arthur's court, the French romances of the Vulgate cycle, particularly those passages devoted to Lancelot's exploits would have afforded him suggestive material, for in them Guinevere's adultery, swathed to be sure in the glow of courtly love, is patent. Arthur himself is degraded by Lancelot's admirers in order to palliate the sins of Guinevere and their hero. One recalls that in the *Vulgate Lancelot* on the night that Guinevere and Lancelot consummate their liaison, in a nearby castle Arthur is enjoying the ultimate favors of a Saxon lady Camille.[29] In *Sir Gawain and the Greek Knight,* however, Lancelot is mentioned only once, and in an inconspicuous place in a catalog of knights (l. 553), no liaison with Guinevere is so much as hinted at, and the poet does not qualify his reverence for the king and queen in the slightest. But the *coup de grâce* to the reformation theory comes in the fact that neither Arthur nor his court show any change in character or behavior as a result of Gawain's adventure nor do they promise such a change in the future.

III

We open a more hopeful line of investigation, I think, by assuming that the explanation for Morgan's presence lurks somewhere in the toils of the plot. She bears all the signs and the *numen* of a *dea ex machina,* and in falling back upon such a device the poet betrays his difficulty in articulating the complex narrative framework of his poem.

From Kittredge's deliberate arranging and sifting of the analogues, it emerges that both the component tales, the Beheading Game or Challenge and the Temptation, at least in the forms that stand in the immediate background of the English poem, were disenchantment stories. In the developed version of the Beheading Game, the hero, after surviving the token return blow and thus proving his courage and fidelity, is asked by the giant challenger to strike off his head for the second time. The hero complies, and the giant by this act is unspelled, resuming his normal human size, appearance and disposition. The Temptation in the form the hypothetical *Gawain* adopted was likewise a test to determine the worthiness of Gawain to be an agent of disenchantment. After the successful accomplishment of the last test, "the host bids Gawain cut off his head. He obeys reluctantly, and the enchantment is dissolved, the knight rising up in his true shape."[30] With good reason Kittredge conjectures that it may have been the common disenchantment theme which prompted the combination of the two tales in the first place (p. 109).

But though itself the product of two disenchantment stories, *Sir Gawain* rejects the *dénouement.* What we should expect if the poet had followed through with the plot to his supposed source and the analogues offered him is that Gawain, having weathered the ordeal of the Green Chapel, would have been asked by the Green Knight to repeat his performance at Arthur's hall and decapitate him again, and when the knight had been unspelled and had explained to Gawain the reason for the strange events in which Gawain had figured, he would have returned with the hero to become a member of Arthur's band.

Instead we have the Green Knight's good-humored explanation of the Challenge and Temptation, and the protagonists part with mutual blessings, Gawain for Camelot, Bercilak for his castle.

Why did the *Gawain* poet reject the conclusion indicated to him by his source and implicit in so many versions of the two stories he was running together? In deference to the poet's abilities, we must suppose that there was some artistic reason behind so important a decision. Perhaps he feared that after the beheading at Camelot and the interrupted beheading of Gawain at the Green Chapel, another beheading would be just enough to make the whole proceeding ludicrous. It seems to me far more likely that the poet's difficulty with the disenchantment action grew out of his major structural problem, the combination of the two stories into a single plot. In those analogues of the Beheading Game which end in disenchantment, the bespelled creature retains his unearthly stature until deflated to common humanity by beheading. Similarly not until the unspelling blow does the tester in the Temptation stories which imply or actually result in disenchantment, *The Carl of Carlisle,* for example, lose his monstrous appearance and imperious tone. In combining the two strands, the English poet—or his French predecessor—made one radical change. The tester in *Sir Gawain* is no longer a giant carl or ogre but a genial, urbane castellan. Bercilak assumes supernatural stature and powers only for the challenge at Camelot and the encounter at the Green Chapel; at his castle he appears in normal human form. His normal appearance at the castle was necessary in order that Gawain detect nothing unusual in his host's behavior, and so could be tested without himself or the reader suspecting that he was undergoing a test at all, and certainly not a test that related to his perilous mission. Thus, in the combined plot, the Green Knight becomes a shape-shifter, changing of his own will apparently from monstrous

ogre to genial human host to monstrous ogre again. Presumably
on his return from the Green Chapel, he changed once more
and again resumed human form.

Kittredge was quite aware of how great an innovation the
shape shifting of the Green Knight was, and he proceeds to
justify the procedure of the French *Gawain* poet, who, he assumes, was the originator of the idea, by saying that since the
gigantic axman of the Challenge was "manifestly a being with
strange powers . . . shape shifting might readily be credited to
him" (p. 108). Unfortunately, Kittredge overlooked the artistic
repercussions of making the Green Knight a shape-shifter. *The
Green Knight's ability to assume human form for carrying out
the Temptation takes away the uniqueness and the climactic
value from that resumption of this human form which Gawain
might have secured for him by a final decapitation.* Nor does
Kittredge's guess that at the end of the French poem Gawain
managed to unspell the Green Knight by some more plausible
mode than decapitation really affect the case because we are
still left with Gawain undergoing a long and anxious trial to
achieve a result which the Green Knight can perform for himself at will (if he is a bonafide shape-shifter) or at a word from
his mistress (if he is the servant of an enchantress). The poet's
only recourse if he wanted to preserve the human host of the
castle test and the pervasive suspense achieved by such a brilliant design was to discard the disenchantment motive in the
last section of the poem.

Dropping the disenchantment *dénouement* naturally entailed
major readjustments in the plot. In the world of *märchen* and
marvelous romances a bespelled person is privileged, and regu-
larly exercises his privilege, to seek out the champion who is
destined to become his unspeller and supervise the tests that
will qualify the champion for unspelling. This principle would
account for the Green Knight's journey to Camelot in the disenchantment versions of the Beheading Game. But if there is to

be no enchantment, some other motive for the journey and the initial action is required. The poet's solution was to make the Green Knight the servant of an enchantress determined to undermine the reputation of Arthur's court, and Morgan for many reasons is the inevitable choice for the role of enchantress. Her hatred for Arthur and Guinevere was notorious. The woods of Arthurian romance are thick with *Morguenetes* and *filleules de Morgain* and fearsome knights on embassies to Arthur's hall to stir up trouble or to entice heroes on doubtful adventures. It is not only in the horn and mantle pieces that Morgan plays the goddess of discord. Since the poet was altering the conclusion that folklore and popular story had conditioned his readers to expect, it was wise that the substituted motive and character accorded so well with the related body of lore on which his story depended, the Arthurian legend. Indeed, Kittredge goes so far as to suggest that the English author's "distinct desire to attach his narrative to the orthodox Arthur saga" (as shown by the chronicle passages at beginning and end) may explain the loss of the disenchantment motive (p. 133). In my opinion, the line of cause and consequence moved in the opposite direction: the loss of disenchantment led to the introduction of Morgan, not *vice versa*. Hulbert's thesis that *Sir Gawain* is ultimately derived from a tale in which the hero is tested for his worthiness to become the lover of a fairy mistress was long ago overwhelmed by Kittredge's superior genealogizing, but it is possible that the English poet knew certain legends in which Morgan, Queen of Fairies, enticed Gawain to undergo such tests, and that the Temptation story in his source had brought these legends and Morgan to mind.[31]

IV

Kittredge's conception of how the plot of *Sir Gawain* evolved, on which the foregoing discussion is based, has been seriously questioned by the Loomis school of Celtic traditionalists. Miss Buchanan argues that *The Carl of Carlisle,* the text from which Kittredge deduced the form of the Temptation story taken over by the French *Gawain* poet, also embodies reminiscences of the Beheading Game.[32] The two plots, according to Miss Buchanan, were combined thus long before the French romance writer took up the story. Her argument does not survive close examination, however. The Temptation, she holds, derives ultimately from a neglected episode of the *Fled Bricrend* which she labels "The Visit to Curoi's Castle." But though Miss Buchanan has pointed out numerous resemblances between this episode and *The Carl of Carlisle,* it is precisely the Temptation scenes which are absent from "Curoi's Castle." These she supplies by the liberal expansion of the Irish storyteller's bare remark that Curoi (Bercilak) "counselled his wife regarding the heroes" who were his guests and that "she acted according to his wish" (p. 326). Taken together with the fact that latterday folktales make Curoi's wife the mistress of Cuchulainn (Gawain's counterpart in the Irish saga), these phrases establish—for Miss Buchanan at least—that an amorous encounter occurred in some less inhibited Irish version of the story. The connection she draws between "The Champion's Bargain," the ultimate source of the Beheading Game, and *The Carl of Carlisle,* is hardly less tenuous. In both stories the giant-host says, "Strike off my head or I'll strike off yours," and in both "the giant is beheaded by his own weapon" (pp. 335–336). One scarcely needs remark that Miss Buchanan has read far too much significance into these two folktale commonplaces.

Professor Loomis supported his disciple's thesis in a lengthy and erudite article on "The Visit to the Perilous Castle," parts of which, however, he has since conceded to be defective.[33] Here he attempted to prove by the traditionalist methodology that the numerous Arthurian versions of the story in which a hero is tested by the sister, daughter, wife, or female dependent of his host at the Perilous Castle are all cognates, going back to a root story which included in combination the two episodes from the *Fled Bricrend* discussed by Miss Buchanan. What makes Loomis' argument not entirely convincing is the elaborate hypothesizing he must use in order to find elements of the Beheading Game in these Temptation stories. In some instances (pp. 1016, 1022, 1025), the mere fact that an ax-bearer interrupts the hero's assignation with dame or damsel seems to him evidence that the Beheading Game has entered the narrative, even though he is dealing with romances written in the period when the *hache* and *guisarme*, rather than the knightly sword, were the standard weapons for household guards and foot soldiers.[34] But particularly in his ingenious reappraisal of the Guingambresil episode in *Perceval* and its German, French, and English relatives, Loomis has shown that Kittredge was much too summary in refusing these analogues a place in the Gawain storycomplex.[35]

More recently, Loomis has changed his ground somewhat and has brought forward an episode in the mabinogi of *Pwyll* as a source of the *Sir Gawain* story.[36] Since he employs this discovery to reinforce his argument that the combined plot had existed before *Sir Gawain*, as well as to offer a new explanation for Morgan's presence in the English romance, his discussion of the Welsh tale is doubly important to us. The *Pwyll* episode is summarized by Loomis as follows:

> Pwyll, Prince of Dyfed (Southwestern Wales), met in a forest glade a huntsman, clad in gray wool, on an iron-gray horse. He revealed himself as Arawn, King of Annwn (the Other-World or Faerye), and admitted that he had suffered defeat at the hands of Hafgan (Summer White), a king from Annwn. When Pwyll agreed to fight Hafgan in Arawn's stead at the end of a year at a ford, Arawn sent Pwyll to his faery palace in his own form. There Pwyll dwelt for a year, sharing the same bed with

Arawn's most beautiful wife, yet turning his face resolutely to
the wall. At the year's end, Arawn fulfilled his bargain, met
"Summer White" at the ford by night in the presence of all their
nobles. It was proclaimed that none should intervene between
the combatants. Pwyll dealt "Summer White" one fatal blow,
and then departed to his own dominion (p. 171).

Now, despite superficial appearances and Loomis's extrapolation from them, there is really no Temptation in the *Pwyll* episode. Pwyll has been transformed into the appearance of Arawn.
Neither Arawn's knights nor the servants at his castle are aware
of the change. Pwyll sleeps in Arawn's marriage bed during
his year of transformation in order to maintain the disguise.
Though Loomis, by way of forcing the parallel with *Sir Gawain*,
comments that Pwyll "spurns" the wife's embraces (p. 171), the
Welsh says nothing about her offering embraces for him to
spurn, unless her simple presence in the bed be so interpreted.
Of key importance is the later conversation between Arawn and
his wife on the first night he rejoins her, a passage which tells
damagingly against Loomis's interpretation.[37] In this scene the
wife expresses her astonishment at Arawn's marital activity after
a year's indifference, a speech which shows that she did not know
her bedmate for a year had not been her husband. There was,
therefore, no collusion between the host and his wife, the chief
requirement for a Temptation story. Not only was there no collusion, there was no test, collusive or otherwise, for it is from
his wife's conversation that Arawn first learns (and only incidentally) of Pwyll's continence. Clearly Pwyll's behavior toward
Arawn's wife was not a test and had no bearing on his success
in combat. If it had been a test, Arawn would have known of
Pwyll's continence from his triumph over Hafgan. Instead,
Arawn seems surprised that Pwyll did not enjoy his wife—he had
explicitly invited him to do so—and interprets the hero's behavior as a gratuitous act of friendship.

After establishing to his satisfaction the Pwyll-Gawain and Arawn-Bercilak relationship, Loomis proceeds by further extrapolation to cast Arawn as the legendary Wild Huntsman, whose traditional mistress in medieval and later folklore was Morgan le Fay (pp. 181 ff.). Morgan, then, if one accepts Loomis's deductions, may have played some role in the story-complex from which *Sir Gawain* derives, a suggestion offered on the basis of other texts by Miss Weston and Hulbert.[38] But to concede Loomis's point helps us only by suggesting yet another reason for the poet's hitting upon Morgan as a means to extricate himself from his plot difficulty; it does not cancel out the fact that in *Sir Gawain* she and her machinations, as Miss Buchanan admits (p. 330), are "feeble accretions."

For though the poet, speaking through Bercilak, would clearly like us to think of Morgan as the "only begetter" of Gawain's adventure, effectually she is not. Her effective life in the poem is local, restricted to the few lines in which Bercilak tells us the reason for his journey to Camelot. It something had been said or insinuated about Morgan or an unnamed enchantress in the challenge scene or if the shriveled hag at the castle had acted in some sinister fashion, Bercilak's explanation might then have carried a measure of plausibility. As the poem stands, his words are inert. The old woman functions solely as a foil to enhance the beauty of Gawain's temptress; nothing of our image of her is altered by what Bercilak has said, no suspicions confirmed. It seems thus less than shrewd to speak seriously of Morgan as "the moving force . . . of the entire plot" when the plot has moved so sturdily to its conclusion without even an allusion to her.

Two lines of Bercilak's (2361–62) further badly undermine Morgan's right to be called the "only begetter" of Gawain's adventure: the speech in which he tells Gawain that he himself was solely responsible for the lady's testing of Gawain. The

Temptation, thus, becomes Bercilak's private prank and is set apart from the Beheading Game inspired by Morgan. Presumably, even had Gawain succumbed to the lady's wiles, he would not have been fatally decapitated but would have only received a deeper wound, since Gawain's contract, so far as Morgan is concerned, is fulfilled when he fearlessly and bravely presents himself for the Green Knight's return blow. One would like to explain these lines away as the vestiges of a previous version of the story. They clearly belong to the new dispensation, however. They could not have come from a disenchantment story, for a bespelled creature would hardly jeopardize his chance for freedom by inventing gratuitous tests to hamper his prospective rescuer.

Try as we may to justify the poet's methods, we cannot get around the stubbornly solid impression that he fails to convince us that Morgan is organic to the poem. She is not, of course, the only thread imperfectly woven into the narrative. An overly literal-minded student may well be given even more trouble by the green lace which Bercilak's lady forces upon Gawain, for the possession of the amulet undoubtedly detracts from his display of courage. Fortunately these few loose threads do not vitiate the poet's achievement in any significant way. No sophisticated reader will be deeply disturbed to realize that *Sir Gawain,* like Gawain, is not quite perfection.

·•❧[8]❧•·

The Meaning of *Sir Gawain and the Green Knight*

ALAN M. MARKMAN

Knights who are at the wars eat their bread in sorrow; their ease is weariness and sweat; they have one good day after many bad; they are vowed to all manner of labour; they are for ever swallowing their fear; they expose themselves to every peril; they give up their bodies to the adventure of life in death. . . . Great is the honour which knights deserve, and great the favour which kings should shew them, for all the reasons which I have told. . . . Of what profit is a good knight? I tell you that through good knights is the king and the kingdom honoured, protected, feared and defended. . . . I tell you that without good knights, the king is like a man who has neither feet nor hands.—Gutierre Díaz de Gámez[1]

Of all the knights who attended Arthur none achieved greater renown than Gawain. In the twelfth century Chrétien de Troyes shrewdly observed that "Devant toz les buens chevaliers / Doit

Reprinted by permission of the Modern Language Association from *PMLA*, LXXII (1957), 574–86. A shorter version of this paper, titled "Romance Hero and Antagonist in 'Sir Gawain and the Green Knight'," was read to the Comp. Lit. II discussion group (Arthurian) of the MLA at its 1955 meeting in Chicago.

estre Gauvains li premiers";[2] some two hundred years later there appeared the excellent Middle English romance, *Sir Gawain and the Green Knight*.[3] It was a forthright declaration of Chrétien's pronouncement. As every reader who has read the romance knows, the account of Gawain's adventures at the castle of Bercilak de Hautdesert[4] and the Green Chapel is a first-rate narrative. It is therefore somewhat surprising to discover that the bulk of Arthurian criticism which has been directed to *Sir Gawain and the Green Knight* has largely overlooked the real source of its extraordinary appeal. Early and late scholars have sought to establish Gawain's origin among the ranks of primitive Celtic gods and to suggest, it would seem, that Gawain's success might perhaps be best accounted for because he is not to be taken for the representation of an ordinary human being, but because he is, on the contrary, either a superhuman or supernatural being. Some critics have been concerned with the Green Knight himself, finding him to be, according to one report, an "unmistakable relation to the Green Man—the Jack in the Green or the wild man of the village festivals of England and Europe," or, in another accounting, a figure modeled on a person who actually lived in the fourteenth century.[5] Other scholars have turned their attention to the sources and provenience of the varied subject matter of the romance. The results of this criticism have been, first, to make of *Sir Gawain and the Green Knight* something of a mythological poem, or else a nature rite; second, to suggest that its hero and antagonist are godlike beings; and, third, to coax the reader's attention away from the hero. All this, I think, would have been very strange to the minds of the unknown poet who composed the romance and the intelligent audience to whom it was given.

The fourteenth century, it is true, lies neatly tucked away in the past, surrounded with some doubts and uncertainties; but yet it is not so remote that we cannot come to an understanding of its people and their literature. As a matter of fact, it ought to be fairly obvious that we have a serious obligation to put ourselves back in time, to see with fourteenth-century eyes, if we can, what people were doing and what they were listening to in, say, 1375. We may safely assume that, like ourselves, the fourteenth-century audience was pleased by stories which told of men in action, and that, like our own authors, their writers and poets were able to communicate experience in a meaningful form. The men, actions, and form which we observe in the fourteenth-century romance may be different from what we have given to us today, but these tales nevertheless will yield positive rewards when they are read carefully. *Sir Gawain and the Green Knight* deserves the very best attention we can give to it as a literary work.

To begin, then, *Sir Gawain and the Green Knight* is, first and last, a romance. It is the especial nature of that particular type of narrative to which we must direct our attention if we are to see in their true perspective the real functions and meaning of its hero, Sir Gawain, its antagonist, Bercilak, and its fundamental mixture of realistic detail and marvelous occurrence. To come at it directly, I suggest that the primary purpose of the poem is to show what a splendid man Gawain is. It is the method of demonstration in the romance, the controlled test, which requires a more careful consideration: its intent seems to be to discover, by pitting a real man against a marvelous, unnatural man, what a perfect knight can do when he is forced to face the unknown. A complementary test, the so-called "Love Test," tries the knight in a very real, natural situation. Finally, I shall point out that it is magic, not mythology or folklore, which informs and directs the marvelous occurrences in the romance. Fitting his central role in the story, Gawain himself furnishes the key which unlocks the mystery. "What," he asks, "can a man do but try?" (v. 565). What is to be elucidated is the

nature of the test, or what may be called the "romance function," that is, the technique which brings the known in contention with the unknown so that, in the half real, half unreal
world of romance, the hero can demonstrate the very best action
which a man can perform. Here, where he did not think to
look for it, is Arnold's Hebraic tone, the message of conduct and
obedience. What a man must do, or, in a word, human conduct,
is the heart of the poem, and our participation in the hero's
test is its source of pleasure.

There is no reason to doubt that, in this romance, Gawain is
the representation of a real man. In the entire poem there is not
a line which ascribes to the hero any superhuman or supernatural quality. Sir Gawain's strength does *not,* like the sun,
wax in the forenoon and wane in the afternoon. His sword does
not gleam like the rays of the sun. His horse, Gringolet, is *not*
considered to be a part of a sun god's apparatus; he is a perfectly
normal battle horse, the large, strong *destrier* so necessary in
feudal warfare. What, then, is the hero? He is the ideal feudal
Christian knight who not only represents the very highest
reaches of human behavior but who also holds out for our evaluation those qualities in a man which his age, and the feudal age
at large, admired most. He is not, to be sure, an average man,
nor is he the counterpart of any single knight who ever lived;
on the contrary, he is the very best knight who sums up in his
character the very best traits of all knights who ever lived. If
we consider the most favorable report of the character of knighthood from, say, Guillaume le Maréchal to Edward, the Black
Prince, we shall find that in the aspect of Gawain presented in
Sir Gawain and the Green Knight there is reflected the ideal of
chevalerie which the feudal age tried to maintain.

In the very first place we should notice Gawain's physical fitness for knighthood. Throughout the feudal age the armored
cavalryman had to possess strength and endurance, he had to

be skilled in the use of his weapons, and he had to be a good horseman. Anything short of proficiency in these qualities would have rendered a knight unfit. In *Sir Gawain and the Green Knight* Gawain represents physical perfection. He is strong enough to wield the Green Knight's tremendous ax; with one blow he decapitates his adversary, driving the steel bit into the floor of Arthur's hall (vv. 421–426). He has both the strength and endurance to complete his arduous journey to the Green Chapel: a lesser man might well have died on such a trip, but Gawain persisted, and, in spite of the severe season (vv. 726–732), managed to survive.* His agility in placing himself in position to attack after the Green Knight had lightly wounded him on the neck (vv. 2315–2319), as well as his handling of the war ax (vv. 421–426), demonstrates the skill at arms which the feudal age demanded of the knight. His many days in the saddle, and especially the concern for his horse which Gawain evinced as he appraised the care shown to Gringolet by his host's men (vv. 2047–2054), illustrate almost too well the horsemanship expected of the knight. Without a doubt, Gawain is shown to be a perfect knight physically.

The nonphysical qualities of the ideal knight which Gawain possesses are courage, humility, courtesy, and loyalty. His courage, of course, is demonstrated, in the first place, by his willingness to accept the monstrous challenge of the Green Knight and, thereafter, by his action at the Green Chapel. (The fundamental motivation for Gawain's intervention is really his sense of duty, or decorum: what a knight must do to help his lord extricate himself from an unseemly situation—in a word, loyalty. But the act demanded great courage too.) Humility becomes any man. Gawain's chagrin, displayed after the Green Knight has ex-

---

* In one sense it might be said that Gawain received supernatural assistance. His prayer to Mary, we know, appeared to be answered almost at once. Yet he had already managed to exist on his own, passing the ordeal of nature's most severe torment.

plained the purpose of their bargain (vv. 2369–2388), and his refusal to claim any glory when he returned to Arthur's court (vv. 2505–2512) show that Gawain was, when he ought to be, a humble man. His courtesy requires no discovery here. His very first words in the romance, as he asks Arthur's permission to accept the challenge (vv. 342–361), and his conduct with the Lady of the Castle are the perfection of knightly courtesy. For Gawain courtesy was a way of life. The strongest part of his character, however, is his sense of loyalty. He is loyal to his lord, Arthur, and he is loyal to his host, Bercilak. He is a man who can be counted on to keep his word. His own declaration to his host, as he explains why he cannot tarry, constitutes the extreme of trustworthiness. "It behooves me," he states, "to move on. I have now at my disposal barely three days, and I would just as soon fall dead as fail in my errand" (vv. 1065–1067). Loyalty, or trust-worthiness, actually underlies every action and thought of the hero; he is the particular man he is because his strong sense of duty compelled him to do what was most needed at the time. Like that other great feudal hero, Roland, Gawain's chief ac-complishment, in the eyes of his peers and lord, was his Ciceron-ian capacity to attend to his nearest duty. A favorite with the ladies, a good companion, a stalwart fighter with a strong right arm, a decoration at any man's board, "The Flower of Knight-hood"—all this Gawain is, but if it were possible for him to step from the pages of romance, our latter-day Charleses and Arthurs would welcome him primarily, I think, because he would be a man who could be counted on to do, in any situation, what most needed to be done. As we found him to be eminently fitted phys-ically for knighthood, so too do we find that Gawain's character illustrates perfection of knighthood.

It is obvious that the feudal age admired these qualities. The best knights in real life were brave, they tried to be courteous, and, on occasion, they made some show of humility. Loyalty, of course, was the keystone of the entire feudal structure: when lord and vassal were loyal to each other, society flourished; when they were not, society collapsed. Appropriately, it is Gawain's loyalty which motivates the action of *Sir Gawain and the Green Knight*. Had he not been loyal to Arthur and Bercilak, had he not been a man of his word, the structure of the romance would have collapsed; indeed, there would have been no romance.

Gawain, to be sure, is something more than a glittering symbol of perfection. He is a man. One of the marks of genius in the romance is the deliberate care which the poet took to make his hero human. His acceptance of the Lady's lace, of course, is the most notable incident in the romance which illustrates his humanity. But his behavior throughout is distinctly human. He even tries to excuse his weakness by declaring, in our human way, that he had been deceived. In anger, not directed to the Lady, but to himself, he tells Bercilak that it had been his fate to share the lot of Adam, David, and Samson. "These men," he declares,

> ". . . wer forne þe freest, þat folȝed alle þe sele
> Excellently of alle þyse oþer, vnder heuenryche
>   þat mused;
> And alle þay were biwyled
> With wymmen þat þay vsed.
> Þaȝ I be now bigyled,
> Me þink me burde be excused."   (vv. 2422–2428)

("were the best of the ancients, the most fortunate, and excellent above all others under Heaven. They were beguiled by women they consorted with; if I am now deceived, I think I might be excused.")

All the more human for this slight fault, Gawain is a likable man who has won the esteem and affection of his fellows (vv. 672–686). He is given, both in the long romance tradition and in this romance, the highest position; he is Arthur's nephew.

His trials and joys are made to seem real enough. Who could doubt that the young knight, so relieved at finding unexpected comfort in Bercilak's castle, so sincere in both his moments of elation and concern, is a human being? His greatness, I think, is defined most clearly when, amidst the long faces of the court retinue who tried to comfort him as he prepared to set out on a search which, it was felt, must lead to certain death, Gawain alone remained calm, and replied to his fellows:

> . . . "Quat schuld I wonde?
> Of destinés derf and dere
> What may mon do bot fonde?"   (vv. 563–565)
>
> ("Why should I hesitate? Against a
> hard and dire fate, what can a man do
> but try?").

Such a man we can all admire. Take him where you will in the romance, Gawain is, for his age, the representation of the very best man who ever lived.

Much has been said about the Green Knight. Bercilak's true nature will be understood, however, only when it is realized that his primary function is to serve as Gawain's antagonist. The Green Knight is not a superhuman or supernatural being. He is an ordinary human being who, as he tells it to Gawain, has been transformed by Morgan le Fay. The full circumstances of transformations such as this are well known to readers of romance. As Kittredge pointed out fifty years ago, what we have in *The Turk and Gowin,* say, represents the more nearly normal romance situation. The Turk, victim of a magic spell, lived for a time as a misshapen creature; his disenchantment could be accomplished only when he was decapitated by the best of all knights.* The *Gawain* poet employed an alternative pattern.

---

* Life, temporarily, as a misshapen creature may be a punishment, a form of "penance," or a disguise. Disenchantment, usually prescribed by the enchanter, may take almost any form; a kiss, a word, or a specific act are common in romance. Disenchantment by decapitation is the most astonishing.

Ordinarily we should witness the disenchantment when Gawain decapitated the Green Knight. Instead of seeing Bercilak arise from the floor of Arthur's hall, however, we observe an even more fantastic occurrence—the Green Knight picks up his own head. But there can be little doubt that the Green Knight had been put under spell. He is not, to be sure, the victim of magic, but the agent of magic, the marvelous man whose single purpose in the romance is to serve as the agent of Morgan le Fay's will. It is a brilliant plan. Since Gawain is the very best man, his opponent, if he is to test the hero severely, must be something more than another ordinary human being. The choice of a man temporarily endowed with the power of magic was the best possible solution. Not only is the hero given a formidable opponent but the adventure itself is also given its indispensable atmosphere of romance.

Although the romance is filled with realistic details which reflect its author's accurate observation of his own time, life, and scene—as a matter of fact, a line-by-line analysis discloses that slightly less than ten per cent of the romance is given over to the marvelous— we must not overlook the nature and purpose of the marvelous occurrences in *Sir Gawain and the Green Knight*. To begin with, everything in the romance which is either strange or untoward, or which cannot be explained rationally, and which I call "the marvelous," is accounted for by the direct manifestation of Morgan le Fay's magical power, the transformation of Bercilak. It is the magical power of Morgan le Fay, power she learned from Merlin (vv. 2446–2452), which gives rise to the romance atmosphere in the poem. All the lines which describe the Green Knight and his horse, the passages given over to the fantastic bargain, and the description of the final meeting of Gawain and the Green Knight, find their ultimate source in Morgan le Fay's power. The Green Lace which Gawain accepts from the Lady is a magic talisman; in another romance it might well have been a ring, or brooch, or a necklace.[6] All marvelous occurrences in the romance, in short, derive from magic, and, as the agent of Morgan le Fay, it is Bercilak's single function to carry out her will. There can be no doubt about it; within the framework of the romance structure of *Sir Gawain and the Green Knight* the nature of the marvelous is magic. And although this particular detail is not given, undoubtedly Morgan le Fay cast a spell upon Bercilak, allowing him to assume a different shape, as the Green Knight, when it served her purpose. Yet even if not more than ten per cent of the romance is given over to the marvelous, the marvelous is, of course, indispensable. It informs and shapes the entire narrative. From the moment the Green Knight enters Arthur's hall until Gawain returns safely to the same hall the action of the romance is severely conditioned by the influence of Morgan le Fay's magic. It is the cohesive force which joins together the two primary motifs in the poem, the "Beheading Test" and the "Love Test." It is the force which compels Gawain to begin his journey, and it is the force which pulls him into Bercilak's castle. It is the force, finally, which constitutes the marvelous atmosphere, which supplies the necessary feeling that everything which occurs is occurring "nowhere," which makes us accept the fundamental precept of romance, namely, that we are, at the same time, both in this world and in another world.[7]

Thus far I have described what I think is the true nature of the hero, the antagonist, and the romance atmosphere of *Sir Gawain and the Green Knight.* How and why the romance is constructed as it is becomes the most important question one can ask about the poem. Not only is it a question, by and large, which Arthurian criticism has neglected, but it also is, I am convinced, the most fruitful inquiry criticism can undertake. Sometimes a simple observation will bear useful results: it is so in the case at hand. A striking difference may be observed between the behavior of the romance hero, the epic hero, and the hero of the modern novel. It seems to be the function of the epic hero to show off, to display his well-known qualities in actions which, for the most part, were already known and admired by the audience which listened to the recitation. The exploits of Achilles, for example, were familiar to all, a part of public knowledge, so to speak. So too was his personality known. There was never a question of what Achilles would or would not do, or why he acted as he did. One's pleasure in the recital of old deeds surely must have come about as a result of perceiving, once again, the familiar champion going through his paces. The epic hero had to earn his stature, no doubt in lays or folk-songs, before he could be given immortality in the epic form. In its best form, such a recital must have been both inspiring and pleasing, and so long as the heroic age persisted, every man must have felt, each time he listened to the recitation, an inti-mate kinship with the great hero. At the other extreme, the hero of the modern novel is, in the beginning, an unknown quantity, and the situations into which he is to be placed are unpredict-able. What is perhaps the most significant of all literary inno-vations, character development, separates a Michael Henchard, say, or a Santiago, from Achilles. Before our very eyes, from page to page as we follow him from one incident to the next, we see the hero of the modern novel grow. The hero of modern fiction has to earn his stature as he goes along. Our pleasure in reading the account of the modern hero's actions surely comes about because we see in his development something of ourself, be-cause, imaginatively and sympathetically, we are the hero.

Midway between the epic hero and the modern hero lies the romance hero. Where we find both the character and the actions of the epic hero known in advance, where we find both the character and the actions of the modern hero unknown in ad-vance, we find that the character of the romance hero is known in advance but his action and behavior are not. My guess is that the romance hero exists to show us the way. We know who the hero is and what he is like, but we do not know what he will do. Gawain is the best man, we know—his carefully established reputation attests no less—the one knight who ought to perform in any situation as well as any man might be expected to. What reason could there be for placing such a man in action other than to test him, to try out our best representative? The romance hero brings his reputation along with him, but he has to earn stature in the romance; he may, as a matter of fact, gain or lose everything as he goes along; he has, indeed, a perilous course to tread, the eyes of readers of all ages watching each step he takes. It is the function of the romance hero, I think, to stand as the champion of the human race, and, by submitting to strange and severe tests, to demonstrate human capabilities for good or bad action. Seldom do we ask ourselves why the romance hero does this or does that: always we ask, "What will he do now?" or "How can he do that?" The romance condition seems to be very much like this: we construct the very best man to represent the ideal human behavior; we ask, then, what could such a man do if he were to be placed in the most trying, the strangest positions; we provide the unnatural incidents of romance to test the hero, because only the unknown can constitute a valid test and, at the same time, generate the universal appeal of the mysterious, the remote. There is no doubt in my mind that the charm and appeal of Gawain is this: of all champions who have set out in romances to show us the way, none has lived up to his reputation so well as Gawain.

Sir Gawain and the Green Knight displays the perfect knight contending against the unknown. No part of its structure can be elucidated if it is considered apart from its proper relationship to the chief aim of the romance, namely, to test Gawain and, in so doing, to project his behavior as a model for the very best human conduct. Two methods are employed in the romance to bring Gawain, the known, into conflict with the un-known. The first, which initiates the action, I call "attraction." Gawain, seated comfortably in Arthur's hall, finds all of a sud-den that the unknown has come to him. The confusion and shock caused by the Green Knight's unexpected entrance could occur only in the romance world. At once the hero and the mys-terious man, the known and the unknown, are brought together, are placed in contention. Everything required for a complete narrative structure is formulated by the time the Green Knight, head under his arm, rides out of Arthur's hall. Our expectation is that, in due time, the hero will set out on his search for his adversary, either find him or not, either keep his part of the bargain and return, or fail and lose his life. Let us think of it as a straight line journey from *A*, Arthur's hall, to *B*, the Green Chapel, and a direct return to *A*. The poem's structural bril-liance is revealed when we recall that the hero does not go directly from *A* to *B*, but goes instead to *C*, Bercilak's castle, before going on to *B*. The second method, used to cause Gawain to turn from his expected route, I call "deflection." The hero is deflected into a second adventure which becomes, as we know, a second test. Having passed his test in the castle, the hero re-turns to his primary objective. After his adventure at *B*, the hero returns, of course, to *A*. Surely one of the most striking indica-tions of skill in the poem is the passage which signals the hero's deflection to the second adventure. It is all done without the hero's knowledge: Gawain does not know, nor could he possibly know, what lies in store for him inside the castle so fortuitously revealed to him. To appreciate this skill we shall have to con-sider, for a moment, the geography of the romance. There are two geographies in *Sir Gawain and the Green Knight:* what can be called "real" geography and what can be called "romance" geography. From the time Gawain rides out of Arthur's hall until, at wits' end and near physical exhaustion, he directs

Gringolet into a thick wood that was "strangely wild" (v. 741), his passage, although beset by "many marvels in the mountains" (v. 718) and "giants" (v. 723), has been in the real world: our normal sense of geography can comprehend the land he traverses, even if it could not guide us directly to follow his path. But at the instant Gringolet enters the "wild wood," he carries his rider into a different world. He has crossed the invisible boundary which separates the real world from the romance world:[8] here, in the heartland of romance, anything can happen; here, the hero will find more than he bargained for. The deflection, of course, is, like all the action of the romance, conditioned by Morgan le Fay's power. For although the poet writes that Gawain prayed for assistance, we know that the prayer was not necessary; the hero would have been drawn to the castle in any event. Had a wide net been spread to snare him, Gawain could not have been more efficiently pulled into the castle. What is more likely than the Christian knight praying? What is more unlikely than immediate manifestation of the efficacy of prayer? Always, in *Sir Gawain and the Green Knight,* the real and the unreal are brought together; always, in romance, such things can happen. It is a delightful irony, as we see it work out, that Gawain should be put to an unlooked-for test while he takes comfort, anticipating the real test some few days later. But, once more, that is the sort of thing we expect in the romance world. Such is the scheme of the structure of the poem, a scheme brilliantly devised to show how the very best knight might be expected to behave when he is pitted against the unknown.

A word or two must be inserted here about the nature of the "Love Test" or so-called "Chastity Test." As other scholars have pointed out,[9] what keeps Gawain from inviting the Lady into his bed, to be blunt about it, is not his chastity, but his strong sense of loyalty. As the guest of Bercilak, Gawain is in the position, for the duration of his visit, of vassal to his host; his host is, for the time, his lord. It would have been a heinous breach of loyalty to his lord had Gawain made love to his lord's wife. Any feudal audience would understand that; the lovely chatelaine, at the hands of Gawain, was inviolable. It is, of course, a severe, extreme test of Gawain's integrity. The hero is placed in a terrifying dilemma. On the one hand he faces the normal sexual impulse of any man; on the other, his sense of propriety and his loyalty to his lord. Because he is courteous, he cannot treat the Lady summarily. To his great credit, and the glory of British literature, Gawain retains both his honor and his reputation. The poet, however, is not without a sense of justice, and Gawain, because he made the slightest compromise, does not leave Bercilak's domain completely unscarred. His chastity was never in the balance, but his integrity was; for the small chink in his otherwise unsullied armor Gawain will pay—he will carry to his grave a slight scar on his neck. The "Love Test" and the "Beheading Test" complement each other. Man's greatest virtue, *Sir Gawain and the Green Knight* tells us, is loyalty, and if we wish to act to our highest capacity, we must be loyal to those who deserve our loyalty. In a word, we must be obedient to our station and social duty. For the medieval man, short of the advice which Holy Mother Church afforded to guide him to heaven, there could be no better injunction.[10]

There are, to be sure, other matters of interest in the romance. The poet's sense of time and pseudohistory, like his use of a dual geography, reinforces the romance atmosphere. Other structural details, the balance of Gawain versus the Green Knight and Gawain versus the Green Knight's wife, say, or the similarity between the bargains arranged by the Green Knight and by his normal self, Bercilak, deserve further attention. I think, however, that they all fit well into the general structural outline I have described. Other elements, the color and number symbolism, for example, as well as the deep sympathy for what we have to call "the sheer joy of living," are important in the poem. Certainly, to look in another direction for a moment, there are overtones in the romance which ought not to be passed over—there are, or may well be, traces of the Celtic world of mythology, of nature rites, of the paradoxical "Northern, or Cold Hell," so-called. Certainly the romance has a positive and healthy Christian tone. I neither deny nor ignore these details; I simply believe they are of secondary importance.

What we need constantly to keep in mind, of course, is the real obligation to read *Sir Gawain and the Green Knight* as a romance. The poem is not just the exposition of a single virtue, say, chastity; to take it so is to underread the romance. Nor is it a Christian declaration of man's imperfection; to take it so is to overread the romance, to take it as primarily a Christian poem. Of course it is a Christian poem, but not exclusively, not even primarily so, as, say, Robert Grosseteste's *Château d'Amour,* or Chaucer's *Second Nun's Tale,* or Richard Rolle's religious lyrics are Christian. What we have at hand, I think, is the matter of the poet's attitude. I believe the *Gawain* poet's attitude (not his intention, which we do not know) is quite clearly that here is a man who goes as far as man can, who shows human capacity for action, who drums into our consciousness the most moral of earthly lessons—we must act as our duty to others dictates. And so it is I see loyalty as the human trait which underlies and informs all the virtues we see in Gawain. In short, of all the components which inform and shape the romance—magic, Christianity, realistic details, the overtones I have alluded to—what comes out of it is not a symbolic knight in shining armor, but a man. Perhaps I have erected a "live horse" to beat—I am really not sure I have not—but the poem, like Gringolet, can carry this additional burden.

What I believe to be the most important in *Sir Gawain and the Green Knight,* put as directly as I can, is that its true mark of genius is its forceful presentation of its human hero, Gawain. He is the point of interest; he indeed comes first. The romance exists to show us what a splendid man he is. We are drawn to him because, as he passes his tests, he shows us our capabilities for human conduct, because, in the best sense of it, he shows us what honest moral conduct is. We shall probably not equal his behavior, but we admire him for pointing out the way. We approach this excellent romance properly, I think, when we see that it is the urgent concern of Gawain to show us something of ourselves, to show us our human capability for right and good action, and, in fulfilling a fundamental requirement of fiction, to show us, in some measure, what it means to be alive in the world.[11]

·•∍[9]∊•·

Gawain's Shield and the Quest for Perfection

RICHARD HAMILTON GREEN

I

Sir Gawain and the Green Knight is an aristocratic romance which embodies the chivalric ideals of the English ruling class in the mid-fourteenth century. It is a highly stylized projection of the image of that class, a marvelous world where the virtuous hero represents the noble ideal and his antagonists the forces which threaten its ascendancy. Social historians have shown that the chivalric tradition, in its outward forms and theoretical formulations at least, persisted long after its institutional vitality had been sapped by economic, political and social change. It remained a characteristic attitude of the upper classes toward public and private secular affairs, partly out of nostalgia for the supposed glory of an earlier age, partly as a means of protection against the threats to vested interests implicit in change, partly as the familiar embodiment of ethical ideals rooted in a more

Reprinted by permission of The Johns Hopkins Press from *ELH*, XXIX (1962), 121–39.

stable religious tradition. One of the most obvious and attractive features of our poem is the clarity with which elegance of courtly manners, magnificence of costume and entertainment, the professional skill of noble pursuits are presented. These are attractive in themselves, and they provided the appropriate literary environment in which the noble virtues which pertained to this conspicuously noble life could be examined and tested.

These virtues of the secular estate: valor and fidelity in the service of one's temporal lord, justice in dealing with the strong and the weak, sobriety and courtesy in the conduct of personal life, piety in the service of God, belonged to, and derived their value and ultimate sanctions from, the medieval doctrine of Christian perfection, both institutional and individual. The chivalric ideal, however modified and tarnished by practice and human imperfection, was the imitation of Christ, the effort to realize in the individual and in society the perfection to which human nature aided by grace could aspire. The dominant image which bound the ideals of chivalric and Christian perfection was the image of the Christian knight, champion of the Church militant on earth, committed to the pursuit of personal virtue and the preservation of the divinely sanctioned social order. Add to this the image of life in the world as a *passage moralisé* in which perfection is an ideal to be sought, but achieved only in another world beyond challenge and frustration, and we have the moral world of the poem.

In this general way, *Sir Gawain and the Green Knight* is a romance which fits our customary expectations: an ideal society in a marvelous world where the virtuous hero represents the temporal and spiritual ideal, flattering and encouraging those whose model he is meant to be. That the English upper classes should feel themselves involved in Gawain's character and fortunes was a consequence of the medieval view of history. He was

Arthur's knight, and Arthur was England's greatest king. The writer of romance, like the writer of chronicle, recorded the legendary events of a past which was seen as a continuing process of fulfillment; both poet and historian dealt imaginatively with tradition because both were primarily concerned with instruction, with providentially given models to be emulated or shunned. But romance is a complex genre and the *Gawain* poem is no run-of-the-mill example of its kind. It is the most skillfully made of the English romances, and the most complex in intention, exhibiting a subtlety of presentation and density of implication which we have only begun to appreciate.[1] It is also late in the history of the genre, and, since it is alive and original in ways that most of its contemporary pieces are not, we should not be surprised if it shows some of the stresses of the period in which it was made.

Because Arthur and Gawain are figures of England's destiny, and provided patterns of individual conduct and its conseqences, the aims of the poet are essentially serious; but I find that the poem reveals a sense of humor which mitigates the seriousness of its themes and adjusts the magnitude of its exemplary hero to the temper of an age which produced the satires of Chaucer and Langland. The burden of my essay will be to examine some of the implications of the poem's comic tone for its central concern with the ideal of secular perfection. This poet is more than propagandist and entertainer; he is the amiably ironic teacher and conscience of the court. His poem manifests approval of the noble life and a lively enjoyment of its elegance. But beneath the brilliant surfaces he finds a dark world of potential failure, and subtly, sometimes comically, he warns of powers of evil which may corrupt even the most virtuous men and institutions. He presents Gawain as the norm against which his audience is asked to measure its own achievement, and he warns against the folly by which even the most exemplary can be corrupted; but his presentation is sympathetic, graceful, informed with a humor that turns in upon itself, because the poet belongs to the society he pictures and has his own stake in the doubtful possibilities of its continued success.

At the very beginning of the poem we encounter the frame of time within which England saw the greatness of its origins and destiny; but the greatness of the past is marred by reminders of failure. Britain's ancient glory is marked by its beginnings in Troy, by the heroic figure of Aeneas, and Brutus the founder of Britain; but Troy was burned to ashes, Aeneas the atheling, the truest on earth, was tainted with treason, and the history of Britain to the time of Arthur has been a succession of war and woe, of bliss and blunder. Arthur is presented as the noblest of British kings, ruling his fair folk in their first age, the most fortunate under heaven, possessing all the weal of the world. Everything is superlative, suggesting at once England's pride in its hero-king and the poet's awareness of an excessive self-confidence deflated by events in the popular history he knew and believed, a confidence that will or ought to be shaken by events within the narrower dimensions of his tale. In Arthur's court are gathered the most famous knights, the loveliest ladies, and in their midst was Guinevere, the *comlokest* that man ever saw. Into this description of lively, beautiful and accomplished people, gathered at Christmas, the time of the First Coming, at the New Year, in their first age, the poet introduces a discordant note, not obtrusive but sufficient to remind his hearers of what they already knew about the legendary Arthur, his beautiful but vulnerable queen, and his Round Table. The great king is "sumquat childgered" and restless, stirred by his young blood and wild brain.[2]

In the midst of the feast there occurs the ominous intrusion of a figure from another world who cannot be ignored, however much he offends against the social proprieties of the occasion.

The Green Knight comes to test the great fame of the court and its knights, the "wisest and worthiest of the world's kind." He is as gracious as he is terrifying; his urbane self-confidence is in telling contrast to the nervous silence of the court. Arthur rises to the occasion, and so, of course, does Gawain; but even the king seems somewhat petulant, and his ungracious challenge to a fight earns the Green Knight's scorn for these beardless childer. As his figure suggests, and as events prove, the Green Knight is no adversary to be overcome by physical prowess. He belongs to the world of mystery, a mixture of benevolence and malevolence, an ambiguous figure of forces beyond man's full understanding and control—as ambiguous as all the agents of divine trial. He has come to test their reputation for wisdom and fortitude of a different sort, the natural and supernatural virtues of the Christian Knight.

The Green Man wants a Christmas game, a test of mortality, but when he describes its rules he is met again by silence and fear. Arthur had wanted a marvel before dinner, but he wanted a marvelous story or some hand-to-hand combat with predictable consequences however painful. He had asked for nothing so mysterious, so fatal as this. The Green Knight breaks the shocked silence with contempt: is this the famous court of Arthur? can the Round Table be overwhelmed by one man's words? He laughs in their faces. With a humility which, as events prove, reflects more social grace than any profounder kind, Gawain volunteers. With this action we move from the wider sphere of institutional virtue to the test of the individual knight, the representative of Arthur's court, of English chivalry and Christian soldiership.

With masterful economy the poet marks the passage of the ecclesiastical and solar year, a figure some critics have used to support eclectic readings which make the poem somehow an account of a vegetation myth.[3] But this procession of seasons,

within the Christian context explicitly and pervasively established by the poet, much more clearly indicates the passage of
time from the First Coming to the Second, from man's undertaking the journey of life to the judgment which is its inevitable
conclusion. The arming of the knight about to undertake his
quest occurs on the morning following the celebration of All
Saints Day on November first, the last great feast of the liturgical year when the medieval church celebrated the final victory
of all those who had achieved the perfection which the Church
Militant on earth still sought. When the ceremonial arming is
completed, Gawain attends Mass and offers his homage at the
high altar. He then returns to the court, takes leave of the king
and the lords and ladies who kiss him and commend him to
Christ. He mounts, takes his helmet, and—climactically—is presented with his shield. With the poet I intend to pause over the
shield and its pentangle, though "tary hit us schulde," because,
as the identification of the hero, it is of the utmost importance
for an understanding of Gawain's character and actions.

The shield is literally a means of physical protection, its heraldic device a conventional means of identification. But both are
symbols, and since the poet leaves no doubt of the importance
of their figurative meanings, we may with profit explore both
the commonplace associations he could take for granted and the
particular meanings he takes pains to specify. This shield and
its device constitute an iconographical instance of extraordinary
importance in the late Middle Ages, unique in its combination
of rarity, elaboration, and focal position in the work as a whole.

For the Middle Ages, the basic figurative meanings of armor,
and especially helmet and shield, were found in Ephesians, chapter 6, a passage so fully glossed in St. Paul's text and so widely
used in medieval literature that to pursue it beyond its specific
reminders for the action here would be pointless. "Be strengthened in the Lord, in the might of his power. Put you on the

armor of God, so that you may be able to stand against the deceits of the devil." That is, put on the virtues of Christian soldiership to stand against the adversaries of the spirit: "for our wrestling is not against flesh and blood; but against the rulers of this world of darkness. Therefore take unto you the armor of God, that you may be able to resist in the evil day, and to stand in all things perfect. In all things take the shield of faith, wherewith you may be able to extinguish all the fiery darts of the most wicked one." An English contemporary, or near contemporary, of the *Gawain* poet, Robert Holkot, writes in his commentary on Wisdom:

> Our shield is our faith. In all dangers take up the shield of faith by which you can extinguish all the fiery weapons of the most evil one. In the history of Britain it is written that King Arthur had a picture of the glorious Virgin painted on the inside of his shield, and that whenever he was weary in battle he looked at it and recovered his hope and strength. So, too, if we wish to triumph in the warfare of this present life, we should bear on the shield of our faith the image of the Virgin with her Son; we should look at her and be confident in her, because from her we derive virtue and strength.[4]

The heraldic charge which appears on the outside of the shield literally identifies the knight who bears it, but it is also, as the poet elaborately makes clear, the symbolic means of identifying his characteristic virtues and aspirations. And since nearly everything that happens in the poem is governed by the behavior of the hero, the device which defines his character is likely to be of pervasive significance for the entire action. The poet himself stresses the importance of the pentangle's symbolism when he explains its meaning and why it "apendeʒ to þat prynce noble." It is, he says, a sign that Solomon set in betokening of truth, by the symbolism that it has.

Hit is a syngne þat Salamon set sumquyle   (625)
In bytoknyng of trawþe, bit tytle þat hit habbeȝ,
For hit is a figure þat haldeȝ fyue poynteȝ,
And vche lyne vmbelappeȝ and loukeȝ in oþer,
And ayquere hit is endeleȝ; and Englych hit callen
Oueral, as I here, þe endeles knot.
Forþy hit acordeȝ to þis knyȝt and to his cler armeȝ,
For ay faythful in fyue and sere fyue syþeȝ
Gawan watȝ for gode knawen, and as golde pured,
Voyded of vche vylany, wyth verteuȝ ennourned
            in mote;   (635)
        Forþy þe pentangel nwe
        He ber in schelde and cote,
        As tulk of tale most trwe
        And gentylest knyȝt of lote.

Fyrst he watȝ funden fautleȝ in his fyue wytteȝ,   (640)
And efte fayled neuer þe freke in his fyue fyngres,
And alle his afyaunce vpon folde watȝ in þe fyue woundeȝ
Þat Cryst kaȝt on þe croys, as þe crede telleȝ;
And quere-so-euer þys mon in melly watȝ stad,
His þro þoȝt watȝ in þat, þurȝ alle oþer þyngeȝ,
Þat alle his fersnes he feng at þe fyue joyeȝ
Þat þe hende heuen quene had of hir chylde;
At þis cause þe knyȝt comlyche hade
In þe more half of his schelde hir ymage depaynted,
Þat quen he blusched þerto his belde neuer payred.   (650)
Þe fyft fyue þat I finde þat þe frek vsed
Watȝ fraunchyse and felaȝschyp forbe al þyng,
His clannes and his cortaysye croked were neuer,
And pité, þat passeȝ alle poynteȝ, þyse pure fyue
Were harder happed on þat haþel þen on any oþer.[5]

Gawain was endowed with all the five fives in the perfect unity
of the endless figure by which they were represented—a wholly
virtuous knight, the best that his society had to offer. The poet's
exegesis is sufficiently enigmatic in itself, but in its narrative

context (apart from an undercurrent of suspicion which I shall take up in a moment) it supports the idea that Sir Gawain is the exemplar of Arthur's court, and so of all England; he is, or ought to be, the model of the secular, militant estate, the ideal of the ruling class, presented for the admiration and emulation of the contemporary audience.

The hero's claim to the perfection indicated by his charge can only be confirmed by the success of the quest which he is about to undertake. But Sir Gawain's most notable action in the course of his trial, the one which breaks the pattern of our easiest expectations, is a failure; the exemplar of chivalric virtue is false, treacherous, cowardly, recreant in that "lewté þat longeʒ to knyʒteʒ" (2373–84). At this moment near the end of the poem, we should recall those earlier ominous signs of youthful pride which suggest, in however low a key, that Arthur's court and its hero are somewhat less perfect than the ideal to which they aspire. If we have not noticed them, it may be that we have found attractive those relatively minor signs of human weakness which establish the congenial brotherhood of the imperfect. As one recent critic has put it, speaking for many: Gawain is a likeable man, all the more human for his slight fault, a model for the very best human conduct in spite of that "slightest compromise," the deceit of accepting the magic girdle.[6] But our poet is not so complacent, and neither is his hero; the ideals of fourteenth-century England were neither as flexible nor as earthbound as that. A feeling of sympathy, like the note of subdued amusement, is in the poem, but neither indicates a lack of commitment to the heroic ideals which Gawain represents and to which noble men must aspire. To recognize the inevitability of partial failure, and to weigh it ironically against reputation and pretentions, is not to transform vice into virtue for the sake of the general comfort. It remained for later ages to reduce human

aspirations to human size, and to exorcize guilt with the reassur-
ances of statistical togetherness. We can only recover the moral
world of a poem devoted to chivalric perfection by recalling
what was meant *then* by perfection. The key to the evidence in
the poem is found in the device inscribed on the shield of
the hero.

II

Little that has so far been written of Gawain's pentangle has
been shown to belong to the age in which the poem was made
or to bear directly on the poet's use of the device.[7] The pentangle is as old as history and as ubiquitous as the gammadion, a
situation which has given readers a false sense of confidence
while obscuring the fact that the device is very rare in the Middle Ages. We have been told that it has been found scratched on
Babylonian pottery, that it is a sign of the Pythagoreans' perfect
number, that it is an alternate to one of the suits in the Tarot
pack, that it is used in Freemasonry and Jewish iconography
on account of its associations with Solomon, and we are reminded that as the *drudenfusz* it appears in *Faust* and elsewhere in German. But all this is early and late, or almost wholly
undocumented, and while some of it may have a remote, or psy-
chologically profound, bearing on our poem, I should like to
explore some possibilities which are nearer the explicit and implicit interests of a skillful and well-informed court poet of the
second half of the fourteenth century.

First, the pentangle, or pentalpha, or pentagram, is called a
sign set by Solomon as a token of truth. The poet could hardly
have chosen a more ambiguous patron for Gawain's virtue. For
Solomon is a figure of perfection; there was no man like him
and his reputation reached the corners of the world (III Kings

4:29–34). He was for the Middle Ages a figure of Christ, the exemplar of wisdom and kingship, of power over demons. But in the Bible, and everywhere in the exegetical tradition, he is a gravely flawed figure, remarkably wise, but in the end guilty of follies that cost him his kingdom; and though he had power over demons, he was ultimately their victim, for his weakness for women turned him away from God and he built temples to the powers of darkness (III Kings 11:1–9). In the late Middle Ages theologians debated whether or not he was saved.[8] Gawain himself, late in the poem after he has acknowledged his failure, associates himself with Solomon's weakness when he comforts himself that others had been driven to folly and sorrow by the wiles of women: Adam, Sampson, David, and Solomon (2414–28).[9]

If Solomon is a dubious figure, so is his pentangle. It is not found in the Bible, not even in the elaborate decoration of his temple, though we do find there significant fives and even a pentagon. Nor is it associated with him in medieval art and literature apart from this poem, with a single exception. It is found in the books of magic associated with his name which were known and occasionally described as idolatrous books of necromancy.[10] Hugh of Saint Cher and others do comment favorably on certain figures of Solomon, inscribed on gems, which had the power of casting out demons, but I have not found these specified as pentangles.[11] The crucial fact is, however, that in the poem the pentangle is not a magic charm with inherent power; it is a sign or token of inner virtue. The test is of virtue, not of magical power; in this romance enchantment belongs to the poet's finely controlled mode, not his subject. Here, with exquisite irony that serves his thematic purposes, the poet transforms a suspect magical sign into an emblem of perfection to achieve the simultaneous suggestion of greatness and potential failure. These suggestions are strengthened if we turn to the

significance of five, and the pentagon, as figures of human
perfection.

The pentagon appears in Dante's discussion of human excel-
lence in the *Convivio*, where he uses the pentagon to illustrate
man's natural perfection.[12] Just as the pentagon is one, but includes potentially the figures which are contained in it, so the
human soul, which is one and rational, includes potentially the
four lower kinds of vital activity which belong to lesser living
things. If the fifth, specifying power of the rational soul, be
removed or subdued by the lower power of the sensual appetites,
we are left with a brute animal, a dead man. Dante takes his
doctrine, and his figures, from Aristotle's *De anima*, and he finds
his specifically medieval elaborations of it in the scholastic commentators, notably St. Thomas.[13] But note that the pentagon
symbolizes *natural* perfection as the philosopher knew it, not
supernatural perfection to which man, by reason of the fall and
the grace of redemption, was called. A pentagon in the Biblical tradition associated with Solomon has a similar significance.
The doors to the Holy of Holies, the doors to eternal life, are
hinged on pentagonal posts five cubits high (III Kings 6:31 32).
Bede's comment, repeated in the *Glossa Ordinaria* and therefore
standard throughout the late Middle Ages, explains that the
pentagonal posts signify the body with its five senses which is
destined to be admitted to heaven, and the five cubits signify
that this destiny can be achieved only by those who serve God
with the five senses of the body and the five senses of the heart.[14]

The number five as symbol is limited in the same way as the
pentagon.[15] In Macrobius and Martianus Capella, and generally
in the Fathers and later commentators, pentads of almost any
sort stand for the senses, and, by extension, for the body and the
sensual appetites. The five senses are limited inasmuch as they
need the government of reason, just as the pentagonal soul is

limited by its dependence on grace. In Durandus' great work on
the liturgy, ritual fives are also found to signify the five wounds
of Christ, the five kinds of mercy necessary for salvation, and
perhaps most significantly, the secular estate as opposed to the
spiritual estate whose number is four.[16]

These traditional views fit well enough the poet's enigmatic
explanation of Gawain's five fives. To be found faultless in his
five wits is to have achieved, at least by reputation and aspiration, natural control over the senses, interior as well as exterior.
Not to fail in his five fingers is a darker, but nonetheless conventional attribute which, so far as I know, has not so far been
satisfactorily explained.[17] Perfection in the five fingers was, in
the Middle Ages, a conventional figure for the five virtues which,
in the words of John of San Geminiano, "are necessary for man
in order that his works should be perfect." The thumb stands
for justice because—as Aristotle and Avicenna had said—justice
works with the other virtues and is equal to them in strength,
just as the thumb works with, and is equal to, the other fingers.
The index finger signifies prudence, the third finger temperance,
the ring finger fortitude, and the *digitus auricularis* figures obedience with respect to the divine will, to human authority, and
to one's own reason.[18] This interpretation points to the natural
virtues, and therefore to natural perfection, and thus it fits the
pattern of the number five, the figure of the pentagon, and the
domain of the five senses. With the five wounds of Christ and
the five joys of Mary we move from the signs of natural perfection to figures of the theological virtues of faith and hope.

For the five wounds there is a pentangle in the Renaissance
which was probably known in the fourteenth century. In Valeriano, Carteri, a Lapide and others the pentangle appears as a
symbol of ὑγιεία, or *salus,* in ancient times a charm against illness
or bodily injury, but in Christian times a figure of salvation be-

cause it is a figure of the five wounds of Christ.[19] Valeriano illustrates the figure with a nude Christ, arms and legs moderately extended with the wounds in hands, feet and breast connected by lines to make a pentangle. Says Cornelius a Lapide: "this pentalpha is God, who is alpha and omega; and Christus Salvator; whence Valeriano justly adapts the figure to the five wounds of Christ." And Valeriano: "But since these stories of the preternatural power and symbolic meaning of the pentagram in antiquity may not seem sufficiently agreeable, I have decided to pass over many stories of this sort, especially since it ill becomes men given to serious things to occupy themselves with such worthless legends. But I certainly cannot pass over the fact that we can accept as signifying true "salvation" *(verae salutis)* the five wounds of Christ . . . which appropriately constitute a pentalpha."[20]

III

In summary, then, the device on Sir Gawain's shield indicates the moral perfection to which the knight as *miles Christi* aspires. The heraldic charge signifies the character of the hero about to undertake the "aniuus viage" which will test his right to the device as it will test the right of the court he represents to its reputation for perfection. But, as we have seen, the sign that Solomon set as a token of truth is fraught with suggestions of human weakness in the face of the powers of darkness; the hero will do well to keep his gaze fixed on the image of spiritual perfection, the "hende heuen quene," painted on the inside of his shield.

Alone, with no companion but God, he undertakes his journey. He is an alien, far from friends, and surrounded by enemies. Against such obvious adversaries as dragons and trolls his valor and piety are sufficient. The real test comes in the familiar social environment of Bercilak's castle where, divested of armor and shield, warm and well fed and admired, he must struggle against the dark powers within himself, aroused and concealed by the softening influences of society. On the final day of his journey, Gawain is keenly aware of the liturgical season. It is the solemn vigil of Christmas, a day of penance and expectation. Still wandering in the wilderness he prays to the Virgin to hear Mass on the great feast, and he cries for his sins.

But after a gracious and admiring welcome at the castle, when he is comfortably settled before the fire in the great hall, Gawain forgets both the perils of the journey and the implications of the season—not to speak of the doom he must face on the octave day. The vigil of Christmas was a day of fast and abstinence, but Gawain is served a fish dinner fit for a gourmet with an insatiable medieval appetite. With amused irony the poet records Gawain's graceful compliments on the feast, and the protests of the waiters: this is a penitential dinner; wait until you see what we have tomorrow. The poet also notes that the hero seemed to have a better and better time as the wine went to his head. After dinner, the lord of the castle, his ladies, and his honored guest go to the chapel for solemn Vespers, and, while I should not want to take too solemn a view of this episode, what goes on in the chapel between the well-fed hero and his host's beautiful wife suggests devotion to something other than the liturgy. Under other circumstances, the lady's bare breast and bright throat might claim even the perfect knight's attentive concern— but not in the chapel. There is laughter in the poet's voice as he contrasts the broad buttocks of the ugly older matron with the beauty of the young wife: she was a "more lykkerwys on to lyk" (966–69).

The courteous flirtation continues next day, the day, as the poet remarks, that "dryȝtyn for oure destyné to deȝe watȝ borne." The tone of the poem at this point surely does not suggest the stern moralist's condemnation, but neither is it a simple celebration of noble manners. It is designed to suggest some softening in the moral fiber of a hero distracted from a quest which will try his virtue to the utmost. It would be gauche of the poet, and so of the critic, to spoil this party, but in the context of the total action it is not amiss to remind ourselves that Gawain is falling somewhat short of the perfection of his five wits and fingers, not to speak of the five wounds, especially since it is just such genteel compromises with heroic and single-minded virtue which will result in his fall within the week.

Nor is the virtue displayed by Gawain in the bedroom as impressive as it has been taken to be by most modern readers. These scenes are high-style parody of a discredited literary convention in striking contrast to the simplicity and coarseness of the analogous scenes in *The Carl of Carlyle*. Here again the note of amusement invests the action and dialogue. Everything is excessive and mildly ridiculous: the great Gawain lies in bed far into the morning while his host is out in the forest engaged in the chivalric exercise of hunting. His wife, a gentle lady, is engaged in a hunt of her own, and with all the *courtesie* of a sophisticated trollop. "Here you are . . . and we are alone," she says, as she sits on his bed. "My husband and his men have gone for the day . . . the door is locked. Since I have in my house the man whom the whole world praises, I shall spend my time well, while it lasts. You are welcome to my body, to use it for your pleasure." If this falls somewhat short of *gentilesse* Gawain's reply is mildly ridiculous enough to complete the parody of *amour courtois:* "In faith, that would indeed be a favor, but I am unworthy to reach for such reverence as you suggest" (1230–44). To read these scenes as though they were a solemn exercise of Gawain's chastity, or a demonstration of his skill as a courtier who will not, whatever the provocation, offend a lady, is to mistake game for earnest. This is a gentle mockery of manners mistaken for morals, and further evidence that Gawain is in fact more vulnerable than he knows.

The poet's handling of Gawain's religious conscience is more subtle, and equally amusing. When, after the third grueling morning of temptation in the bedroom, he accepts the magic girdle because he thinks it can preserve him from death, he breaks his faith as a knight to his host, to his fearful antagonist, and most of all to himself. The pentangle is shattered and its place taken by a new sign, now indeed a magic charm—or so he hopes—which he will later call "a token of untruth," the analogue of the foul skin of the fox in the parallel symbolism of the hunt. At once the hero wants to go to confession, and in the scene which follows the poet adds to his pervasive comic irony an extraordinary revelation of medieval psychology. This is no ordinary confession; it is the last chance for a doomed man. Gawain confesses "the more and the mynne," his great and small sins, and he is said to be shriven so clean that Judgment Day should come in the morning—as, of course, it will. But he has repressed the only serious sin of which we can imagine him guilty; and, if it does not seem serious to us, it will to him when he has to face it at the Green Chapel, and that is sufficient to make it so. But face to face with his confessor in the castle he cannot acknowledge it, even to himself, for to do so would be to lose the protection he thinks it offers. To suppose, as a recent interpreter of the confessional scenes does, that Gawain makes an invalid confession, and faces the perilous confrontation at the Green Chapel in bad conscience, is to think worse of the hero than the poem as a whole permits.[21] There are moral issues which the rational mind will not face, or face dispassionately, when survival seems to be at stake and when so many mitigating circumstances can be invoked to cloud the issue.

The irony of muddled conscience is sustained through the New Year's journey to the green mound and to the end of the quest. When his guide suggests flight, Gawain gallantly refuses, because, he says, "Ful wel con dryʒtyn schape / His seruaunteʒ for to saue" (2138-39). And later, "To Goddeʒ wylle I am ful bayn, / And to hym I haf me tone" (2158-59). Does his hand stray unconsciously to the supposedly magic girdle; and do we, who know of its existence, smile sympathetically at this exemplary Christian knight who hedges his bets against impending doom? Only when he is confronted directly with the evidence of his *untruth* does Gawain acknowledge the flaw in his virtue. And, as essentially good men will, especially those who tend to overconfidence in virtue, he is overwhelmed by shame and greatly exaggerates the degree of his failure. He accuses himself of cowardice, treachery, and untruth—and, significantly, of disgrace to his class, recreancy in the "larges and lewté þat longeʒ to knyʒteʒ" (2374-88).

But the Green Knight will not condemn him, nor will the poet, nor will the reader. Sir Gawain is one of the best who ever walked, but here he lacked a little in fidelity to that perfection to which he aspired, and for which he stood. In this self-discovery the hero made a beginning in the necessary virtue of humility. Will Arthur's court profit by the lesson? The poem suggests that it probably will not. The knight who went out to vindicate the honor of the court bore on his shield the sign that Solomon set as a token of truth; he returned with new knowledge of his limitations, carrying the girdle about his neck as a token of untruth. But the lords and ladies of the court, still somewhat *childgered* and given to pride, laughed loudly and decided amiably that the knights of the Round Table would wear the green lace in honor of Gawain. Will the fourteenth-century courtiers profit by the lesson? They will at least have been reminded of the ideal to which they were called, and of the weakness which afflicts even the best. But the poem has not demanded tears or terror. Amid the relieved laughter of the knights and ladies one sees the wry smile of the amiable poet: it is enough if some of the laughter is directed at themselves.

·· ⊰[10]⊱ ··

Structure and Symmetry
in *Sir Gawain*

DONALD R. HOWARD

No one who reads *Sir Gawain and the Green Knight* fails to notice its elaborate, symmetrical structure. Everywhere in the poem is balance, contrast, and antithesis. Things are arranged in pairs—there are two New Year's days, two "beheading" scenes, two courts, two confessions; or in threes—three temptations, three hunts, three kisses, three strokes of the ax. These intricacies are unobtrusively integrated with events and themes; and perhaps just for that reason, critics have taken note of them only piecemeal and in passing, often with reference to the poem's mythic or symbolic content.[1] In what follows I intend to examine the narrative units based upon structural parallels in *Sir Gawain,* and to suggest in what way they coincide with the divisions of the poem marked by the ornamented and colored capitals of the manuscript. To do so, however, I shall have to turn first to the symbolism of the poem; for what I wish to argue

Reprinted by permission of the author and The Mediaeval Academy of America from *Speculum*, XXXIX (1964), 425–33.

See also Stoddard Malarkey and J. Barre Toelken, "Gawain and the Green Girdle," *JEGP*, LXIII (1964), 14–20.

is that its most protracted structural parallel depends upon the juxtaposition of two symbols, the shield and the girdle.

I

Everyone from Mary McCarthy to C. S. Lewis has expressed caveats about literary symbolism, and it is true, symbol-hunting is an easy game with no particular criteria of corrigibility. In the study of medieval literature there is the added problem of a vast body of symbolism based on the four-level method of interpreting Scripture.[2] It is reassuring, therefore, to have at least one medieval work in which the symbols are identified as such by the author. No one has ever questioned the fact that the pentangle shield and the green girdle in *Sir Gawain and the Green Knight* are symbols. They are neither "Freudian" nor "patristic." Rather, the author tells us in ll. 619–665 what the pentangle means, and there is precedent in medieval lore for that symbolic meaning. Likewise with the magic girdle, when Gawain keeps it at the end of the poem he says in so many words that it is to be a "syngne of my surfet" to remind him of the "faut and þe fayntyse of þe flesche crabbed."[3]

Yet I think no one has examined the way in which these two symbols are juxtaposed and paired, so that their meaning, to use Northrop Frye's language, comes about through the centripetal force of their relationship within the whole literary structure.[4] Gawain's journey to the Green Chapel, we know, is made in two stages. Hence there are two descriptions of the arming of the knight, one when he leaves Arthur's court (ll. 536–669), the other when he leaves Bercilak's castle (ll. 2011–41). The earlier passage begins with Gawain's statement of his indifference to his destiny—"Quat schuld I wonde? / Of destinés derf and dere / What may mon do bot fonde?" (ll. 563–565); it ends with the description of the shield. The later passage, however, ends with a description not of the shield but of the girdle, which Gawain wears "to save himself."

Thus the girdle, within the symbolic structure of the poem, becomes a substitute for the shield. By shield I mean the shield itself, not its painted allegory. Critics often treat the shield and its pentangle device as a single object, which of course they are. Yet the symbolism of shield and girdle is symbolism of a different kind from that of the pentangle. The pentangle has an *assigned* symbolic value; it is put into the poem in order to stand for an abstraction, like Sansfoy and Sansloy, or Sin and Death. It tells us that Gawain is the "pentagonal man," the ideal knight.[5] The shield and girdle, however, take their symbolic meaning from the situation, the use they are put to, the attitudes and emotions which people show towards them, and their juxtaposition one against the other. They remain just as much girdle and shield as Desdemona's handkerchief remains a handkerchief, or Eve's apple an apple. While the pentangle is a painted sign—it appears on the knight's cote-armor as well as on his shield[6]—the shield and girdle are real objects, and function in the poem as living, articulate symbols, dynamically paired.

The pentangle shield of course evokes the chivalric ideal. As part of the knight's armor, it is not surprising that it has symbolic meaning, for a knight's garments and gear, like a priest's vestments, were often given symbolic values.[7] Yet the description of the arming of Sir Gawain gives no symbolic meaning to anything *but* the pentangle. All his articles of clothing and armor are described in the most worldly terms—they are of costly silk, of bright fur, of well-worked and highly polished steel adorned with gold. His helmet, the last garment he puts on (kissing it as a priest might kiss the stole), has a silk cover embroidered with the best gems and encircled with costly diamonds. His garments and armor are also *useful*—they are "alle þe godlych gere þat hym gayn schulde" (l. 584). The poet has concentrated all his powers on the lush description and saved the symbolism of moral values until the end, where it is more pointed and dramatic. By arranging his material in this way, he has underscored an essential fact: that a knight's valor is dependent on worldly means. The practice of chivalry presents the knight with the problem of using the world's goods for worldly ends and yet adopting those virtues which will keep him from loving the world itself.

After hearing Mass, Gawain puts on his helmet and takes up the shield (the manuscript at this point makes a subdivision with a colored capital).[8] On its inside is the image of the Blessed Virgin, which will remind Gawain of her five joys and so renew his courage. On its outside is the pentangle or "endless knot," representing Gawain's perfection in his five senses and his five fingers, his faith in the five wounds of Christ and the five joys of the Virgin, and his possession of the five knightly virtues— franchise, fellowship, purity, courtesy, and pity.[9] (These virtues, as Professor Engelhardt has shown,[10] correspond in a general way to the chivalric virtues of piety, valor, and courtesy, and so represent his religious, military, and courtly obligations.) Hence the shield, with its images on either side, functions in two ways—to the knight as a devotional reminder, to the world as an emblem of his inner moral perfection. It is at base a worldly object, a part of his warlike gear, designed at once to protect his body and remind him of his immortal soul, so that it suggests at once his knightly valor and his spiritual indifference to destiny. To the world, the shield shows what spiritual strength lies beneath Gawain's rich trappings; to Gawain, it shows what ultimate spiritual meaning lies beneath the world's bright lures. Yet it is to have this devotional and spiritual meaning precisely in those moments when he is most the knight, when he is most given to worldly deeds and most reliant upon the shield as a made object. It thus points to the proper attitude for a knight:

to be indifferent to one's life in the world and yet preserve it, to use the world well and yet love it little.[11]

After the temptations, when Gawain is ready to leave the castle for the Green Chapel, the poet again describes the arming of the knight. This time, however, he says nothing about the shield; instead, he ends by explaining why Gawain wears the girdle:

> Bot wered not þis ilk wyȝe for wele þis gordel,
> For pryde of þe pendaunteȝ, þaȝ polyst þay were,
> And þaȝ þe glyterande golde glent vpon endeȝ,
> Bot for to sauen hymself, when suffer hym byhoued,
> To byde bale withoute dabate of bronde hym to were
>   oþer knyffe   (ll. 2037–2042).

As the shield is emblematic of Gawain's knightly virtue, the girdle is emblematic of his fault. The whole movement of the story hangs upon his yielding to temptation, accepting the girdle, and having his failing revealed to him. In the end, Gawain himself makes the girdle a symbol of his "surfet" and of the weakness of the flesh. Now a girdle was an ordinary article of clothing, a belt or cincture from which one hung objects like keys or a purse. Because of its function, it was a convenient symbol for worldliness—the Oxford English Dictionary in fact reports such a metaphorical usage in the fifteenth century. *This* girdle, however, has the added lure of being rich and finely wrought in its own right: it is made of green silk, embroidered about the edges, and hung with pendants of highly polished gold.[12] More than that, it has powers of its own—not merely an emblematic meaning, like that of the shield's device, but remarkable "costes þat knit ar þerinne" (l. 1849), magical properties to save the wearer from being slain. The author carefully reminds us that Gawain accepts the girdle for these powers, not for its

richness. He goes so far as to tell us what the knight thought
before accepting it:

> Þen kest þe knyȝt, and hit come to his hert,
> Hit were a juel for þe jopardé þat hym iugged were,
> When he acheued to þe chapel his chek for to fech;
> Myȝt he haf slypped to be vnslayn, þe sleȝt were
>   noble   (ll. 1855–58).

And Gawain, when he proposes to wear it as a memento of his
failing, himself denies any interest in either its worth or its
beauty:

> 'Bot your gordel' quoþ Gawayn "God yow forȝelde!
> Þat wyl I welde wyth good wylle, not for þe wynne golde,
> Ne þe saynt, ne þe sylk, ne þe syde pendaundes,
> For wele ne for worchyp, ne for þe wlonk werkkeȝ,
> Bot in syngne of my surfet I schal se hit ofte,
> When I ride in renoun, remorde to myseluen
> Þe faut and þe fayntyse of þe flesche crabbed,
> How tender hit is to entyse teches of fylþe . . .   (ll. 2429–36).

Gawain has taken the girdle, then, not to own it for its value
or wear it for its beauty, but simply to save his life.[13] It is as
worldly an object, and used for as worldly an end as the shield;
but unlike the shield, it is magical, it is used solely for a selfish
reason, and its acceptance requires that he act dishonorably
either to the lady or her husband if he is to keep it. He is guilty
not because he desires "to sauen hymself," but because in order
to do so he uses worldly means in the wrong way.

Even after he has taken the girdle, however, the knight continues to profess submission to God's will. When tempted by his
guide to flee he declares, "Ful wel con dryȝtyn schape / His
seruaunteȝ for to saue" (ll. 2138–39), and again, "I wyl nauþer
grete ne grone; / To Goddeȝ wylle I am ful bayn, / And to
hym I haf me tone" (ll. 2157–59). So, when he sees the Green
Chapel, he says, "Let God worche! . . . My lif þaȝ I forgoo, /
Drede dotȝ me no lote" (ll. 2208–11). In these utterances we

must not think him hypocritical. While he has taken the girdle and presumably held some hope for its efficacy, he has not deserted, but compromised, the chivalric ideal and its religious requirements. He is, in fact, never wholly sure of the girdle's powers. At the first stroke of the ax he flinches; and on the third stroke, when his neck is nicked, he bounds up and throws into place—his shield.

Gawain's indifference to "destinés derf and dere" is, we need to remember, the self-abnegation not of the cloistered monk but of the active knight. "What may mon do bot fonde?" (l. 565) he had asked—what can one do but *try*. He is admirably suited to put his destiny to the test: he is devoted to the articles of faith and has the virtues appropriate to the ideal Christian knight. The problem is to maintain the fine balance between this religious ethos and the unavoidable necessity of using worldly means to preserve life and accomplish knightly deeds. Hence he accepts the girdle not for any active pride which revolts against God, nor for avarice, nor covetousness, nor for vainglory, but for instinctive self-preservation, the central, involuntary worldliness of fallen man, through which even the best is easily tempted. This perfectly understandable weakness, however, leads him into other transgressions—the breaking of his oath to the lord, the false confession, the last failure of courtesy to the Green Knight. Once he has upset that finely balanced indifference to the world, those of the chivalric virtues which govern worldly action become in part unattainable. The poem suggests in this way how the worldly aims of chivalry and the other-worldly aims of the Christian life are ideally interrelated, but, for fallen man, potentially incompatible.

II

The poet suggested these distinctions by treating as symbols articles which were naturally part of his story. The girdle and shield are juxtaposed as two kinds of worldliness: the girdle an illicit and self-centered means of holding on to life; the shield an allowable, self-abnegating use of the world's goods in the service of the highest Christian ideals. These two symbols, paired so that they reflect the moral choice which confronts the hero, initiate two sequences which form a major structural parallel in the poem. The main action, beginning with Gawain's departure in the second division, falls into two stages—the events at the castle, and those at the Green Chapel.[14] The one comprises Sections II and III; the other, Section IV. No one, I think, has noticed that these two sequences are matched by an elaborate parallelism. The same kinds of events, in exactly the same order, occur in either part, and they center upon the three temptations in the first sequence and the three strokes of the ax in the second, with a confession following in each. These parallel contrasts are used artistically to distinguish Gawain's temptation and fall from his punishment and pardon. We shall see this best if we represent the contrasts in diagram:

Sections II–III	Section IV
(1) Arming of the knight, and description of the shield (ll. 536–669)	Arming of the knight, and description of the girdle (ll. 1998–2041)
(2) Journey to the castle (ll. 670–762)	Journey to the Green Chapel (ll. 2069–2159)
(3) Description of the castle (ll. 763–810)	Description of the Green Chapel (ll. 2160–2211)
(4) Three temptations (ll. 1126–1869)	Three strokes of the ax (ll. 2212–2330)
(5) Confession to the priest (ll. 1876–1884)	Confession to the Green Knight (ll. 2378–2438)

This structural design coincides with the four manuscript divisions marked by ornamented capitals, the four "sections" of the poem observed in editions. Now the last three of these are subdivided by small ornamented capitals, so that the whole falls into nine units.[15] These nine units seem to be based on a principle of suspense; they mark off blocks of information. The four major divisions, on the other hand, mark the major episodes of the story—the opening scene, with the beheading episode and challenge; the passing of a year, and Gawain's journey to the castle; the temptations; and the second "beheading" scene, followed by the explanation and Gawain's return to court. The opening scene is kept as a single unit with no internal division— a kind of prologue to the mission which Gawain must undertake. The work begins and ends with a reference to the fall of Troy and the founding of Britain, so that the events at Arthur's court are seen in the perspective of history as a point out of the past to which the reader draws up close and then away.[16] This sense of the sweep of time is matched within the poem by the lines on the passing of the year, at the beginning of the second division (ll. 491–535), which divide the prologue from the main action—the first New Year's feast with its beheading episode from the journey which Gawain must make a year later.

The second division of the poem is therefore a kind of intermezzo between the challenge and Gawain's journey. It comprises the description of the year's passing, Gawain's preparations to leave, the description of his armor with the passage on the pentangle, his voyage through the wilderness, and his arrival at the castle. The smaller capitals of the manuscript make two divisions within it, one beginning with the description of the shield (l. 619), the other with his arrival at the castle (l. 763). In the castle, a great dinner is set with many dishes and fine sauces, which Gawain calls a feast; it is a fish dinner, though, since Christmas Eve is a fast day, and he is drolly reminded that these culinary splendors are a penance—"Þis penaunce now ȝe take, / And eft hit schal amende" (ll. 897–98). After dinner the company hears evensong, and in the chapel Gawain sees for the first time the beautiful young lady with her ugly, aged companion.[17] On the next day there is a true Christmas feast; after it Gawain learns that the Green Chapel is nearby, and agrees that while waiting to leave he will exchange what he wins in the castle for what the lord wins hunting. Throughout, there is a fine balance of contraries: the revolution of the seasons, the warlike shield and its religious emblem, the unpleasant journey and the agreeable life of the castle, fasting and feasting, youth and age, beauty and ugliness, and at last the agreement to give what each has gained.

This tendency to match and contrast things is a dominant feature of the poem's style. It is, with respect to the purely verbal element, a feature encouraged by alliterative verse; a dozen examples come to mind—"bliss and blunder," "brittened and brent," "stad and stoken." As we have seen, it sustains the structural unity not only in the two beheading scenes juxtaposed at beginning and end, but in the parallels, diagrammed above, between the events at the castle (Sections II–III) and those at the chapel (Section IV). These parallels contribute to the almost ritual symmetry of the whole, and they give to the later sequence a dreamlike aura of familiarity. Each of them contrasts in its own way, and each contrast contributes to the mystery and wonder of the final scene:

(1) In both parts, the arming of the knight before the journey is described in detail. In the earlier passage, the description ends with the lines on the pentangle shield. But when Gawain leaves the castle for the Green Chapel, the shield is not mentioned; instead the passage ends with a description of the girdle and a reminder that he is wearing it not for avarice or vainglory, but only to save his life.

(2) In both parts he must undertake a journey. In the earlier journey there is positive danger from beasts and giants; there is

cold and hardship. In the shorter journey to the Green Chapel there are no physical dangers, but there is a spiritual one: his guide tempts him to flee. The description of the mist which hovers about the place and of the streams flowing through it creates an atmosphere of eerie uncertainty, very different from the explicit perils of the earlier passage: here, the perils are to come at the *end* of the journey.

(3) In both parts, the building is described as the knight comes upon it. The castle is on a knoll, surrounded by a park, and is built in the very newest style of late fourteenth-century architecture.[18] It is so new, and so idealized, that it seems almost illusory; its pinnacles, the author tells us, seemed as if cut out of paper (l. 802).[19] The Green Chapel, on the other hand, is ancient and gnarled, in part subterranean—such a place as the devil at midnight would say his matins in—like a cave or the crevice of an old crag, overgrown with grass. It is at the fork of a roaring stream, and the air is split with the ominous, and comic, whirring of a grindstone.

(4) The three temptations are of course paralleled by the three strokes of the ax. The temptations are carried out with an exuberant humor in which the daily hunting and the exchange of winnings serve as humorous parallels. The hunts themselves contrast with the temptations in intensity and aggressiveness, and the animals hunted suggest those qualities which Gawain must conquer—timidity, ferocity, and cunning.[20] The relation between Gawain and the lady reverses the courtly love code, in which the God of Love was said to be irresistible; in fact, in *Sir Gawain,* the lady offers to be the knight's servant (l. 1240).[21] The enviable but ridiculous position of the hero was a familiar one, to be sure, but it is heightened by the ritual exchanges. The kisses increase in number daily. The whole is recounted in a tone of suppressed mirth; while there is great suspense over the outcome of the temptations, the reader is encouraged to feel

that he really knows what is going on. The lord's replies on receiving the kisses are richly ambiguous, for it is never wholly clear whether or not he knows what his wife has been up to. And the romping style of the passage makes the reader feel that he knows something of the *kind* of outcome, though he knows no details.

But at the Green Chapel, the three strokes of the ax are short and suspenseful. We know something is going to happen; we hear a noise, *as if* someone were grinding a scythe! But when Gawain gets under the ax, we are completely in the dark. Even when his neck is nicked on the third stroke and he bounds up in self-defense, we are puzzled. When he accepted the girdle, we knew exactly what had happened; here, we are more confused than ever. We know the facts, but they make no sense.

(5) The explanation of course follows at once. As soon as Gawain's fault is revealed to him he flares up at the knight, flinging the girdle at him. Then he confesses his fault. This confession, as John Burrow has shown, parallels his confession to the priest after Gawain has taken the girdle. That earlier confession was really invalid; but in the second confession (though made to the Green Knight) he is genuinely contrite, he makes an honest confession (ll. 2379–86), he promises to do better (ll. 2387–88), and of course he does public penance by wearing the girdle. The court's judgment of his sin, however, is far less severe than his own—he twice confesses covetousness, although this is specifically denied in the poem. He wears the girdle as a sign of the weakness of the flesh, and the rest of the court join him in wearing a green band across their chests. Agreeing to do so, the king comforts him and the rest laugh.

This analysis of the narrative structure indicates that the significant manuscript divisions are the ornamented capitals which mark the four major divisions. The five small capitals which mark subdivisions do not systematically correspond to narrative units. They seem to serve for emphasis, and were probably placed in accord with the author's—or scribe's—sense of dramatic rhythm. One precedes the description of the shield (l. 619); another marks Gawain's arrival at the castle (l. 763). In the third section, one marks the beginning of the second temptation (l. 1421), and another follows Gawain's confession (l. 1893). In the fourth section, there is a small capital at the beginning of the "beheading" scene (l. 2259). If we divided the poem into nine sections (without regard to the size of the capitals), its structure and symmetry would be obscured. All of this lends significance to a fact which has generally been ignored: at each of the three internal divisions marked by the larger capitals, the scribe has left one ruled space, and through each of these spaces the illuminator has extended the red ornamentation across the page in an identical design. There is no similar spacing or ornamentation elsewhere within the text of *Sir Gawain* or of the other three poems preserved in the same manuscript.

This elaborate parallelism, with its multiple contrasts, helps produce the gamelike, ironic tone of *Sir Gawain*. Its effect is comic. The ritual balance of incidents does, in the end, what comedy always does—it purges extremes of conduct and brings the reader comfortably back to a norm; it restores the *status quo*. Gawain returns to the starting-place, and, however chastened, is greeted with laughter which dispels his sobriety. The symbolism of shield and girdle suggests an essential and inescapable conflict between chivalry and Christianity; but this conflict is treated throughout in a spirit of amused and ironic detachment, as if the poet meant to suggest that these contrarieties of medieval thought, being irreconcilable, should be taken in good humor as a condition of life in an imperfect world. The mysterious and marvelous, which in tragedy remain ultimately incomprehensible, are here explained rationally away; we are asked not so much to *feel* the hero's experience as to think about it, to understand. The symmetrical world of the poem is at once unreal and substantial—far in the past and idealized, and yet plainly the world of real human conduct, of uncertainty and self-deception. It is too neatly balanced to be like the flux of history itself, yet it is an unpredictable world full of surprises; and, from the long view, it is ordered and right.

·◦❳[11]❲◦·

Myth and Mediaeval Literature:
Sir Gawain and the Green Knight

CHARLES MOORMAN

It seems obvious that much of the current interest in the place
of myth in literature, as manifested in an ever-increasing number of books and articles on the subject, stems from the fact that
myth study can be said to be the logical successor, not in terms of

Reprinted by permission of the author and the editor from *Mediaeval
Studies*, XVIII (1956), 158-72.

For studies of seasonal imagery in *Gawain*, see John Speirs, "Sir Gawayne
and the Grene Knight" in his *Medieval English Poetry: the Non-Chaucerian
Tradition* (London, 1957), pp. 215–51; William A. Nitze, "Is the Green
Knight Story a Vegetation Myth?", *MP*, XXXIII (1936), 351–66; Ananda K.
Coomaraswamy, "*Sir Gawain and the Green Knight*: Indra and Namuci,"
Speculum, XIX (1944), 104–25; Derek A. Pearsall, "Rhetorical *Descriptio*
in *Sir Gawain and the Green Knight*," *MLR*, L (1955), 129–34; and Theodore
Silverstein, "The Art of *Sir Gawain and the Green Knight*," *University of
Toronto Quarterly*, XXXIII (1964), 258–78.

For studies of color symbolism, see Joseph F. Eagan, S.J., "The Import of
Color Symbolism in *Sir Gawain and the Green Knight*," *St. Louis University
Studies*, series A, vol. I (1949), 11–86; A. H. Krappe, "Who *Was* the Green
Knight," *Speculum*, XIII (1938), 206–15; D. W. Robertson, "Why the Devil
Wears Green," *MLN*, LXIX (1954), 470–72; Dale B. J. Randall, "Was the
Green Knight a Fiend?", *SP*, LVII (1960), 479–91; Robert B. White, Jr., "A
Note on the Green Knight's Red Eyes," *ELN*, II (1965), 250–52; and William
Branford, "Bercilak de Hautdesert: An Interrogation of the Green Knight,"
English Studies in Africa, VII (1964), 54–64.

literary influence, but of "intellectual fashion,"[1] to the New Criticism. It will be conceded that the New Critics have achieved their ends; they have succeeded in making even the most conservative academicians concentrate their efforts, both in print and in the classroom, toward bringing their peripheral studies of aesthetics, sources, biography, and literary history to bear directly upon the illumination of a text in hand. The myth critics, on the other hand, bid fair to returning the serious study of literature to a point of view which the New Critics originally banded together to attack. These mythographers have forsaken that basic doctrine of the New Criticism which insisted on the integrity of the individual work of art, and have returned for inspiration to those sections of the library given over to myth, folklore, anthropology, psychology, and comparative religion.

A glance at the critical barrage directed at *Sir Gawain and the Green Knight,* and for that matter in almost any other piece of medieval literature, which seems particularly susceptible to this sort of treatment, will show how the myth critic has shifted the focus of interest away from purely literary values and back again to the most sterile sorts of source hunting and parallel finding. Just as the typical nineteenth-century academician regarded *Sir Gawain and the Green Knight* only as a storehouse of information on mediaeval armor, architecture, and venery, so do the myth critics insist that the poem is only a repository of myth patterns and thus direct their efforts to elucidating Gawain's relationship to the British Jack-in-the-Green, the Celtic sun god, and the omnipresent vegetation god. A very brief review of two of these myth-minded critical treatments of *Sir Gawain and the Green Knight* should serve to demonstrate that, despite their pieties in theory, the myth critics have in practice shown that they believe that once they have discovered the myth pattern inherent in a piece of literature, they have illuminated and settled once and for all the critical problems presented by that particular work.

Our first critic, the late Heinrich Zimmer, is a follower of C. G. Jung, the disciple of Freud. The Jungian school takes as a point of departure Jung's concept of a "collective unconscious" in which mythological archetypes "correspond to certain *collective* structural elements of the human psyche in general, and like the morphological elements of the human body, are *inherited.*"[2] The Jungian critic thus first "circumscribes" the central archetype present in the work (which can never be exactly described because "it does not refer to any thing that is or has been conscious"[3]), demonstrates its universality by bringing to light a number of parallel manifestations of the myth, and finally, by way of conclusion, states that in this particular poem we find an unconscious manifestation of the archetype. Professor Zimmer follows this general pattern rather closely in examining *Sir Gawain and the Green Knight* in the course of a volume entitled *The King and the Corpse,*[4] the unifying thesis of which is, as I understand it, that the hero's quest is essentially a psychiatric process by means of which the innocent hero, in undergoing the *rite de passage* which initiates him into the life of the whole man, gives up his conscious self and intellectual identity in order to be guided by his brute instincts to the bottom of his personality and there unite conscious and unconscious, intellectual and animal existences.

In his extended discussion of *Sir Gawain and the Green Knight,* Zimmer finds that the archetypal pattern which the poem reflects is that of the initiation of the hero, the *rite de passage,* which in turn involves the death-rebirth archetype: "Through the valley of death he [Gawain] is conducted to the aloof and lonely sanctuary of life renewed, and then, having withstood the trial, is reborn."[5] But while no one would deny that the poem involves testing and initiation, it is difficult to understand in reading Zimmer's analysis just how this general statement of theme, applicable surely to a great many myths, is entirely and consistently relevant to a particularly finished and beautifully articulated fourteenth-century poem. For example, in order to superimpose his death-rebirth archetypal pattern on the poem, Zimmer states that the Green Knight represents Death and his wife Life.[6] Zimmer bases these statements on the facts that (1) "in folklore and fairy tales the dead not uncommonly carry their heads under their arms . . . ," that (2) "pale green is the color of livid corpses," and that (3) Life is traditionally Death's bride.[7] It seems evident to me that Zimmer goes too far afield in his speculations here. It would be wiser, and certainly more justifiable in terms of the poem, (1) to assume that the Green Knight picks up his head and tucks it under his arm because Gawain has just hacked it off and it is rolling about the hall, (2) to note that in English poetry (Zimmer cites Tibetian art at this point) the color green is traditionally associated with Life, if indeed it represents any one thing consistently, rather than with Death,[8] and (3) to object that the assignment of a symbolic role to Bercilak's Lady, not on the evidence of any personal characteristics, but simply on the grounds of her marriage, is at best a highly arbitrary business.

The rest of Zimmer's discussion consists not, as one would expect, of a detailed analysis of the progress of the romance, but instead of a helter-skelter examination of the myth pattern as it appears in the probable sources of *Sir Gawain and the Green Knight.* The reason for this retreat into the sources of the poem is evident: Zimmer states that "in the present version the point of the challenge, temptation, and trial is not made quite clear. The romance seems to miss something of its own suggested depth. . . . One cannot even be sure that the thirteenth and fourteenth century French and English poets . . . consciously intended the reading that inevitably emerges. . . ."[9] In short, the poem and the myth do not agree. As an example of the *Gawain* poet's ignorance of his proper duties as myth recorder, Zimmer points out that the presence of Morgan le Fay in the poem may be attributed to the fact that "themes that must once have been enacted on a higher mythical stage now appear obscured and encumbered with the trappings of chivalric pride and family intrigue."[10] But it must be clear to even the most casual reader of the poem that since Morgan is, according to the poet, the instigator of the testing device and thus the prime mover of the plot-action, she cannot be done away with quite so easily and on grounds as tenuous as these without materially distorting the intent of the poet and the structure of the poem.

In short, Zimmer refuses to deal with the poem on its own terms; if Morgan le Fay, or if anything else for that matter, does not fit in with the myth and the archetype, then it is denounced as a late addition or put down as an example of the poet's failure to understand the myth involved, and so done away with as irrelevant to the proper study of the poem. This, it seems to me, is to underestimate gravely the skill, the understanding, and the intent of the poet and, worse than this, to ignore completely the literary qualities and the integrity of the text itself.

Our second critic, John Speirs, though offering a more carefully wrought analysis, makes the same mistake in emphasis. Speirs begins his discussion of the poem[11] by attacking those scholars and editors of the poem who have, according to him, "ignored its uniqueness" and deliberately refrained from examining the "object, the English poem as what it positively is."[12] So far, nearly everyone would agree with Mr. Speirs' aims, if not with his language and tone. Yet what is the next point made in the analysis? Morgan le Fay is dismissed from serious consideration since she, as a character in the poem, is not "realized as Lady Macbeth is realized."[13] What Mr. Speirs apparently cannot see is that none of the characters in the poem, including Gawain himself, is "realized as Lady Macbeth is realized"; since the *Gawain* poet is a mediaeval romancer, and not an Elizabethan dramatist, he quite naturally does not "realize" his characters as Shakespeare does. Had he done so, he would have violated every canon of the art which he so skillfully practiced. Aside from this consideration, Mr. Speirs suffers, as did Professor Zimmer, from the mistaken notion that it is possible to add or subtract the parts of a poem regardless of all considerations of mechanical, much less organic, unity. In short, although Mr. Speirs states that he intends to look at the poem "as what in itself it is,"[14] he begins his analysis by deleting the character who motivates the entire action and in doing so eliminates the only explanation given us of what actually happens in the poem; Bercilak's statement of the meaning of the test becomes a "bone for the rationalizing mind to play with and be kept quiet with."[15] Yet four lines later, Speirs speaks of the poem as a "great unified work of art."

Mr. Speirs next proceeeds to more fertile matters of discussion. The poem is a "midwinter festival poem,"[16] and he immediately sends us away from the poem and off to the source books. The Green Knight is not Death this time but the "Green Man . . . the Jack in the Green or the Wild Man of the village festivals of England and Europe," who is in turn the "descendent of the Vegetation or Nature God of . . . almost universal and immemorial tradition whose death and resurrection mythologizes the annual death and rebirth of nature. . . ."[17] This conclusion could have been foreseen, since Mr. Speirs, judging from his outlook and from the sorts of evidence he brings forward and the authorities he cites, is a thorough-going ritualist, a disciple of the Cambridge school represented chiefly by Frazer, Miss Harrison, Cornford, Murry, and Miss Weston. Thus the long analysis which follows corresponds to the basic party line of the group, summarized by Stanley Edgar Hyman as the belief that myth is the "spoken correlative of a ritual, the story which the rite enacts or once enacted,"[18] and contains the usual Celtic mythologist talk about Gawain, none of which is particularly applicable here. For instance, we are told that Gawain's traditional role was that of "the hero, the agent who brought back the spring, restored the frozen life-processes, revived the god—or (in later versions) cured the king."[19] How this can be said to illuminate the poem, I cannot see. In *Sir Gawain and the Green Knight,* Gawain is indeed the hero, but he unfreezes no life-processes (he himself is almost frozen, as a matter of fact), revives no god, cures no king.

The rest of Speirs' analysis is, for the most part, made up of strange attempts to find ritualistic backgrounds for details of the poem,[20] and Speirs goes on to make the usual and expected identifications: the old woman is the "old year" and Bercilak's Lady is the "new year."[21] The hunts are "symbolically the doing-to-death of the qualities of the natural man which Courtesy has to vanquish"[22] (this in spite of the fact that Speirs does not consider the poem to be about Courtesy and Chivalry at all), which symbolic hunts in turn are said to be related to "animal sacrifices of fertility rituals."[23] The Green Chapel is the "secret source of life"[24] (this in spite of the fact that it is the "corsedest kirk" that Gawain ever saw). And so it goes.

Mr. Speirs ends his analysis by reminding his readers how studiously he has avoided the "error of regarding it [the poem] simply as a recorded myth, the record of the story of a ritual."[25] Yet it is hard to see that Speirs has in fact avoided such a pitfall. He has certainly said nothing illuminative concerning the poem, except to cite as a general theme "a kind of adjustment, if not reconciliation between man and nature" and to add, lest this seem vague, that "in a more limited sense, the courtly order has been put to the test of nature."[26] Yet even here it is hard to see just how this statement of theme fits the facts of the poem (the mixed nature of Gawain's success; the function of Morgan le Fay in the action) and the facts of Speirs' own interpretation (the relation between the testing of the courtly order, the Old and New Year symbolism, and the vegetative god). I cannot understand how Mr. Speirs' analysis, for all its ingenuity and sincerity, accomplishes anything other than to repeat what essentially has always been said of the poem—that Gawain undergoes a series of tests and that this testing is the theme of the poem.

So might, with illustrations, run the case against myth criticism as currently practiced. There is, however, a more sensible, and, I believe, a more productive attitude toward the place of myth in literature. Like these critics, I believe that the application of the fruits of myth study to literature furnishes the critic with a tool of interpretation by which he can arrive quickly and with great precision at the heart of a piece of literature. Yet I believe also that it is impossible to leave the problem, as do these critics, at the stage of identification; the myth is not the poem, and we must always remember that a definition must contain both *genus* and *differentia,* both identification and separation. In literary scholarship, it has never been sufficient to delineate a source; the scholar must show how that source is used in the work at hand, how it itself becomes a tool of creation. To be able to show how the poet uses myth and, in doing so, to concentrate not on the identity of the myth, but on its function, not on its closeness to the known pattern, but on the changes which the poet effects in that pattern, not on origin, but on use would seem to me to constitute the proper aim of the myth critic.

It would seem that any criticism following such a strategy must rest *ab initio* upon two major assumptions concerning the nature of myth itself: (1) that myth is in itself meaningful (the problem of myth origin); (2) that myth is used in literature, whether consciously or unconsciously, for a meaningful purpose (the problem of myth transmission). The first of these assumptions has been sufficiently examined to have become almost self-evident; no matter whether a critic holds to the ritual, the euhemerist, the Jungian, or to any variation of these doctrines, he will agree that myth is in some fashion and to some degree meaningful. Moreover, it seems to me that the critic has the right to hold to and use any reasonable theory of myth origin as long as the method of critical analysis which he raises on the structure of that theory is capable of throwing light upon a literary text.

The second of these two assumptions, that involving myth transmission, has a closer relationship to the problem of the function of myth in literary art. Here I would propose a distinction. I can understand very easily the use made of myth by modern artists who share our own ideas of the nature and composition of myth, by, for example, Yeats, Auden, Eliot, and Charles Williams. Theirs is a conscious and knowing use of myth; when Yeats speaks of a "Ladaean body" and Eliot of the "bloody wood," they hope by allusion to myth to bring to a poem, usually for purposes of identification and comparison, the whole context of the myth of which they refer. What Eliot wishes us to understand in that brief allusion to the "bloody wood" in *Sweeney among the Nightingales* and to apply to Sweeney's situation in the tavern is not simply the story of the ritual assassination of the priest-king at Nemi, but the consciousness of a whole complex of meaning which is itself represented by the murder of the priest-king and which takes on a still further relevancy and meaning when seen in relation to the complex of meaning, or lack of meaning, represented by Sweeney. In short, those modern writers who use myth use it consciously, with a clearly defined purpose, and, in the works of the men mentioned above at any rate, with good effect.

The writers of the Middle Ages present an entirely different problem, different not only in degree, but in kind, which has as yet not been sufficiently recognized, let alone dealt with. Here the use of myth seems to me to be in the great majority of instances unconscious. For example, we can say that the references to figures of the Christian myth (whether the *Gawain* poet would in fact consider these Old Testament characters "mythical" does not here affect the point) in the following passage from *Sir Gawain and the Green Knight* are designed to do little more than serve as ordinary metaphorical references, used here as "authorities" in typically mediaeval fashion to make a traditional antifeminist point about the nature of women:

> Bot hit is no ferly þaȝ a fole madde,
> And þurȝ wyles of wymmen be wonen to sorȝe,
> For so watȝ Adam in erde with one bygyled,
> And Salamon with fele sere, and Samson eftsoneȝ—
> Dalyda dalt hym hys wyrde—and Dauyth þerafter
> Watȝ blended with Barsabe, þat much bale
>   þoled   (2414–19).[27]

But while the use of myth in this passage is perfectly clear, can it be said that the ancient myth of initiation which underlies the poem as a whole is used consciously by the poet?[28] John Speirs states, without evidence, that it is.[29] I assert, using the same evidence, that it is not, and pending the discovery of concrete proof, I would maintain that mine is the more satisfactory point of view. Yet it is clear that the *rite de passage* pattern is repeated in essence, if not in detail, in *Sir Gawain and the Green Knight* and that some theory of transmission must be brought forward to explain the phenomenon.

I would at this point prefer to fall back upon what might be called common sense rather than upon metaphysics or psychology in suggesting a possible explanation. The *rite de passage,* in all its tremendously varied forms, would appear to represent an almost universal theme, appearing as it does over and over again in myth and in formal literature. It is not necessary, however, to be a follower of any school of myth interpretation to explain its universality. Certainly there would appear to be relatively few general literary themes which are of real importance to the human spirit. Of these, the passage of the soul through its difficulties to its triumph, *ad astra per aspera,* through the valley of the shadow of death on to the Celestial City, is constantly observable, clothed in an immense variety of forms, both in our own personal experience and in the vicarious experience of literature. The passage of the spirit, seen in its most articulate and naked form in the progress of the myth hero in the quest, is part of the general experience of being human. Thus, in the initiatory rites of savages, in the Holy Week of the Christian year, in the great myths of all peoples, this natural and omnipresent human problem and hope is elevated, by symbolic action, to universal and archetypal and, in most cases, religious heights. It seems entirely natural to me, therefore, that this theme should appear at all times and in all places and that it should appear in literary forms in which it would seem to be unconscious in that it is given a local habitation and a name instead of being transcribed in the broad and general terms which are natural to philosophy but alien to art. Myth therefore becomes, if nothing else, a touchstone useful in isolating and labeling the characteristics which this universal theme inherently assumes in art and useful also in defining the particular form, the nature of the *differentia,* which the pattern manifests in the work in hand.

In the Middle Ages, the prevailing use of the allegorical, rather than the symbolic, method would seem to bring nearer the surface of the literary work this unconscious mythic quality which to some degree underlies all literature.[30] Thus it is that these myth patterns become comparatively easy to trace in the literature of this period. Here again I would suggest a further partition for purposes of analysis. It would seem to me that this general theme (called variously death-rebirth, initiation, withdrawal-return) appears in one dominant form in the literature of the Middle Ages—that of the journey. It is apparent that mediaeval literature is full of accounts of journeys: Dante travels through the realms of the dead; travelers find their way into the Celtic underworld; pilgrims "seken straunge strondes," and, most important of all, hundreds of knights traverse hundreds of fields and forests in quest of objects strange and high. That all of these journeys are variants of a single basic pattern—the pattern of the archetypal journey-initiation-quest—appears to me at this time to be a possibility.[31] The application, therefore, of the journey myth, seen in terms of its initiatory, *rite de passage* aspect, to the specific journeys of mediaeval literature would be a useful task, provided always that the critic bear in mind that he must refrain from identifying myth and literature, that he must not neglect *differentia,* once he has established *genus.* No one would claim, of course, that such a line of action would further illuminate *The Divine Comedy,* where the pattern is revealed in such elevation and clarity as to render obvious its workings and its effects.[32] But that this method of critical analysis should throw light on the works of Chrétien de Troyes, on *Pearl* and *Piers Plowman,* on Malory seems to me to be more than sufficient justification for undertaking the labors of the task.

This is, to say the least, a long preamble of a tale. Yet in demonstration I would attach at this point an analysis of *Sir Gawain and the Green Knight.* I would hope that this analysis will have two virtues in its favor: (1) that it attempts to treat myth, and more particularly this peculiarly important journey myth, in *Sir Gawain and the Green Knight* according to its function in the poem and (2) that it attempts to use myth as a tool, in conjunction with other tools of structure and imagery, in arriving at some statement of the theme of one of the most puzzling of all poems. We may very well begin with the structure of the poem.

The whole poem is very neatly enveloped by a framing reference to the noble Trojan ancestry of the British race and, more significantly, by the reveling at the court of King Arthur which begins and ends the poem. Thus, the narrative is enclosed within an envelope which brings the reader full circle from New Year's through the seasons to New Year's, and from Arthur's court to the Green Chapel to Arthur's court again. Gawain's adventure with the Green Knight is self-contained and so made to stand independently from the Arthurian material generally. *Sir Gawain and the Green Knight* can in no sense be said to be an episode in a longer chronicle concerning the history of the Round Table; it is a complete action in itself, containing as it does no references, either direct or indirect, to other incidents in the familiar Arthurian cycle. In this regard, the tone of the poem is also at least superficially alien to the tragedy and corruption which are a part of the kingdom's later history. It is, for the most part, a Christmas poem, filled with revelry and holiday celebrations in each of its four fits. The poem is dominated by the Christmas colors: the Green Knight, the white snow, the red and gold of Gawain's trappings. If we are to find in the poem any coherent theme, we must thus take into account first of all the facts (1) that the poem is self-contained and (2) that it is at least superficially a gay Christmas poem.

It will also be seen that, in each of the sections, the main action is surrounded and enveloped by a picture of Christmas revelry and courtly life which serves to make the poem an almost continuous Christmas celebration. Certainly the court scenes serve to link the fits together by maintaining parallel structure and by establishing thereby a remarkable consistency of tone. There are festal meals in each fit: Arthur's New Year's celebration in Fit I, the welcoming dinner which Bercilak gives to

Gawain in II, the knightly dinners at Bercilak's castle in III, and Arthur's celebration at the return of Gawain in IV. There are also descriptions of the arming of knights in each fit: the Green Knight in Fit I, Gawain in II, the hunters in III, and Gawain again in IV. There are also many parallel incidents which serve to make connections backwards and forwards in the poem and so serve to keep the major action of the poem constantly before the reader. For example, the slaughtering of the captured animals suggests the beheading game; the exchange of gifts at the end of each day in the castle and the New Year's gift game at Arthur's court suggest the exchange of blows; each of Gawain's two journeys suggests the other by the repetition of the description of the terrain. These, like the descriptions of arms and dress, serve both to maintain structural unity and to establish the background of pomp and splendor upon which a great deal of the action takes place.

The elaborate nature descriptions, however, all of which are done on a gigantic scale—the three journeys of Gawain, "fer floten fro his frendeʒ" (l. 714), the hunting scenes, the description of the Green Chapel—contrast with the courtly scenes and so keep before the reader an atmosphere which shifts continually from the pleasant court life to the wild roughness of the world outside the court. We shall return to this point. Moreover, since so much of the poem (well over half) is taken up with this sort of descriptive detail, it, like the form of the poem, must be taken into account in any statement of the theme of the poem. For example, Professor Henry Savage has already pointed out the very close parallels which exist between the hunting descriptions and the temptation scenes in Gawain's bower.[33] In the hunting scenes, it is clear that the nature of the hunted animal—the shy deer, the aggressive boar, the deceitful fox—suggests very powerfully the tactics which Gawain uses to put off the Lady's advances; he first attempts to put her off by evasion, then by demanding her intentions, and finally, to save his life, by accepting and hiding the green girdle. Such interpretation shows quite clearly that the balanced structure of the poem and the great abundance of balanced descriptive material—the feasting, arming, and nature passages—must be relevant to the theme of the poem.

The *Gawain* poet has also constructed a clear series of parallel incidents within the poem which serve to link the adventures of Gawain into a meaningful and balanced pattern. The function of many, if not all, of these parallel incidents is, I think, to establish for purposes of comparison two levels of courtesy and chivalry within the poem, that of Arthur's court and that of Bercilak's castle. It is at this point that we may best introduce the function of the initiation myth in the poem.

It is clear from the beginning that Gawain's task is spiritual rather than physical. It is usual to state, of course, that almost any given quest in the mediaeval romance is undertaken in behalf of a worthy cause and so has as its aim a non-physical and thus, in a sense, "spiritual" goal. But aside from such obvious exceptions as the Grail quest in the Arthurian cycle, the knightly quest is undertaken primarily in the service of the secular ideal of chivalric duty and not from any purely religious or spiritual motives. However, the quest of Gawain in this poem, although emanating from the chivalric virtue of loyalty to one's oath, is described in such terms as to transform it into a semi-religious quest for what can only be described as a spiritual object or set of values. Briefly stated then, the journey of Gawain to the domain of the Green Knight amounts, in mythical terms, to a *rite de passage* by which Gawain is initiated into a full understanding both of himself and of the values by which he lives and, by way of that knowledge (to return to the terms of the poem), to an understanding of the true nature of the chivalry of Arthur's court. Certainly the stages of the initiatory rite, as seen by

Van Gennep[34] and the other commentators, are reflected in the poem; Gawain, having received what Joseph Campbell designates a "call to adventure,"[35] journeys forth from his usual world (Arthur's court in the poem) and retires into a strange land, where he undergoes various tests (the assaults of the Lady) and receives a gift of great value to his people (the green girdle). He returns bearing this saving gift, but is scorned and so is unable to redeem his people by means of this curative device.[36] The application of these general stages of the *rite de passage* to the poem will, I think, become clearer in detailed analysis.

Gawain's quest is plainly intended to be taken as a spiritual task. As Professor Denver Baughan points out, Arthur is not able to qualify for the adventure; he can only swing the Green Knight's ax wildly about, unable to strike with it.[37] Gawain alone can deal the blow effectively. The element of magic in the poem reinforces this interpretation; the beheading game is from the beginning no ordinary chivalric adventure. Since this is true, it is likewise clear that Gawain's search for the Green Chapel becomes a spiritual quest; note that Gawain can find the castle of Bercilak only after he has prayed that he find "sum herber þer heȝly [he] myȝt here masse" (l. 755) and that he discovers the castle *immediately* upon ending the prayer with the words "Cros Kryst me spede" (l. 762). Gawain's journey becomes, in a sense, the journey of the individual towards a spiritual ideal higher than himself, made alone through the valley of the shadow "ne no gome bot God bi gate wyth to karp" (l. 696). Gawain's quest is also shown through imagery to be essentially religious in character. The pentangle device on Gawain's arms is described in great detail and in religious terms (ll. 620–69). He is said to undertake the journey "on Godeȝ halue" (l. 692). Few people live in the wilderness through which Gawain rides "þat auþer God oþer gome wyth goud hert louied" (l. 702). Gawain prays to Mary on his journey (ll. 737–39), and it is clear that Gawain is under the Virgin's special protection (l. 1769) and that his fate is in the hands of God (ll. 1967, 2136 ff.). Gawain twice says that in keeping his tryst with the Green Knight he is obedient to God's will (ll. 2156 ff., 2208 ff.) and in his final interview with Bercilak, Gawain receives what sounds like religious absolution from the Green Knight (ll. 2390 ff.).[38]

As I have said, the *Gawain* poet clearly contrasts the two courts. In the beginning, Arthur's company receives high praise:

> With alle þe wele of þe worlde þay woned þer samen,
> Þe most kyd knyȝteȝ vnder Krystes seluen,
> & þe louelokkest ladies þat euer lif haden,
> & he þe comlokest kyng þat þe court haldes;
> For al watȝ þis fayre folk in her first age,
>   on sille   (ll. 50–55).

Guinevere is:

> Þe comlokest to discrye
> Þer glent with yȝen gray;
> A semloker þat euer he syȝe,
> Soth moȝt no mon say   (ll. 81–84)

There is certainly no sign of corruption or bad blood here. But when we compare these descriptions of Arthur's court with the later descriptions of Bercilak's court, it becomes apparent that Bercilak's court is just as elaborate as Arthur's and in several major respects closer to the courtly and chivalric ideal. First the lady of the castle:

> Ho watȝ þe fayrest in felle, of flesche & of lyre
> & of compas & colour & costes of alle oþer,
> *& wener þen Wenore, as þe wyȝe þoȝt*
>   (ll. 943–45, my italics).[39]

Second, Bercilak's court boasts the finer hospitality. Compare Arthur's welcoming of the Green Knight, who has said that he comes in peace (see l. 266):

> . . . 'sir cortays knyȝt,
> If þou craue batayl bare,
> Here fayleȝ þou not to fyȝt'   (ll. 276–78)

with the Green Knight's welcoming of the armed Gawain:

> 'I-wysse, sir, quyl I leue, me worþeȝ þe better
> Þat Gawayn hatȝ ben my gest at Goddeȝ awen fest'
> > (ll. 1035–36).

Arthur, we note, is almost rude and certainly high-handed, since the unarmed Green Knight has said nothing about fighting and, in fact, carries the holly branch of peace (ll. 206, 265). On the other hand, Gawain, armed to the teeth, is accepted as a guest and the modest court is delighted to have him (ll. 916–19).

It can be shown, moreover, that this contrast between the courtesy and chivalry of Arthur's court and that of Bercilak's furnishes the real motivation for the Green Knight's challenge. In his final explanation, Bercilak tells Gawain that he was sent to Arthur's court by Morgan:

> For to assay þe *surquidre,* ȝif hit soth were,
> Þat rennes of þe grete renoun of þe Rounde Table
> > (ll. 2457–58, my italics).

He announces to Arthur upon his arrival at Camelot that he cannot remain long:

> Bot for þe los of þe, lede, is lyft vp so hyȝe,
> & þy burȝ & þy burnes best ar holden,
> Stifest vnder stel-gere on stedes to ryde,
> Þe wyȝtest & þe worþyest of þe worldes kynde,
> Preue for to play wyth in oþer pure laykeȝ,
> *& here is kydde cortaysye, as I haf herd carp,*
> *& þat hatȝ wayned me hider, i-wyis, at þis tyme*
> > (ll. 258–64, my italics).

Thus, since the testing of the courtesy and chivalry of the Round Table is the cause of the exchange of blows, the differences between the two courts, seen in conjunction with the spiritual nature of the quest, become of considerable importance in determining the theme of the poem.

In an important threefold parallel, moreover, the Green Knight and his lady heap aspersions upon the courtesy and chivalry of Arthur's court by exposing it to irony. First, when none of the knights of the Round Table rises to meet his challenge, the Green Knight says:

> 'What, is þis Arþureȝ hous,' quoþ þe haþel þenne,
> 'Þat al þe rous rennes of þurȝ ryalmes so mony?
> Where is now your sourquydrye & your conquestes,
> Your gry[n]del-layk & your greme & your grete wordes?
>
> (ll. 309–12).

Second, when Gawain is adamant in resisting the overtures of the lady, she doubts that the man before her is the courtly Gawain of whose *gentilesse* she has heard:

> 'Now he þat spedeȝ vche spech, þis disport ȝelde yow!
> Bot þat ȝe be Gawan, hit gotȝ [not] in mynde.'
> . . . .
> 'So god as Gawayn gaynly is halden,
> & cortaysye is closed so clene in hym-seluen,
> Couth not lyȝtly haf lenged so long wyth a lady,
> Bot he had craued a cosse bi his courtaysye,
> Bi sum towch of summe tryfle at sum taleȝ ende'
>
> (ll. 1292–3, 1297–1301).

Third, when Gawain flinches at the Green Knight's first feint, Bercilak says:

> 'Þou art not Gawayn,' quoþ þe gome, 'þat is so goud halden,
> Þat neuer arȝed for no here by hylle ne be vale,
> & now þou fles for ferde er þou fele harmeȝ;
> Such cowardise of þat knyȝt cowþe I neuer here   (ll. 2270–73).

It would seem that the Green Knight, like his lady, finds something wanting in the courtesy and the chivalry of the Round Table. In each case these ironical thrusts follow passages in which the Green Knight and his lady have heaped extravagant praise upon the Round Table and upon Gawain. Thus, it would seem that the difference between the two courts is further reinforced by having Bercilak and the lady first praise the chivalry of the court of Arthur and then, having tested it by their own standards, find fault with it.

In arriving at a statement of the probable theme of the poem, then, we must keep before us at least four major aspects of the form of the poem—the fact that the poem is a self-contained action, the fact that the poem follows in general outline the pattern of the hero's *rite de passage,* the poet's balanced use of court life and nature description, and the prevailing contrast between the court of Arthur and the court of Bercilak.

I have said that the self-contained form and Christmas tone of the poem belie any theory which places great emphasis upon the tragic later history of the court. Yet it is equally clear that even in the heyday of the Round Table, as seen in *Sir Gawain and the Green Knight,* there are disturbing elements which it will be best to list for the sake of clarity:

1. The Arthurian court generally, and Gawain in particular, are subjected at crucial moments to a searching irony which they cannot answer except by raging (ll. 316–22, 2284–85).

2. Arthur is plainly incapable of responding to the Green Knight's challenge (ll. 330–31), and although Gawain is the only knight capable of undertaking the quest, yet even he only partly succeeds in resisting the temptations set before him and so returns to the court, his victory tainted with dishonor.

3. Guinevere is singled out for attack by Morgan (ll. 2456–58), and she clearly suffers by comparison with Bercilak's lady (ll. 943–45).

4. Most puzzling of all, Morgan le Fay, whatever her design, fails, since although Arthur is humiliated by his failure to strike the blow, Guinevere, whom Morgan wished to kill by fear, remains alive.

If we allow ourselves for a moment to hold the assumption that the *Gawain* poet knew the legend in its entirety,[40] we will be able, I think, to fit these pieces of evidence into a meaningful pattern.

Morgan, a former mistress and student of the friendly magician Merlin (ll. 2448–51), is attempting to reform Arthur's court,[41] to "assay þe surquidre" and the "renoun" of the Round Table, by exposing it to the irony of a civilization, far more courtly and chivalrous, represented by Bercilak. Morgan's plan for reform takes the form of an exchange of blows, a knightly game, to be followed by a series of temptations designed to test the spiritual qualities of the company. Arthur, presumably because of his pride, cannot even qualify for the test, and only Gawain, because of his modesty the best of the knights (l. 354), can meet the challenge. Gawain, representing the best qualities of the court, embarks then upon an initiatory spiritual quest, a *rite de passage,* undergoes the necessary dangers and temptations, and returns bearing with him the green girdle which is a symbol both of his success and, ironically, of his failure. But even though Gawain's mission is not completely successful, it would seem that Morgan's plan had succeeded since Gawain has supplied the court with a strong object lesson in the value of chastity and faithfulness. Yet this is obviously not the case since Guinevere, whose death was an integral part of the plan, still lives. Then too, strangely enough, Gawain goes into an extended antifeminist harangue, presumably aimed at Bercilak's lady (ll. 2414–28). Yet we know that the responsibility for the failure of the mission lies solely with Gawain, that he accepted the girdle to save his own life, and that the Lady, far from being an evil temptress, was acting out a part written for her by Morgan and is, in fact, even more gracious than Guinevere. The anti-feminist discourse must thus be aimed at Guinevere herself.

The point, I think, is this. The testing of Gawain is designed to warn the court of two potential dangers, sexual wantonness and unfaithfulness, which threaten its existence and which Morgan is attempting to remove. Wantonness is personified in the figure of Guinevere, who, we remember, is later to bring about the downfall of the court by her affair with Launcelot. Unfaithfulness, a breach in the chivalric code of loyalty, is manifested in the court itself, which later will indulge in the personal feuds which culminate in the treachery of Mordred. Thus, Morgan's plan fails on both counts because Arthur, though himself humiliated, is able to comfort and protect the queen (ll. 470–75), and Gawain, though able to resist the temptations of the Lady which are designed to test in him these two qualities, cannot keep complete faith with Bercilak. Both dangers remain in the court, and it is obvious from the knights' laughter (ll. 2513–15) that the court does not take seriously the green girdle, the gift of great value, which is a warning against both. Only the initiated Gawain perceives the danger.

The *Gawain* poet, I maintain, is presenting us, within a deliberately limited form, a microcosm, or better said, a semi-allegorical presentation of the whole history and meaning of the Round Table. Morgan attempts reform; Gawain fails in keeping faith with Bercilak; treacherous Guinevere remains alive. The form of the poem is thus quite consciously limited in time and in space in order to facilitate a unified and complete presentation of the progress of the Round Table; only in a single, complete adventure could the poet achieve any unified design which would reflect the whole of the tragedy. In this sense the poem is semi-allegorical in method in that we are not presented with a segment of the action, but with a miniature version of the whole action. The gay light tone, which reflects the ignorance and pride of Arthur's court, is maintained throughout the scenes which take place within the safe precincts of Camelot, but once the poem moves to the outside world, the tone changes radically. The journeys are always difficult and dangerous, the terrain rugged and foreboding. The scene of the final encounter, the Green Chapel, is, to Gawain, the "corsedest kyrk" that he ever saw (l. 2195). Certainly, the prevailing tone is that of Christmas, but we must remember that the court is in "her first age" and that all the knights are ironically ignorant of Morgan's attempts to forestall the fate which will overtake them and ignorant also of the dangers outside the court which must be a part of any spiritual quest. Only the returned Gawain, who has himself made the initiatory journey, sees the imminent destruction which he expresses in his condemnation of women, and which he attempts to forestall by the institution of the green baldric.

Thus, the limited form of the poem, the gaiety of the court contrasted with the terrors of nature, the *rite de passage* and the prevailing contrast between the two courts all combine to give us the central theme. That some such purpose as this lies behind the romantic façade of the poem is further demonstrable by an examination of those features of the poem which the *Gawain* poet adds to his source materials. Professor Kittredge lists those elements which were "certainly added or greatly elaborated by the English author" as:

> the learned introductory stanza summarizing the fabulous settlements of Western Europe . . . ; the description of the Christmas festivities (i, 3) and that of the Green Knight (i, 7–9); the challenge (i, 12–13) and the speech of Gawain (i, 16); the highly poetical stanzas on the changing seasons (ii, 1–2); the very elaborate description of the process of arming a knight (ii, 4–6), with the allegorical account of the pentangle of virtues (ii, 7);

Gawain's itinerary,—Logres, North Wales, Anglesea, Holyhead, the wilderness of Wirral (ii, 9); the winter piece (ii, 10); the justly celebrated account of the three hunts (iii, 1ff.).[42]

The first of these additions, the introductory stanza, serves to introduce (1) the theme of treachery in the allusion to Antenor and (2) more importantly, the theme of change, of the alternation of happiness and sorrow in the history of England:

> Where werre & wrake & wonder
> Bi syþeȝ hatȝ wont þer-inne
> & oft boþe blysse & blunder
> Ful skete hatȝ skyfted synne   (ll. 16–19).

This theme of the alternation of "blysse & blunder" is immediately reinforced:

> And quen þis Bretayn watȝ bigged bi þis burn rych,
> Bolde bredden þer-inne, baret þat lofden,
> In mony turned tyme tene þat wroȝten;
> Mo ferlyes on þis folde han fallen here oft
> Þen in any oþer þat I wot, syn þat ilk tyme   (ll. 20–24).

In discussing Gawain's acceptance of the Green Knight's challenge, the poet says:

> Gawan watȝ glad to be-gynne þose gomneȝ in halle,
> Bot þaȝ þe ende be heuy, haf ȝe no wonder;
> For þaȝ men ben mery in mynde quen þay han mayn drynk,
> A ȝere ȝernes ful ȝerne, & ȝeldeȝ neuer lyke,
> Þe forme to þe fynisment foldeȝ ful selden   (ll. 95–99).

Thus, at the very beginning of the poem, we can see the English poet adding to his source materials passages which emphasize the theme of change, the alternation of "blysse & blunder" in the history of England. Moreover, when seen in the light of the whole history of Arthur's court, these remarks of the poet seem perfectly applicable to a poem which deals with the court in "her first age," ignorant of the treachery and civil war which will indeed change its "blysse" to "blunder."

The "description of the Christmas festivities [at both courts] (i, 3) and that of the Green Knight (i, 7–9); the challenge [including the failure of Arthur] (i, 12–13) and the speech of Gawain" were necessary if the poet was to carry through his contrasting of the court of Arthur with that of Bercilak. For example, Christmas and New Year's Day, called by the poet a second Christmas (l. 65), would seem to be primarily social occasions at Arthur's court; while we have references to the singing of carols (l. 43) and to the "chauntre of þe chapel" (l. 63), there is no indication in the poem that the Christmas season has any special religious significance to Arthur's court; in fact, even Arthur's priests join in the general merriment (l. 64). On the other hand, we get a full description of the "hersum" Christmas Evensong at Bercilak's castle including the observation that the knights "seten soberly samen þe seruise-quyle" (l. 940). Moreover, Bercilak tells Gawain that he will be better off "þat Gawayn hatȝ ben my gest at Goddeȝ awen fest" (l. 1036). In much the same way, the description of the Green Knight reinforces the contrast between the two courts by pointing out that Arthur immediately challenges the unarmed stranger to combat. Again, the challenge and Gawain's humble acceptance speech were added in order to point up Arthur's prideful attempt to deliver the blow and consequent failure and Gawain's humility in accepting and fulfilling the challenge.

The descriptions of the changing seasons may well have been added (1) as unifying and transitional devices and (2) as a means of supplying imagery of natural flux and change which would serve to remind the reader of the alternation of "blysse & blunder" which the poet had introduced at the beginning of the poem. The description of the arming of Gawain may serve to emphasize the contrast between the two courts by pointing up

Bercilak's kindly welcoming of the armed Gawain. The description of Gawain's pentangle was almost certainly added in order to reinforce the spiritual quest theme of the poem. Finally, the descriptions of the journey and of winter emphasize the contrast between the warmth of the court and the wildness out of doors, and the hunting scenes furnish parallels and commentaries on the temptations of Gawain, who has remained home from the hunt.

Professor Kittredge states also that the *dénouement* of the poem, Gawain's return to Arthur's court, "shows plain traces of innovation."[43] Gawain's return to the court, "full of shame," is "contrary to custom, for the old French poets are loath to let Gawain come off from any adventure without the highest credit."[44] It would seem clear that the poet wished this obviously non-traditional conclusion to be regarded seriously. It is important to the poem as a whole that our final view of Gawain should be that of an initiated and matured penitent rather than of a stainless conqueror. The poet states that the king and the court laughed loudly at the king's decision that all the knights wear green baldrics (ll. 2513–14); we are not told that Gawain laughed with them. This ending also relates Gawain's adventure to the whole Arthurian court and so serves to reinforce the theory advanced here that the poet is writing not simply an isolated adventure of Gawain, but a highly compressed allegorical commentary on the entire Arthurian history.

What then is the relevancy of myth to *Sir Gawain and the Green Knight*? To begin with, whatever else it may be, the poem is not itself a vegetation or seasonal myth; it is first of all a highly sophisticated and skillfully wrought mediaeval poem. Thus it is of no critical value to say simply that *Sir Gawain and the Green Knight* is a record, or a manifestation, or a form of the *rite de passage* and let the matter rest with that identification. What the critic can say, I think, is that the myth of the hero's journey from innocence to knowledge underlies the poem and to a large extent determines its specific structure and theme. The critic can thus use myth both as a point of entrance and as a means of analysis; myth becomes (1) a means of coming directly and with dispatch to the structural and thematic core of a literary work and (2) a yardstick by which the critic can measure the uses to which the poet puts the myth in terms of a specific metaphor and theme. In short, having discovered the myth core of a piece of literature, the critic must go on to examine in their own right the other literary aspects of the work, most of which he will find in turn to be determined by the central archetype. If I am right, the *Gawain* poet is using the myth of the hero's quest to develop a theme which lies at the core of mediaeval literature: that the tragedy of the Round Table, and of the secular society of which it is a symbol, was inevitable and that the seeds of that tragedy were present even in the "first age" of the youthful and joyous court at Christmas time.

Notes

PEARL

1. THE *Pearl:* AN INTERPRETATION OF THE MIDDLE ENGLISH POEM

1. London 1839, for the Ballantyne Club, pp. XLVII – L.

2. In "Early English Alliterative Poems in the West-Midland Dialect of the Fourteenth Century." Ed. by R. Morris. London 1864. There are revised editions dating from 1869, 1885, 1896 and 1901.

3. Pearl. An English Poem of the Fourteenth Century. Ed. with a Modern Rendering by I. Gollancz. London 1891.

4. E. Kölbing, Englische Studien XVI. 268–273, a review of Gollancz's edition. The debate R. Morris–Gollancz in the Academy (No. 999, 1001, 1003 and 1005, 39, 602; 40, 36, 76, 116). F. Holthausen, Zur Textkritik me. Dichtungen, in Herrigs Archiv, Vol. XC, p. 144–8.

5. The Pearl. A Middle English Poem. Ed. with Introduction, Notes, and Glossary by Charles Grosvenor Osgood. In the Belles Lettres Series. Boston 1906.

6. Pearl. An English Poem of the Fourteenth Century. Edited with Modern Rendering, together with Boccaccio's Olympia, by Sir Israel Gollancz. London 1921, in the Medieval Library. Gollancz's edition of the Pearl in "Select Early English Poems" (Milford, Oxford University Press) is only a large paper edition of the same.

7. Cp. Gollancz's introduction p. L. But dozens of Gollancz's changes compared to the 1891 edition follow simply Osgood.

8. Cp. e. g. J. R. Hulbert's review in Modern Philology. Vol. XXV. (1927), p. 118–9.

9. Mittelenglische Sprach- und Literaturproben. Berlin 1917, pp. 114–4, an edition of ll. 1–360.

10. In Fourteenth Century Verse and Prose (Oxford 1925, p. 59), a well annotated edition of lines 361–612 (p. 59 seq.).

11. In Modern Philology VI (1908), 197 seq. on ll. 215/6.

12. Some Notes on the Pearl, PMLA March 1922. Vol. XXXVII, pp. 52–93, and More Notes on Pearl. PMLA. Dec. 1927. Vol. XLII, pp. 807–31.

13. Notes on the Pearl. MLR (1920). Vol. XV, pp. 298–300.

14. Early English Text Society. Vol. 162, 176 plates, compare the review by W. W. Greg in the MLR. Vol. 19, p. 223.

15. Alliterative Poetry in Middle English. The Dialectical and Metrical Survey. Manchester University Press. 1930, p. 262 seq.

16. Gollancz in his editions in rhymeless verses. A. R. Brown in Poet Lore V, 434–6, rendering of ll. 158–172. F. T. Palgrave, Landscape in Poetry. London 1897, pp. 115–7, rendering of st. 4 in metre. S. Weir Mitchell, Pearl, rendered into Modern English Verse, New York 1906. 46 stanzas mostly from the first half, also Portland, Maine, 1908, in the "Bibelot." C. G. Coulton, Pearl rendered into Modern English, London 1906 in the metre of the original (also 1921). Charles G. Osgood, The Pearl rendered in Prose. Princeton 1907. Two poor translations by Sophie Jewett (New York 1908) and Marian Mead (Portland, Maine 1908). Jessie Weston in "Romance, Vision and Satire" (London 1912). W. A. Neilson and K. G. T. Webster in Chief British Poets of the Fourteenth and Fifteenth Centuries, London 1916, a prose-translation by Professor Webster. The German translation by Otto Decker, Schwerin 1916, the Italian by Frederico Olivero (Milano e Turino 1927), with a good introduction.

17. J. P. Gilson: The Library of the Henry Savile of Banke. A paper read before the Bibliographical Society Nov. 18, 1907, London 1909, proves that the MS comes from this library (1568–1617, Banke in Yorkshire).

18. Morris, introduction to his edition, F. Knigge, Die Sprache des Dichters von Sir Gawain and the Green Knight, der sogenannten Early English Alliterative Poems and De Erkenwalde. Marburg 1885. W. Fick, Zum mittelenglischen Gedicht von der Perle. Eine Lautuntersuchung. Kiel 1885. Schwahn, Die Conjugation in Sir Gawayn and the Green Knight und den sogenannten Early English Alliterative Poems. Strassburg 1884.

19. "The 'West Midland' of the Romances" in Modern Philology XIX. 1921–2, p. 9 and p. 11.

20. Ibidem p. 16.

21. Ib. p. 12.

22. Historische Grammatik der Englischen Sprache. Leipzig 1921. Vol. I. I, 47.

23. Ib. § 33, § 357, Anm. 1; § 397, Anm. I; § 399, Anm. 1; § 408, Anm. 3; § 460, Anm. 1.

24. "Sir Gawain and the Green Knight and the West Midland" in PMLA, Vol. XXXVII (1922), p. 503, especially p. 505 and 519.

25. Loc. cit. p. 85–6.

26. Ib. p. 257 seq. compare A. Brandl's unfavorable review in Herrigs Archiv. Vol. 86 (158) 1931, p. 293. "Die grosse Dialektkarte ist nicht ernsthaft zu nehmen" etc.

27. In "The Dialects of the West Midlands" in "Review of English Studies." Vol. 3 (1927), p. 327 seq.

28. Cp. on this R. Huchon's "Histoire de la langue anglaise," Vol. II, 235 who studies the vocabulary and comes to the conclusion: "Il tend à se constituer ainsi une langue littéraire spéciale, qui se superpose à l'idiome courant, le dépasse et diffère de lui par la tonalité et par l'orgine des matériaux employés." Also H. L. Savage's opinion (ed. of St. Erkenwald, p. XXXIII).

29. The best summary for the evidence of common authorship of these poems in Prof. Menner's edition of *Purity* (Yale University Press. 1920). Additional points in Oakden loc. cit. p. 251 seq. On the sources of *Gawain* cp. G. L. Kittredge: A. Study of Gawain and the Green Knight. Cambridge, Mass. 1916. The idea of a French source for *Sir Gawain* has been contested by E. v. Schaubert, Der englische Ursprung von Sir Gawain in "Englische Studien," Vol. 57, pp. 330–446. If her thesis should be accepted, the common authorship of *Gawain* and *Pearl* would become rather doubtful.

30. *St. Erkenwald*, Yale Press, 1926, p. XLVIII seq. cp. C. Horstmann, "Altenglische Legenden" (Neue Folge), Heilbronn 1881, p. 266.

31. The Huchown theory was advocated mainly by George Neilson e. g. in "Huchown of the Awle Ryale, the Alliterative Poet" (Glasgow 1902), or "Cross-links between Pearl and the Adventures of Arthur" in "Scottish Antiquary" 16, p. 67–78. Already M. Trautmann destroyed the theory in "Der Dichter Huchown und seine Werke," Anglia I, 190–49. Best discussion by H. N. McCracken "Concerning Huchown" PMLA. Vol. XXV (1910, p. 507 seq.).

32. The Strode theory advanced by Gollancz in his editions (p.

XLVI of the 1921 ed.), in the DNB under Strode and the CHEL I (1901) p. 320 seq. Carleton Brown (The Author of the Pearl Considered in the Light of his Theological Opinions in PMLA. Vol. XXIX, pp. 146–8) destroys the theory completely.

33. PMLA. Vol. XLIII (March 1928), p. 177–9.

34. E. g. Jusserand, Legouis, Wülker, H. Hecht, Snell, Saintsbury, V. Mathesius etc.

35. Quoted according to "Geschichte der englischen Literatur." 2nd ed. Strassburg 1899, p. 406–7.

36. 1921 ed., p. XLIII.

37. Ib. p. XLIV.

38. PMLA. Vol. XIX (1904), pp. 115–153.

39. Ib. p. 145.

40. PMLA. Vol. XIX (1904), pp. 154–215.

41. Cp. below p. 27.

42. Loc. cit. p. 201.

43. Ib. p. 202.

44. Osgood's ed. p. XXVIII.

45. Ib. p. XXXIV.

46. Ib. p. XXXVI.

47. Osgood points to ll. 35–50 of "Purity."

48. "Purity," ll. 13–124.

49. "In Defence of the Pearl," in "Modern Language Review." Vol. II (1907), p. 39.

50. "Recent Studies of the Pearl" in "Modern Language Notes." Vol. XXII (1907), p. 21.

51. Cambridge History of English Literature I, 331.

52. Ib. p. 320.

53. PMLA. Vol. XXIV (1909), pp. 585–675.

54. Ib. p. 618.

55. Ib. p. 631.

56. University of Washington Publications in English. Vol. IV, No. 1. April 1918. Seattle, Washington, 45 pp.

57. Ib. p. 36.

58. Ll. 1205–6 of the Pearl.

59. Cp. the severe, but just review by Professor C. Brown in the "Modern Language Notes." Vol. XXXIV, p. 42–3.

60. In "Journal of English and Germanic Philology." Jan. 1921. Vol. XX, 1–21.

61. Ll. 885–7 of the Pearl. cp. below p. 23.

62. D. Appleton, New York 1925, pp. 226.

63. Ib. p. 22.

64. Ib. p. 89.

65. Ib. p. 90.

66. Ib. p. 208.

67. Ib. p. 191.

68. Ib. p. 175.

69. PMLA, Dec. 1925. Vol. XL, pp. 814–27.

70. Canto XXVIII.

71. In "Modern Language Notes." Vol. XLII. 2. (1927), pp. 113–6.

72. B text of the Canterbury Tales 11. 1769–75. Skeat's Chaucer. Vol. IV, p. 185.

73. Ll. 243–4 of the Pearl.

74. Ed. of the Pearl 1921, p. XLII and CHEL I, 331. "Privy" in l. 12.

75. Ll. 483–5 of the Pearl.

76. Ll. 473, 483–5.

77. Any text-book of dogmatics shows this e. g. J. Pohle, Lehrbuch der Dogmatik II, 566, II, 665 etc. From Corinthians I, 13, 9 it can be concluded that the blessed inhabitants of heaven shall see everything clearly in God, what on earth is only an object of theological faith. The absence of envy and competition is inforced in our poem by a comparison with the relation between members of the same body. (ll. 457 seq.), a comparison which descends also from 1 Corinthians (6, 15 and Ch. 12) and which is e. g. elaborated by St. Augustine in "De Civitate Dei" (XXII, 30).

78. "My wreched wylle" in l. 56, "del and gret daunger" in l. 250, "strot" in l. 353.

79. L. 1176.

80. In "De Causa Dei contra Pelagium" ed. 1618. Preface, quoted in Brown loc. cit.

81. Psalm 24. 10, quoted by Augustine in the letter to Paulinus written in 417, No. 186.

82. Augustinus, Tractatus 3 in Jovinianum n. 9.

83. Cp. the letter of Augustine quoted above, besides "De Civitate Dei" XXI, 16. In Evangelium Joannis Tractatus 41, 5, also Chrysostomus, homilia de Adam et Eva; Cyprianus epistola 59, ad Fidum etc.

84. De Peccatorum Meritis et Remissione, Liber I. Caput 9. Migne, Patrologia Latina, Vol. 44, p. 114.

85. Augustine, Letter to Mercator No. 193, dating from 418, also to Bishop Bonifacius, No. 98, written in 408, and De Peccatorum Meritis etc. Lib. 1, cap. 19 and lib. 3, c. 2.

86. Sermo 14 de verbis Apostoli.

87. Cp. the list of authorities quoted in Suarez, De gratia VI, 1, 7, Moguntiae 1621, p. 2, and Canisius, Opus catechisticum, Parisiis 1585, p. 413.

88. In Cap. Maiores. Decret 1, 3 tit. 42 de baptismo, quoted by Pohle, Lehrbuch der Dogmatik II, 554.

89. Clement, de summa Trinit. et fide cath. quoted ib.

90. Sermo 66 super Cantica and Epistola ducentesima quadragesima ad Hildefonsum comitem, de Henrico haeretico, printed e. g. in S. Bernardi selectarum epistolarum Liber unicus, Parisiis 1614, p. 351. Bernardus uses the passage "Sinite parvulos venire a me," which the Pearl poet also uses in ll. 718 seq.

91. Sess. 5, canon. 5 de Baptismo and sess. 7 can. 13 de Baptismo. Suarez summarizes the decisions thus: Concilium definit infantes baptizatos vere computari inter fideles, intelligit autem inter fideles justos. Et constat, quia sunt digni regno coelorum. De Gratia, VII, 8, 6, p. 88.

92. Canisius, Opus catechisticum, Parisiis 1585, p. 413. Suarez, De gratia VI, 3, 6 (p. 8), and Gabriele Vasquez, Commentarium ac Disputationum in primam secundae S. Thomae tomus secundus. Antverpiae. MDCXX, disp. CCII. Cap. VI, p. 610–11.

93. L. 417 of the Pearl.

94. Ll. 655–8.

95. L. 660.

96. Brown loc. cit. p. 137.

97. Ll. 447–9, 601–4, 863–4 etc. ll. 601–4 quoted.

98. L. 885.

99. L. 1121.

100. Ll. 675 and 685/6.

101. Epistola No. 167. n. 3. "Induti sunt sancti justitia (Job 29, 14) alius magis, alius minus."

102. John 14, 2.

103. 1 Cor. 15, 41.

104. Commentary to Matthew. Homilium 64. ad Ch. XX, 1–16.

105. Contra haereticos, Lib V, 36, 1–2.

106. Ib. IV, 36, 7.

107. Augustinus, De Sancta Virginitate cap. 26. Migne, Patrologia Vol. XL, col. 410. The same interpretation in "In Joannis Evangelium" Trac. LXVII, cap. 14. Migne, Patrologia Vol. XXX, col. 1812. Canisius loc. cit. p. 1115.

108. Libro Quarto dialogorum, capite tregesimoquinto, quoted by Canisius, loc. cit.

109. Libri IV Sententiarum Dist. XLIX. Paris 1. Q VI. Ed. 1668. Vol. II, p. 533.

110. Summa Theologica I–II. V, 2.

111. Petrus Lombardus, Dist. XLIX Pars I. Migne, Patrologia. Vol. CXCII, col. 957, Duns Scotus, In Lib. IV Sententiarum Dist. L. Qu. V. (ed. 1639, tom. X, pp. 641 and 651). Prosper, De vita contemplativa lib. I, cap. IV, quoted by Canisius, loc. cit. p. 1670.

112. Cp. note 73.

113. "Modern Language Notes" XLII, 2 (1927), pp. 113–6.

114. Quoted in R. Stroppel, Liturgie u. geistliche Dichtung 1050–1300. Frankfurt 1927.

115. In L. dist. 41 Qu. 1, quoted according to Pohle, loc. cit. II, 479.

116. L. 269.

117. L. 221 and cp. l. 1103–4.

118. l. 785.

119. L. 743–4.

120. The last verse of the poem l. 1212.

121. Matthew XII, 46.

122. Episcopus Sardensium, cp. about him A. Harnack, Geschichte der altchristlichen Literatur I (1893), p. 246–55, the passage from Clavis LXVI quoted in J. B. Pitra, Spicilegium Solesmense. Tom. II, 341. Parisiis 1855. Pitra quotes a passage, where the Pearl is also among the ninety-two names of Christ, from a Parisian cod. 36 f. 164, 165 III, 447, and passages from Phoebadius Barcinonensis, Eucherius, a bishop of Lyon, etc. Osgood (his ed. p. 82) quotes Augustine, Chrysostomus, Ephren the Syrian for this interpretation.

123. Bonaventura (1221–1257) in serm. 3 dom. 17 p. Pent. in Opera Omnia. Tom. 7 Lugduni 1668, t. 3, p. 199 A and sermo 6 in Rogat. Rupert of Deutz quoted by Osgood p. 82 from Patr. Lat. Vol. 169, col. 1202. Hrabanus Maurus (died in 856) quoted by Pitra loc. cit.

124. Homilia in Evangelia 11, 2 quoted by Osgood p. 82–3.

125. Patrologia Lat. Vol. 184, col. 1069, quoted by Osgood loc. cit.

126. Ad. litt. XII, art. 46, quoted by Pitra loc. cit.

127. Chaucerian and other pieces. Ed. by W. W. Skeat. Oxford 1897, p. 145.

128. Venetiis 1565. Apud Paulum Baleonium. Pars Quarta, Caput XXIV, Sermo I, preached in 1471, p. 232.

129. PMLA. Vol. XII (1897), p. 326–40.

130. Oakden loc. cit. p. 235, 241.

131. I am thinking especially of the new study of poetical language and meter based on functional linguistics initiated in Russia and happily continued by members of the Prague Linguistic Circle.

P. S. — *C. O. Chapman's* recent article "The Musical Training of the Pearl Poet" in PMLA Vol. XLVI. (March 1931) p. 177–81 collects references to music, especially to Church music in the works of the poet. From his detailed knowledge of the latter, Chapman concludes that the poet attended a choristers' school in his youth. Though there is nothing to contradict this theory, a number of other ways to acquire this knowledge can be imagined.

2. THE MEANING OF THE MIDDLE ENGLISH *Pearl*

1. *Alliterative Poetry in Middle English,* II, 70.

2. Sr. Madeleva, *Pearl: A Study in Spiritual Dryness,* pp. 192–193; and Sr. Mary Vincent Hillman, "Some Debatable Words in *Pearl* and Its Theme, *MLN,* LX, 243.

3. St. 61, especially ll. 729-732: "Þer is þe blys þat con not blynne / Þat þe jueler soȝte þurȝ perré pres, / And solde alle hys goud, boþe wolen and lynne, / To bye hym a perle watȝ mascelleȝ." Cf. D. W. Robertson, *MLN,* LXV, 159.

4. Cf. Sr. Madeleva's views, op. cit. My debt to Sr. Madeleva is considerable and hereby is gratefully acknowledged. My theory was full grown before Sr. Mary Hillman's interpretation was published.

5. *Pearl,* ed. E. V. Gordon (Oxford, 1953), 1–12.

6. S. P. Chase, *The Pearl . . . in Modern Verse,* translates *erbere* as "garden plot." Gollancz in his ed. of 1921, *Pearl, An English Poem of the XIVth Century, Edited with Modern Rendering,* translates it "garden" and insists upon this meaning, but obscures it by adding, "The poet is thinking of the graveyard as a garden." Gordon glosses *erber(e)* as "a grassy place in a garden, often among trees."

7. *Songs and Hymns of the Earliest Greek Christian Poets,* tr. Allen W. Chatfield, p. 106.

8. Emile Mâle, *Religious Art in France in the Thirteenth Century,* tr. Dora Nussey, p. 214.

9. A commonplace. See. e.g., Aquinas, *Summa Theologica,* "Treatise on Man," Q. 102, Art. 4: St. Athanasius, *The Incarnation of the Word of God,* Newly Translated into English by a Religious of C.S.M.V. (1947), pp. 28–29.

10. Ed. Samuel Clegg, 1919, p. 57.

11. *Giles and Phineas Fletcher's Poetical Works,* ed. F. S. Boas, Vol. I, p. 21. Cf. Donne, "The Harbinger to the Progress," in *The Progress of the Soul,* ll. 9–11.

12. Migne, *Patrologia Latina,* CLXXIII, 164.

13. For the *Pretiosa margarita* of the parable as eternal life or blessedness, see Gregory the Great *(PL,* LXXVI, 1115); Bede *(PL,* XCII, 69); Rabanus Maurus *(PL,* CXII, 996); Walafridus Strabo *(PL,* CXIV, 133); Bruno Astensis *(PL,* CLXV, 192); Hugh of St. Victor *(PL,* CLXXV, 794); and at least five other writers in *PL.* Cf. D. W. Robertson, *MLN,* LXV, 160.

14. Noted by Gollancz, 1921 ed., pp. xxvii–xxciii; Sr. Madeleva, op. cit., p. 95; Sr. M. V. Hillman, p. 243; D. W. Robertson, p. 160. Richard Delbrueck in *The Art Bulletin,* XXXIV (June 1952), 142, discusses the pearl as an early Christian symbol of "the soul redeemed, the Christian purified through baptism." For Patristic and medieval testimony see Cornelius á Lapide's celebrated digest, *Commentaria in Scripturas Sacras,* XV, 334; *The Book of the Knight of La Tour Landry,* ed. T. Wright *(EETS,* o.s. 33), p. 158; Sermon 84 in *Select English Works of John Wyclif,* ed. T. Arnold, I, 286-287.

15. *Sum. Theol.,* "Treatise on Man," Q. 102, Art. 2.

16. Here, e.g., are excerpts from St. Bernard's Sermon 81, *Cantica Canticorum,* ed. Samuel Eales, pp. 495–496: "Life is indeed the soul which is living, but it lives not other whence than from itself, and on this account we speak of it with propriety, not so much as living, as being itself life. . . . The soul of man alone can reach the higher life, in as much as it is seen to have been constituted as life by Him who is Life. . . . God is Life; the soul also is Life; it is then like unto God, but it is not equal to Him."

17. *Catholic Encyclopaedic Dictionary,* articles on "Original Sin" and "Grace"; *Dictionaire de Théologie Catholique,* article on "Inno-

cence." Edwin Wintermute's statement, *MLN,* LXIV (Feb. 1949), 83–84, is right as far as it goes: "The pearl means sanctifying grace, the possession of which is essential to the enjoyment of the Kingdom of Heaven." Cf. W. K. Greene, *PMLA,* XL, 814–827: *Pearl* "as a whole was designed to illustrate the doctrine of Divine Grace."

18. Louisa Twining, *Symbols and Emblems of Early and Mediaeval Christian Art,* pp. 141, 142–146; F. R. Webber, *Church Symbolism,* 2nd ed. rev., p. 362. Cf. Mâle, p. 250, on miniatures of the Assumption depicting the soul of the Virgin as a child borne in Christ's arms. In El Greco's *Burial of the Count of Orgaz* the departing soul is a babe carried heavenward by an angel. Cf. the souls in Abraham's bosom.

19. For a general treatment of the motive see Mary A. Ewer, *A Survey of Mystical Symbolism,* and W. R. Inge, *Christian Mysticism,* 5th ed., Appendix D. The Atonement as a divine romance is well handled by R. W. Battenhouse, *PMLA,* LXI, 1049–51. For the Redemption in terms of chivalric romance see Sr. Marie de Lourdes le May, *The Allegory of the Christ Knight in English Literature,* Catholic Univ. (1932); and W. R. Gaffney, *PMLA,* XLVI, 155–168.

20. *The Goodman of Paris,* tr. Eileen Power, p. 60. Cf. Chaucer's "Melibee" and its source. Melibeus' daughter Sophie, wounded by his three enemies (the world, the flesh, the devil), is equated with his own soul.

21. P. S. Allen, *Medieval Latin Lyrics,* p. 223.

22. St. Bernard, *Sermons on the Canticles,* tr. by a Priest of Melleray, I, 306, in a glowing account of the soul in her jeweled nuptial garments, specifies that her gems are pearls, symbolizing virtues. For other references to the jewels of the soul as virtues, see Hugh of St. Victor, *The Soul's Betrothal Gift,* tr. F. Sherwood Taylor (1945), pp. 22–23; Albertus Magnus, *De Laudibus B. Mariae Virginis,* lib. XII, 4.9.7., as cited by Fletcher, *JEGP,* XX, 11:Honorius of Autun, *PL,* CLXXII, 859–860, 966.

23. *Dante's Drama of the Mind,* pp. 9–10.

24. Cf. Sr. Madeleva, p. 132: The maiden of the vision "is the personification of his [the poet's] own soul in the state of such potential perfection . . . as is congruous to it at this time of his life."

25. *PL,* CLXXXIII, 158, quoted by C. S. Baldwin, *Medieval Rhetoric and Poetic,* p. 174.

26. *Three Medieval Centuries in England (1100-1400),* p. 275, n. 21. Cf. ibid., pp. 174, 272, 275.

27. "Quia omnes homines fuerunt ille unus homo, scilicet Adam" (*De Peccatorum Meritis,* Cap. 10, as quoted by Lapide, XVIII, 99).

28. *Sum. Theol.,* II (2nd number), Q. 81 (tr. by the Fathers of the English Dominican Province), p. 401.

29. "A Sawley Monk's Version of Grostete's 'Castle of Love'," in *Minor Poems of the Vernon MS. (EETS,* O. S. 98), Part I, ed. C. Horstmann.

30. Aquinas, *Sum. Theol.,* III (3rd number), Q. 74, Art. 3.

31. Sermon 59 in *Select English Works,* I, 179. This figure appears in beauty in Masefield, *The Everlasting Mercy,* and in recent poems by Thomas Merton; it is a commonplace with the Latin Fathers: *PL,* XXXVII, 1279, 1730; LI, 314; LXXV, 1150; CXII, 926, 1440; CXC, 256, e.g., Cf. Piers Plowman's acre.

32. Edmund Gardner *(Dante and the Mystics,* p. 284) reports that high festivals were regarded as specially propitious for revelations and spiritual consolation. Adam Davy in his series of visions about Edward II dreamed by the ecclesiastical calendar (O. F. Emerson, *A Middle English Reader* (1948), pp. 227–232).

33. *St. John Damascene on Holy Images,* tr. Mary Allies, pp. 160–161, apostrophizing Mary in her Assumption: "Thou art a spiritual Eden, holier and diviner than Eden of Old, The heavenly Bread of Life . . . took flesh of thee." Again St. John of Damascus describes her in the Assumption as "the living garden of delight, wherein the condemnation was annulled and the Tree of Life planted" (quoted by Gardner, op. cit., pp. 212–213).

34. See, e.g., Yrjö Hirn, *The Sacred Shrine,* pp. 438, 446–448; Lapide, VIII, 76, 81, 142, 240; St. Peter Damian, *PL,* CXLV, 938; St. Bernard, *Sermons on the Cantica Canticorum,* ed. Eales, pp. 259–270; Alanus de Insulis, *PL,* CCX, 95, 109.

35. Cf. Carleton Brown, *Religious Lyrics of the Fourteenth Century,* p. 12.

36. Alanus, *PL,* CCX, 64–65: 'Campus dicitur humana Christi natura . . . Hujus campi flos fuit Christus' ("Elucidatio in Cantica Canticorum").

37. Ibid., col. 91. Cf. n. 37 above.

38. Lapide, VIII, 90.

39. St. Bernard, *PL,* CLXXXIII, 1059–60 (quoted by Erich Auerbach, *Speculum,* XXI, 479–80, who also attributes the figure of the

garden as the Resurrection to Gregory the Great and Richard of St. Victor).

40. Origen, *PG,* XI, 99, 375, as cited by Mâle, p. 134. H. R. Patch, *The Other World,* pp. 136, 143, 145–147, 153, cites Cyprian, Isidore of Seville, Bede, Rabanus Maurus, and St. Bonaventura as treating the Terrestrial Paradise as a type of the Church.

41. Patch, pp. 139, 153. Bernard of Silvester, *De Mundi Universitate* (ed. Carl S. Barach and Johann Wrobel, 1876), Lib. I, Part III, l. 3., devotes ll. 360–414 to the medicinal plants in the Earthly Paradise.

42. *PL,* CLXXII, 423, 425.

43. Cassiodorus *(PL,* LXX, 1078, 1105), Augustine *(PL,* XLIII, 153–55, 227–28), Gregory *(PL,* LXXV, 799; LXXIX, 513), Alcuin *(PL,* C, 653), Rabanus *(PL,* CXI, 530), Hugh of St. Victor *(PL,* CLXXV, 275), *St. Ambrose 'On the Mysteries,'* tr. T. Thompson (ed. J. H. Srawley, pp. 71–72); Lapide, VIII, 73–74, 77–78, 87–88, 238–240, 641.

44. *Paradiso,* XII, 70, 104; XXVI, 64; XXXI, 97; XXXII, 39; cf. XXIII, 71–72. The Church Militant fittingly appears in the *Commedia* in the hilltop setting of the restored Earthly Paradise *(Purgatorio,* XXIX, XXX, XXXII).

45. Gardner, p. 290; Ewer, p. 61.

46. Lapide, VIII, 641. Cf. XV, 566; XVI, 606, and Giles Fletcher, "Christ's Triumph and Death." For the Garden of Gethsemane as the Church, see also *PL,* VIII, 59.

47. *Pearl, Cleanness, Patience and Sir Gawain,* reproduced in facsimile from the unique MS. Cotton Nero A. X. in the British Museum, introd. Sir. I. Gollancz, *EETS.*

48. In his 1921 edition of *Pearl,* pp. xviii, 119, n. 41.

49. Among ME vision poems, hill-settings are found also in *Piers Plowman, Winner and Waster, The Vision of Life and Death, The Shepherd on a Hill He Sat,* and *Quia Amore Langueo.*

50. The incomplete subject-indices of Migne's *PL* yield some dozen references to *mons* as *Ecclesia* and numerous references to *mons* as *Christus.* In *Pearl* 678–79, the rendering of Ps. XXIV.3–4 ("Lorde, quo schal klymbe thy hygh hylle," etc.), "hygh hylle" translates the Vulgate *montem Domini,* which is glossed as *Ecclesia* in the 12th-century *Allegoriae in Sacram Scripturam (PL,* CXII, 1000–1002), formerly attributed to Rabanus Maurus.

51. See D. W. Robertson and Bernard F. Huppé, *Piers Plowman and Scriptural Tradition,* pp. 35–37.

52. See note 46, above.

53. Lapide, VIII, 55–57.

54. Lapide, XV, 615 (cf. I, 26, 84; VIII, 499), attributes this opinion to Origen, Tertullian, Athanasius, Epiphanius, Ambrose, Augustine, Cyril, "and others of the Fathers, Jerome excepted." Cf. representations of the Crucifixion in medieval and Renaissance art with Adam's skull beneath the Cross.

55. Lapide, XV, 615: "Unde St. Ambrosius, in Cap. xxxiii Lucae, docet Christum [fuisse] in Golgotha crucifixum quia congruebat, inquit, ut ibi vitae nostrae primitiae locarentur, ubi fuerant mortis exordia."

56. Patch, p. 135 and n. 6.

57. See, e.g., Oelsner's note to Dante's *Purgatorio,* XXXII, in the Modern Library ed. of the *Divine Comedy,* p. 388.

58. For Grail legends see D. Kempe, *The Legend of the Holy Grail, EETS,* 95, pp. xxvi-xxxvii. For religious visions and the Terrestrial Paradise see Patch, pp. 26, 88, 96, 97, 100, 103, 105, 111, 113, 115, 132, 137, and Arnold Van Os, *Religious Visions,* pp. 30, 31–32, 36, 64, 67, 72, 80, 162, 166, 171, 253. For fragrance in symbolic gardens see n. 60 below.

59. *The Catholic Missal,* arranged for daily use by Rev. Chas. J. Callan and Rev. John A. McHugh (1934), Introd., p. 31.

60. Aquinas, *Sum. Theol.,* III (3rd no.), Q. 83, Art. 5; Lapide, VIII, 77–78, 85, 90; *Select Metrical Hymns and Homilies of Ephraem Syrus,* pp. 116–117; *St. John Damascene on Holy Images,* p. 197; Cassian, "Conferences," quoted by Ewer, p. 51.

61. Christ's dual nature? His human nature, sometimes symbolized by field or garden (n. 34 above)? Wyclif said in a sermon *(Select English Works,* I, 286): "The manheed of Crist is o margerite that worshipith his Chirche and confortith mennis hertis."

62. Sr. Madeleva, p. 132.

63. *PL,* CXII, 852.

64. Thomas Merton, "Poetry and the Contemplative Life," *Figures for an Apocalypse* (1947), pp. 95–111. This exposition, based on the Augustinian psychology, "the traditional substratum of Christian mystical theology" (p. 103), also looks back to the testimony of Gregory

the Great, Aquinas, John of the Cross, Teresa of Avila, Ruysbroeck, Bonaventura, and Bernard, and agrees with the views of Bonaventura and the Victorines (Hugh and Richard), which I quote below. See especially Merton, pp. 103–104, 108.

65. *PL,* CXCI, 1662, as quoted by Sr. Rita Mary Bradley, "Backgrounds of the Title *Speculum* in Mediaeval Literature," *Speculum,* XXIX (Jan. 1954), 111–112; cf. 106–108.

66. R. E. Brennan, O.P., *A History of Psychology from the Standpoint of a Thomist,* p. 58.

67. W. R. Inge, *Christian Mysticism,* p. 141 and n. 2.

68. Ibid.; cf. Sr. Rita Mary Bradley, p. 108, quoting St. Basil.

69. See n. 22 above.

70. See n. 7 above.

71. *The Cypress Grove,* pp. 52–58.

72. The medieval baptismal services in England are described by H. B. Swete, *Church Services and Service Books before the Reformation,* pp. 138–143; Wm. Maskell, *Monumenta Ritualia Ecclesiae Anglicanae* (2nd ed., 1882), I, 3–43.

73. "The solemn renewal of this promise [the renunciation of Satan and his works and pomps] is a favourite exercise of piety, often undertaken in common at the end of a mission or retreat" *(Catholic Encyclopaedia,* article on "Baptismal Vows").

74. *PL,* XXXV, 1571. Cf. D. W. Robertson, *MLN,* LXV, 158, who defines "world" in this utterance of Pearl's as "cupidity for temporalia."

75. Lines 1113–16: "þaȝ þou be man fenny / And al to-marred in myre, whyl þou on molde lyves, / Þou may schyne þurȝ schryft þaȝ þou half schome served, / And pure þe wiþ penaunce tyl þou a perle worþe."

76. See *OED* under *betake* and cf. F. A. Patterson, *The Medieval Penitential Lyric,* pp. 87, 120; C. Horstmann, *Yorkshire Writers,* I, 236; *Minor Poems of the Vernon MS.,* I, 231 (lines 363–366); *The Wycliffite New Testament,* ed. Henry H. Baber, Luke 23.46.

77. *Sum. Theol.,* III, Q. 73, Art. 3.

78. "Grace" *(Catholic Encyc.):* "The Friendship with God is one of the most excellent effects of grace. . . . According to the Scriptural concept (Wisdom, VII. 14; John XV. 51) this friendship resembles a mystical matrimonial union between the soul and its Divine Spouse" (Matt. IX. 15; Apoc. XIX. 7).

3. *Pearl:* SYMBOLISM IN A GARDEN SETTING

1. See Tobler-Lommatsch, s.v. *erbier.*
2. Cf. Froissart, *La Prison Amoureuse,* 1391.
3. C. Estienne and J. Liebault (1572), p. 116; English version by R. Surflet (1616), p. 333.
4. *The Boke of Curtasye,* 399 ff.
5. Surflet, p. 235; W. Lawson, *The Country Housewifes Garden* (1618), p. 18.
6. *Phil. Soc. Trans.* 1858.
7. On the seasonal headpiece, see also G. V. Smithers, *King Álisaunder,* II (EETS. 237), pp. 35 ff.
8. With the wording in *Pearl* compare *Sir Gawain,* 167, þe golde ay inmyddes, of plaiting where gold thread takes part in some regular pattern of alternation along with the colored hair. Of interest, as supplying some kind of analogue to the *Pearl* passage, is Milton's *Paradise Lost,* IV. 699 ff.:

> each beauteous flow'r,
> *Iris* all hues, Roses and Jessamin
> Rear'd high thir flourisht heads between, and wrought
> Mosaic.

9. For the examples from Hugh of St. Victor, see *Sermones Centum,* VI (Migne, *Patrologia Latina,* CLXXVII. 914), and *Sermo de Assumptione B. Mariae* (ibid. 1218 ff.). Philip's lyric is in *The Oxford Book of Medieval Latin Verse,* no. 253.
10. Charles d'Orléans, *Poésies,* edited by P. Champion (1923), Rondeaux, CCLVII. 4 f.
11. Machaut, *Poésies Lyriques,* edited by V. F. Chichmaref (1909), Les Chansons Baladées, XIX. 19 ff.
12. *Romaunt of the Rose,* 2801 ff.; Machaut, *Le Confort d'Ami,* 2187 ff.
13. Chichmaref, op. cit., La Loange des Dames, CXIV. 9 ff.

4. PRECIOUS METAL AND GEM SYMBOLISM IN *Pearl*

1. E. V. Gordon (ed.), *Pearl* (London, 1963), I, ll. 1–2. Subsequent quotations will have their line references in parentheses.
2. Ian Bishop, "The Significance of the 'Garlande gay' in the Alle-

gory of *Pearl,*" *Review of English Studies,* VIII (February, 1957), p. 14.

3. Emile Mâle, *Religious Art in France in the Thirteenth Century,* trans. Dora Nussey (New York, 1913), p. 214. See also Marie P. Hamilton, "The Meaning of the Middle English *Pearl,*" cf. Chapter 2 of this volume, p. 40.

4. William H. Schofield, "The Nature and Fabric of *The Pearl,*" *PMLA,* XIX (1904), p. 188. See also Dorothy Everett, *Essays on Middle English Literature* (London, 1959), p. 90.

5. *The Peterborough Lapidary* in *English Mediaeval Lapidaries,* eds. Joan Evans and Mary S. Serjeantson, E.E.T.S., O.S., #190 (1933), p. 73.

6. A. Welby Pugin, *Glossary of Ecclesiastical Ornament and Costume* (London, 1868), p. 211.

7. Howard R. Patch, *The Other World* (Cambridge, Mass., 1950), p. 190.

8. Milton R. Stern, "An Approach to *The Pearl,*" *Journal of English and Germanic Philology,* LIV (October, 1955), p. 689.

9. Patch, op. cit., p. 190.

10. *The London Lapidary of King Philip* in *English Mediaeval Lapidaries,* eds. Joan Evans and Mary S. Serjeantson, E.E.T.S., O.S., #190 (1933), p. 28.

11. Stern, op. cit., p. 689.

12. *The London Lapidary of King Philip,* p. 28.

13. *The Sloane Lapidary* in *English Mediaeval Lapidaries,* eds. Joan Evans and Mary S. Serjeantson, E.E.T.S., O.S., #190 (1933), p. 121.

14. *The North Midland Lapidary of King Philip* in *English Mediaeval Lapidaries,* eds. Joan Evans and Mary S. Serjeantson, E.E.T.S., O.S., #190 (1933), p. 41.

15. *The London Lapidary,* p. 20.

16. Joan Evans, *Magical Jewels of the Middle Ages and the Renaissance, Particularly in England* (London, 1922), p. 76.

17. *The London Lapidary,* p. 23.

18. Wendell S. Johnson, "The Imagery and Diction of *The Pearl:* Toward an Interpretation," *English Literary History,* XX (September, 1953), p. 169.

19. A. C. Spearing, "Symbolic and Dramatic Development in *Pearl,*" cf. Chapter 5 of this volume, p. 105.

20. *The Peterborough Lapidary,* p. 76.

21. F. Edward Hulme, *The History, Principles, and Practice of Symbolism in Christian Art* (New York, 1909), p. 162.

22. Ibid., p. 149.

23. *The London Lapidary*, p. 24.

24. George F. Kunz, *The Magic of Jewels and Charms* (Philadelphia, 1915), p. 284.

25. *The London Lapidary*, p. 23.

26. Ibid., p. 29.

27. Ibid., p. 30.

28. Ibid., p. 20.

29. *The Sloane Lapidary*, p. 121.

30. *The London Lapidary*, p. 30.

31. Gordon, op. cit., p. 79.

32. *The London Lapidary*, p. 19.

33. Gordon, op. cit., pp. 79–80.

34. *The London Lapidary*, p. 22.

35. Ibid., p. 27.

36. Ibid., p. 28.

37. Gordon, op. cit., p. 75.

38. *The London Lapidary*, pp. 19–20.

39. Ibid., p. 29.

40. Sister Mary Madeleva, *Pearl: A Study in Spiritual Dryness* (New York, 1925), p. 165.

41. *The London Lapidary*, p. 29.

42. Ibid.

43. Ibid., p. 26.

44. Ibid.

45. Johnson, op. cit., p. 179.

46. Gordon, op. cit., p. 81.

5. SYMBOLIC AND DRAMATIC DEVELOPMENT IN *Pearl*

1. Sister Mary Madeleva, *Pearl: A Study in Spiritual Dryness* (New York, 1925); M. P. Hamilton, "The Meaning of the Middle English *Pearl*," cf. Chapter 2 of this volume.

2. D. W. Robertson, "The Pearl as a Symbol," *MLN*, LXV (1950), 155–61; M. R. Stern, "An Approach to *The Pearl*," *JEGP*, LIV (1955), 684–92.

3. I do not catalog them here, since they are summarized in most

recent articles on *Pearl*. There is a useful brief analysis in the article in this journal by Stanton de Voren Hoffman, "The *Pearl:* Notes for an Interpretation," *MP,* LVIII (1960), 74–75.

4. M. W. Bloomfield, "Symbolism in Medieval Literature," *MP,* LVI (1958), 73–81.

5. This and all subsequent quotations from *Pearl* are taken from the edition of E. V. Gordon (Oxford, 1953).

6. *Pearl,* ll. 937–60.

7. And the case of the distinction between the two Jerusalems surely casts doubt on Hoffman's contention that "in the poem we find together several meanings of the pearl figure and . . . they are kept distinct" (op. cit., p. 76). If the poet had wished to keep several meanings of the symbol distinct, would he not have distinguished among them explicitly, as he does between the Old Jerusalem and the New?

8. Cf. W. H. Schofield, "Symbolism, Allegory, and Autobiography in *The Pearl,*" *PMLA,* XXIV (1909), 585–675: "a learned man of the fourteenth century was so used to interpretations of the pearl that the word could hardly be mentioned without a great many rising to his memory instantly" (p. 639).

9. Ibid., p. 588.

10. Moorman seems to me right in insisting that within the drama of the poem the role of the narrator is at least as important as that of the Maiden (see Charles Moorman, "The Role of the Narrator in *Pearl,*" *MP,* LIII [1955]), but I cannot agree with him when he remarks that "we are never allowed to see and judge the experience presented by the poem objectively and for ourselves but are, instead, forced, by the point of view which the poet adopts, to accept the experience of the vision only in terms of its relationship to him" (p. 74). Here and elsewhere in this article, though not consistently, Moorman fails to allow for any difference between the narrator and the poet: thus at one point he refers to "the poet's immediate grief" (p. 75). For evidence that the poet sometimes invites us to "judge," not merely to "accept," the narrator's experience, see below.

11. Op. cit., pp. 589 ff.

12. *Pearl,* note on ll. 1–4.

13. Schofield, op. cit., suggests some connection with the feast of the Assumption of the Virgin, and with St. John's Great Reaper (p. 616, n. 2).

14. For the traditional elements of the *locus amoenus* motif, see

E. R. Curtius, *European Literature and the Latin Middle Ages*, trans. W. R. Trask (New York, 1953), pp. 183–202.

15. See Gordon, op. cit., p. xxxiv and note on l. 228.

16. And see W. S. Johnson, "The Imagery and Diction of *The Pearl*," *ELH*, XX (1953). "The result is an emphasis upon a ubiquitous sense of contrast between the nature of heaven and the nature of earth, the revelation of which seems, for our present reading, to be the poem's main purpose" (p. 163).

17. This seems to me a more plausible interpretation of the lines than A. L. Kellogg's suggestion *(Traditio,* XII [1956], 406–7) that the allusion is to the doctrine of *creatio ex nihilo,* a reading which does not seem to explain *þef* or *cler.*

18. It might be compared with the *Vita de Dowel* section of *Piers Plowman,* which consists largely of sermon-like speeches from various personified abstractions, and in which Piers himself appears in the B text not at all, and in the C text only once, and that briefly. There are many similarities between *Pearl* and *Piers Plowman,* despite their great difference in length (cf. n. 19 below).

19. Such an attempt would be rather similar to that of the Dreamer in *Piers Plowman* to distinguish the various "names" of Liberum-Arbitrium and their "causes":

> "Ʒe ben as a bischop," quath ich·al bordynge that tyme,
> "For bischopes blessed·thei bereth meny names,
> *Presul* and *pontifex*·and *metropolitanus,*
> And other names an hepe·*episcopus* and *pastor.*"
> "That is soth," he seide·"now ich seo thy wil
> How thow woldest know and conne·the cause of alle here
>   names,
> And of myne, yf thow myghtest·me thynketh by thy speche!"
> "Ʒe, syre," ich seyde, "by so·that no man were a-greued,
> Alle the science vnder sonne·and alle sotile craftes
> Ich wolde ich knewe and couthe·kyndeliche in myn herte!"

(Ed. W. W. Skeat, 2 vols. [Oxford, 1886], C. XVII, ll. 202–11.) And the attempt would perhaps seem to the *Pearl* poet to deserve a rebuke similar to the one Langland's Dreamer receives:

> "Thanne art thow inparfyt," quath he·"and on of Prydes
>   knyghtes;

For such a luste and lykynge·Lucifer fel fro heuene;
   Ponam pedem meum in aquilone, et ero similis altissimo.
Hit were a-geyn kynde," quath he·"and alle kynne resoun
That eny creature sholde conne al·excepte Cryst one"
(Ibid., ll. 212–15).

20. Dorothy Everett, *Essays on Middle English Literature* (Oxford, 1955), p. 93.

SIR GAWAIN
AND THE GREEN KNIGHT

6. THE TWO CONFESSION SCENES IN *Sir Gawain and the Green Knight*

1. Ed. I. Gollancz (Early English Text Society, 1940).
2. W. A. Pantin, *The English Church in the Fourteenth Century* (1955), p. 192.
3. J. de Burgo, *Pupilla oculi* (Paris, 1518), part V, chap. 3, sec. A.
4. J. Bromyard, *Summa predicantium* (Venice, 1586), p. 119.
5. De Burgo, V, 5, A. Compare *Piers Plowman* (B text), V, 276–85; and see R. W. Frank, *Piers Plowman and the Scheme of Salvation* (1957), pp. 106 ff.
6. Noted by Gollancz in his edition of the poem. Gollancz also suggests that Gawain's confession is to be read as "sacrilegious," but his argument is strange. See his note to l. 1880.
7. I follow Gollancz' interpretation of this line—"let me under-stand your will, i.e. what do you want me to do now? Gawain, having confessed, asks for penance"; though it is possible that the phrase means "let me win (or regain) your goodwill" (so Tolkien and Gordon in their edition. See *Cursor mundi*, ll. 24824–25: "þa þat he had na giftis tille Wiþ hotis faire he overtoke þaire wil"). The Green Knight's reply suggests that in either case the reference is to doing penance.
8. It is probable that the phrase "penaunce apert" has the specific sense "public penance" here. The *Pupilla oculi* (V, 1, B–H), in common with most authorities of the period, distinguishes three kinds of penance—solemn, public, and private—a distinction which is explained in the early thirteenth-century penitential of Robert of Flamesbury as follows: "Paenitentia alia solemnis, alia publica, alia privata. So-lemnis est quae fit in capite jejunii, quoniam cum solemnitate in

cinere et cilicio ejiciuntur paenitentes ab ecclesia . . . Publica et non solemnis est quae fit in facie ecclesiae sine supradicta solemnitate, ut perigrinatio. Privata est illa quae quotidie fit privatim coram sacerdote." The *Pupilla oculi* states that public penance is imposed "ut pro peccato publico publicam habeant medicinam." Gawain's sin would have been considered public in the sense that it affected the well-being of others *(MED* and *NED* give examples of the word "apert" used to render the Latin "publicus" in this sense, e.g., "Glotonye, lecherie, and othere synnis, prevy or aperte").

9. *Inferno,* V, 9. I refer here to the Green Knight as he is during and after the "discovery" scene. Criticism of the poem has sometimes failed to notice that the Green Knight, although he has only two *physical forms,* has three distinct *personae*—the "aghlich mayster" (fit one, and fit four up to l. 2330), the genial host (fits two and three), and what I here call the "conoscitor" (the latter part of the fourth fit).

10. See Greta Hort, *Piers Plowman and Contemporary Religious Thought* (n.d.), pp. 142 ff.

11. *Chaucer's "Parson's Tale,"* ed. Robinson, vss. 1062–63.

12. I follow Gollancz in taking "werke" to refer to the "workmanship" of the embroidered girdle. The phrase "wylyde werke" seems clearly to be parallel with "wlonk werkkeȝ" (l. 2432) in the closely related passage quoted below. "Wylyde" could mean either "cunning" (from "wile"—so Tolkien and Gordon) or "choice" (from ON "vildr" —so Gollancz). If the former, the phrase might be compared with *Piers Plowman,* Prologue, l. 162—"colers of crafty werk."

13. Compare: "Corsed worth cowarddyse and couetyse boþe" . . . (l. 2374) and

> "Þis is þe laþe and þe losse þat I laȝt haue,
> Of couardise and couetyse þat I haf caȝt þare;
> Þis is þe token of untrawþe þat I am tan inne" . . .

(ll. 2507–9).

14. Robert Mannyng, *Handlyng Synne,* ed. F. J. Furnivall (Early English Text Society, 1901–3), ll. 11551–56. The French original has "harte"—"halter"—for the English "wyþþe."

7. MORGAN LE FAY IN *Sir Gawain and the Green Knight*

1. *Histoire littéraire de la France,* XXX (Paris, 1888), 73.

2. G. L. Kittredge, *A Study of Gawain and the Green Knight* (Cambridge, Massachusetts, 1916), p. 136.

3. Op. cit., p. 131.

4. J. R. Hulbert, *"Syr Gawayn and the Grene Knyʒt," Modern Philology*, XIII (1915–16), 454, 462.

5. "The Role of Morgan le Fay in *Sir Gawain and the Green Knight*," *ELH*, XVII (1950), 241–251.

6. *Sir Gawain and the Green Knight*, eds. J. R. R. Tolkien and E. V. Gordon (Oxford, 1936), l. 231. All quotations from *Sir Gawain* will be taken from this edition.

7. *Sir Gawain and the Green Knight*, ed. Sir Israel Gollancz, with introductory essays by Mabel Day and Mary S. Serjeantson, *EETS*, 210 (London, 1940), p. 102. Cp. G. J. Engelhardt, "The Predicament of Gawain," *Modern Language Quarterly*, XVI (1955), 224 n.

8. *Beowulf and Sir Gawain and the Green Knight*, transl. G. H. Gerould (New York, 1935), p. 141.

9. *The College Survey of English Literature*, eds. B. J. Whiting *et al.* (New York, 1942), I, 118.

10. *Fled Bricrend;* see Kittredge, p. 12.

11. Baughan, p. 247; Kittredge, p. 132.

12. *Vulgate Versions of Arthurian Romances*, ed. H. O. Sommer (Washington, 1908–16), IV, 140 ff.

13. B. J. Whiting, "Gawain, His Reputation, His Courtesy and His Appearance in Chaucer's *Squire's Tale*," *Mediaeval Studies*, IX (1947), 196 ff.

14. L. A. Paton. *Studies in the Fairy Mythology of Arthurian Romance* (Boston, 1903), p. 13.

15. *Works*, ed. Eugène Vinaver (Oxford, 1947), II, 597 (Caxton, X, 17).

16. *Lestoire del Saint Graal*, Sommer, op. cit., I, 451–2; *Livre d'Artus,* Sommer, VII, 164; Paton, op. cit., pp. 62, 225 ff.; cp. Tolkien and Gordon, p. 115.

17. *Les Prophécies de Merlin,* ed. L. A. Paton (New York, 1926–7), I, 413–414; *Le Roman en Prose de Tristan,* ed. Eilert Löseth (Paris, 1891), p. 360; *Malory,* ed. Vinaver, II, 641–643 (Caxton, X, 37).

18. *Merlin,* eds. Gaston Paris and Jacob Ulrich, *SATF* (Paris, 1886), I, 166.

19. On evil significance of colors used to describe Morgan, see J. F. Eagan, "The Import of Color Symbolism in *Sir Gawain*," *Saint Louis University Studies,* I (1949), 75–76.

20. Paton, *Fairy Mythology*, pp. 25 ff.

21. Ibid., pp. 60 ff.; cp. *Livre d'Artus*, Sommer VII, 135 f.

22. *Roman de Troie*, ed. Constans, *SATF* (Paris, 1904), I, 434 f., ll. 8023 ff. Cp. Paton, *Fairy Mythology*, p. 21 and R. S. Loomis, "Morgain la Fée and the Celtic Goddesses," *Speculum*, XX (1945), 183–186, 202.

23. Sommer, IV, 117 ff.

24. *Huon de Bordeaus*, eds. F. Guessard and C. Grandmaison (Paris, 1860), ll. 9, 10, 379–380, 382; Paton, *Fairy Mythology*, pp. 50, 61, 124.

25. *Merlin*, eds. Paris and Ulrich, II, 189, 212–213; cp. *Malory*, ed. Vinaver, I, 149 f. (Caxton, IV, 13).

26. Löseth, *Tristan*, p. 137.

27. *Brun de la Montaigne*, ed. Paul Meyer, *SATF* (Paris, 1875), ll. 3253, 3399; Löseth, *Tristan*, pp. 96, 118; Paton, *Fairy Mythology*, pp. 17–18, 74 ff.

28. Löseth, *Tristan*, pp. 191 ff.; *Les Prophécies de Merlin*, ed. Paton, I, 414; cp. *Malory*, ed. Vinaver, II, 643 ff. (Caxton, X, 38).

29. Sommer, III, 409–411.

30. Kittredge, p. 106.

31. See J. L. Weston, *The Legend of Sir Gawain* (London, 1897), pp. 45 ff. and Hulbert, *Modern Philology*, XIII, 458 ff.

32. Alice Buchanan, "The Irish Framework of *Gawain and the Green Knight*," *PMLA*, XLVII (1932), 315–338.

33. *PMLA*, XLVIII (1933), 1000–1035. Professor Loomis has generously written me that he now realizes that "the Temptation then in the various stories owed little to the role of Bláthnat [Curoi's wife] in 'The Visit to Curoi's Castle' and far more to the Welsh traditions of Pwyll and Arawn's wife and the Breton traditions of Morgain." His 1943 article cited below marks the shift of opinion.

34. See Volkmar Bach, *Die Angriffswaffen in der Altfranzösischen Artus- und Abenteuer-Romanen* (Marburg, 1887), pp. 45–47, 127–130.

35. *PMLA*, XLVIII, 1024 ff. Cp. 1009 ff., Loomis' notes to Ulrich von Zatzikhoven, *Lanzelet*, trans. K. G. T. Webster (New York, 1951), pp. 171–173, and his *Arthurian Tradition and Chrétien de Troyes* (New York, 1949), pp. 417–420. The Guingambresil episode was put forward as the source of *Sir Gawain* by Miss M. C. Thomas, *Syr Gawayne and the Green Knight* (Zurich, 1883); Kittredge dismisses her work, p. 294.

36. "More Celtic Elements in *Gawain and the Green Knight*," *Journal of English and Germanic Philology*, XLII (1943), 170 ff. Reptd. in *Wales and the Arthurian Tradition* (Cardiff, 1956), pp. 77 ff.

37. *Mabinogion,* trans. Gwyn and Thomas Jones (London, 1949), pp. 6–8.

38. See note 31.

8. THE MEANING OF *Sir Gawain and the Green Knight*

1. *El Vitorial,* trans. Joan Evans, *The Unconquered Knight* (London, 1928), p. 61.

2. *Erec und Enide,* ed. W. Foerster (Halle, 1890), vv. 1691–1692.

3. All citations of the text are from the Gordon and Tolkien edition (Oxford, 1925); translations are my own.

4. The form *Bercilak* appears to be better supported than *Bertilak;* see R. L. Smith, "Guinganbresil and the Green Knight," *JEGP,* XLV (1946), 15 ff.

5. J. Speirs, " 'Sir Gawain and the Green Knight'," *Scrutiny,* XVI, iv (1949), 277; H. Braddy, "Sir Gawain and Ralph Holmes the Green Knight," *MLN,* LXVIII, iv (1952), 240–242.

6. We scarcely need to be reminded that it is not a "love token." Incidentally, I do not think, as Roger S. Loomis suggested some time ago ("More Celtic Elements in Gawain and the Green Knight," *JEGP,* XLII [April 1943], 149, 153), that Bercilak was wearing that same lace about his waist when he appeared as the Green Knight at Arthur's court. The lace, to be sure, belonged to Bercilak (vv. 2358–2359), but it appears more likely, if indeed he took it to Arthur's hall, that it was wrapped around his ax helve, not about himself. (Cf. the lace, vv. 1829–1833, with the description of the ax, vv. 217–220). At any rate, he survived Gawain's blow because of Morgan le Fay's power; he would not have needed an additional magical warranty. If, as I think, Bercilak did not rely on the lace, the lace then becomes an object of curiosity indeed, for it is a magic talisman never put to the test. Since Gawain, as it turns out, has no opportunity to rely on it either, we have no grounds for belief in its efficacy. We may perhaps conclude that a man who relies on his own integrity and honor has no need of a magic talisman.

7. The power of Morgan le Fay has apparently overwhelmed at least one reader. D. E. Baughan, in "The Role of Morgan Le Fay in *Sir Gawain and the Green Knight,*" *ELH,* XVII (1950), 241–251, insists the poem is "an apotheosization of chastity." To make his case, Baughan argues that the "Beheading Test" and the "Love Test" illus-

trate the same virtue, the hero's chastity. There is no need, of course, to suppose that only one virtue in man must be held out for our evaluation; the poem is not that restricted: Baughan, it seems, works it out this way: the Lady of the Castle tests Gawain's chastity; the "Beheading Test," ideally, ought also to test Gawain's chastity; therefore Bercilak's intent, imposed upon him by Morgan le Fay, was to demonstrate that Arthur was unchaste, and so failed to decapitate Bercilak, and that Gawain, because he was chaste, succeeded in striking off Bercilak's head. Unfortunately, there is no authority in the text for such a reading. The passage Baughan refers to, "Now hatȝ Arthure his axe, & þe halme grypeȝ, / & sturnely stureȝ hit aboute, þat stryke wyth hit þoȝt" (vv. 330–331), states that Arthur, the Green Knight's ax in his hands, "grips the helve and whirls it about sternly as if he intended to strike with it." Baughan wants to read "... struck with it." (Baughan, p. 246: "the poet gave the account something of Morgan's magic so that it seems almost as if Arthur did not strike.") But it is not possible to read "þat stryke wyth hit poȝt" struck with it; literally, the phrase is rendered "that thing he seemed to strike with." (ME þynken<OE þyncan, imp. vb., "seem, appear." The Gawain poet, had he meant "struck," would have written stroke, as he did in v. 671.) The "many and seemingly insoluble questions that have been raised regarding the plot" (Baughan, p. 251) are not to be answered by forcing the text to say something it does not.

8. In the romance an imaginary boundary is established between the "real" world and the "romance" world, the principal action usually taking place inside the romance world. It may be an obvious feature of terrain, such as the mysterious mound into which Gawain and the Turk disappear (The Turk and Gowin, ed. Hales and Furnivall, Percy Folio MS., vv. 66–68), or an inconspicuous line of brush where a strange knight lurks, waiting to snare Arthur (The Weddynge of Syr Gawen and Dame Ragnell, ed. Laura Sumner, Smith Coll. Stud. in Mod. Lang. [Northampton, Mass.], V, iv, 1924, vv. 44–45). Whatever its nature, this boundary exists, and the hero must cross it to reach his goal. Once across the line inside the romance world, geography, on purpose, is obscure. We could, for example, follow Gawain's route for a time, but we would have no more chance of finding Bercilak's castle than Master Wace had of finding faeries in the forest of Broceliande.

9. Principally J. R. Hulbert, " 'Sir Gawayn and the Grene Knyȝt'," MP, XIII (Dec. 1915; April 1916), 433, 691, et passim.

10. G. J. Engelhardt, in "The Predicament of Gawain," *MLQ*, XVI (Sept. 1955), 218–225, however, sees in the poem a lesson more suited to the pulpit than to the castle hall. With Engelhardt's judgment I have no quarrel. By restricting his inquiry to the predicament of Gawain, he draws attention to the force and tension of the extreme dilemma which the hero, in his test at the castle, has to face. Further, his explication of what he calls the "pentagonal" Gawain is masterly. But when I apply Engelhardt's demonstration—essentially the consideration of Gawain's "predicament . . . in terms of the three virtues (valor, piety, and courtesy) that would govern the three domains of activity . . . in which the complete knight . . . might demonstrate his perfection, or . . . his *trauþe*" (p. 219)—to the total structure of the poem, I find that *Sir Gawain and the Green Knight* becomes, not a moral romance, but a theological dissertation, a Christian demonstration of the imperfection of man. The poem thus turns out to be "a humane and sympathetic presentation designed to reveal how human and imperfect is even a supposedly perfect knight such as the pentagonal Gawain" (p. 225, n. 14, §2. Note the justice of Engelhardt's objection to Baughan's reading of vv. 330–338; §1 of this note is utterly convincing.) I may have misread Engelhardt, but I detect here a denigration of the hero, not unlike what we see in certain of the Welsh lives of 'the saints, in which Arthur, Bedivere, and Kei are knocked down a peg. It is, I think, unfair to Gawain. Where we ought to congratulate the hero for his superior quality as a man, Engelhardt seems to chastise him for his failure to equal the behavior of Christ. So far as we can determine the poet's intention (design), I should prefer to state that the poem is a "humane and sympathetic presentation" of a guide for human conduct, of a model man. Gawain is a splendid man, to be sure, but not an impossible one. The poem seems to tell us that we must do our duty, and that we must not avoid action because we might be forced to place our life, or our soul, in jeopardy. It also seems to tells us that we are allowed an occasional slip, provided we learn humility. We need not, I think, look to *Sir Gawain and the Green Knight* as a reminder that, after all, only Christ could spurn Satan.

11. In the last 5 or 6 years, accompanying a wholesome revival of interest in medieval life and literature, *Sir Gawain and the Green Knight* has received its share of attention. Apart from the Baughan and Engelhardt articles which I had to take some account of, the following works deserve notice: John Speirs, "Sir Gawain and the Green Knight," *Scrutiny*, XVI, iv (1949), 274–300; Dorothy Everett, *Essays on*

Middle English Literature, ed. Patricia Kean (Oxford: Clarendon Press, 1955), pp. 75–77, et passim; H. L. Savage, *The Gawain-Poet* (Chapel Hill: Univ. of North Carolina Press), 1956.

9. GAWAIN'S SHIELD AND THE QUEST FOR PERFECTION

1. For a full account of the present state of *Gawain* studies, including a judicious evaluation of current interpretations, see Morton W. Bloomfield, *"Sir Gawain and the Green Knight:* An Appraisal," *PMLA,* LXXVI (1961), 7–19. Since Bloomfield's appraisal will undoubtedly be the point of departure for future studies of the *Gawain* poem, a clear statement of the main difference between his approach to the poem and mine may be helpful at the outset. Bloomfield agrees with George Kane *(Middle English Literature* [London, 1951], pp. 73–76) that the conduct of the hero is not the main concern of the poem: "What is the poet's first intention? Although I do not agree with Kane that it is the decorative and visual which the poet wishes to elevate I think he is making an important point—that the ethical side can be overvalued. I do not believe the poem was written fundamentally to present us with a good man who emerges somewhat stained or humbled from his encounter with the world of evil or of the supernatural. The humor, suspense, and tone of the poem belie the centrality of this interpretation" (p. 17). My own view is that these are precisely the qualities of the poem which modify, embody, and shape the poem's central moral concern.

2. What ensues is no "chyldys game." See William Matthews, *The Tragedy of Arthur* (Berkeley and Los Angeles, 1960), pp. 161–63.

3. The most influential reading based on vestiges of pagan myth and ritual is found in John Speirs, *"Sir Gawain and the Green Knight,"* *Scrutiny,* XVI (1949), 274–300. Bloomfield puts succinctly the most serious objection to such criticism as it has so far been applied to this poem: *"Sir Gawain* is one of the few undoubtedly aristocratic poems of the English Middle Ages extant. It would be surprising if in this courtly and Christian atmosphere of a poem perhaps written entirely or partly in high style, we could find alive mythic and ritualistic elements" (p. 14). This does not, of course, suggest that Christian myth and ritual are not immediately and pervasively *alive* in the poem. Many details of the poet's figurative representation of Christian ideas need further historical and critical investigation.

4. *M. Roberti Holkoth in librum Sapientiae praelectiones CCXIII*

(Basel, 1586), lect. 36, p. 127. The "History of Britain" referred to by Holkot is probably that of pseudo-Nennius. This text was called to my attention by Professor R. E. Kaske whose generous learning is felt elsewhere in this essay.

5. The text cited is that of J. R. R. Tolkien and E. V. Gordon (Oxford, 1925).

6. Alan M. Markman, "The Meaning of *Sir Gawain and the Green Knight*," cf. Chapter 8 of this volume. Markman's thesis is bluntly stated: "To come at it directly, I suggest that the primary purpose of the poem is to show what a splendid man Gawain is" (p. 161). Markman properly finds that ". . . human conduct is the heart of the poem . . ." and that Gawain represents ". . . the ideal feudal Christian knight . . ." (p. 162), but his reading of the poem is quite literal and his notions of the ideals of human conduct are much more modern than medieval. George J. Engelhardt, in "The Predicament of Gawain," *MLQ*, XVI (1955), 218–25, establishes the moral issue which is central to the poem's action and characterization by showing that, in spite of reputation and real virtue, the hero does succumb to the world's imperfection. My own interpretation may be regarded as an elaboration of Engelhardt's assessment of the poem's subject, and a substantial modification of his treatment of the poet's tone and historical meaning.

7. In addition to the brief and general notes supplied by editors and translators of the poem, see V. S. Hopper's discussion in connection with his general treatment of the number five. *Medieval Number Symbolism* (New York, 1938), pp. 123–25. Among those who have interpreted the pentangle in the terms established by the poem, Engelhardt comes nearest the poet's interpretation, but he finds it to be simply "the symbol of the complete man, whose integrity admits no imperfection" (pp. 218–19). His only documentation of the concept of the *eques pentagonalis* is a reference to Edgar de Bruyne on this variation of the medieval *homo quadratus* in *Etudes d'esthétique médiévale*, II (Bruges, 1946), pp. 348–50; but de Bruyne finds no pentangles from Vitruvius to Leonardo da Vinci. We might call attention to the pentagles, used as aids to drawing in the tradition which extends from Vitruvius to the late Renaissance, found in the sketchbook of Villard de Honnecourt (1225–50). See Theodore Bowie, *The Sketchbook of Villard de Honnecourt* (Bloomington, 1959), plates 35, 36, 37, 39. However, Erwin Panofsky observes that, in spite of medieval concern for "the God-ordained correspondence between the universe and man," medieval theories of proportions had degenerated into a

code of practical rules which had lost all connection with harmonistic cosmology. "The History of the Theory of Human Proportions as a Reflection of the History of Styles, " *Meaning in the Visual Arts* (Garden City, N.Y., 1955), pp. 83–91. In my opinion, philosophical uses of the analogies between geometrical figures and natural relations (e.g. Dante's comparison of the pentagon and the soul: see below, pp. 84–85) are related more closely to the *Gawain* poet's use of the pentangle.

Robert Ackerman, in a recent article on Gawain's shield *(Anglia,* LXXVI [1958], 254-65), attempts to associate Gawain's five fives with the sacrament of Penance and the vernacular penitential literature of medieval England. He fully documents the conventional use of the sins of the five senses as categories for the examination of conscience, but his efforts to show a similar connection for the other pentads are unconvincing.

8. Henri de Lubac, *Exégèse médiévale,* I (1959), pp. 285–90.

9. Chaucer's Parson attests the conventionality of this ancient pattern of human imperfection: "Ful ofte tyme I rede that no man truste in his owene perfeccioun, but he be stronger than Sampsoun, and hoolier than David, and wiser than Salomon," *The Parson's Tale,* I. 955. The Venerable Bede, in his commentary on Proverbs 7.26, has much the same catalog of strong men who were deceived by women: *Et fortissimi quique interfecti sunt ab ea.* Ut ipse Salomon sapientissimus virorum, ut Sampson fortissimus, ut David mansuetissimus a mulierum decipula, ut Origenes ab haeretica doctrina, quem post apostolos Ecclesiae magistrum fuisse, quandiu recte sapuit, qui negaverit, errat, *Super Parabolas Salamonis Allegorica Expositio,* I, vii (PL 91, col. 964).

10. Lynn Thorndike gives abundant evidence for the association of Solomon and magic in the late Middle Ages. Among writers of the thirteenth century, he cites William of Auvergne, bishop of Paris, who declares that there is no divinity in the angles of Solomon's pentagon, and that the rings and seals of Solomon are a form of idolatry and involve execrable consecrations and detestable invocations and images. *De legibus,* ch. 27. Albertus Magnus (in *Speculum astronomiae,* ch. 2) lists five treatises current under the name of Solomon as evil books of necromantic images. *A History of Magic and Experimental Science,* II (New York, 1923), esp, p. 280. C. C. McCown, in his edition of the Greek text of *The Testament of Solomon* (Leipzig, 1922), says that books of magic attributed to Solomon flourished in the Middle Ages, and that the most popular was the *Clavicula Salomonis,* in which there

are many "pentacles," or magical drawings (p. 100). Against these books, he cites a steady line of condemnation. The only text of the *Clavicula* I have been able to see (S. L. MacGregor Mathers, *The Key of Solomon the King* [London, 1889], in the Houdini Collection of the Library of Congress) is edited from seven MSS, the oldest being no earlier than the end of the sixteenth century. McCown's edition of the Greek *Testament* is based on Harleian MS 5596, among others, written in the fifteenth century. In a late recension of the *Testament* the seal engraved on Solomon's ring is a pentagram, a type identified by Mc-Cown as belonging to the western tradition of the ring (p. 86). In summary, such evidence as I have seen indicates that, in the late Middle Ages in the West, the pentangle was associated with Solomon, and both with magic, in a popular tradition which was condemned by the Church. The *Gawain* poet's adaptation of the pentangle seems to be wholly original.

11. "Excogitavit etiam characteres quosdam, qui inscribebantur gemmis, quae antepositae maribus arrepitii cum radice quadam Salomoni monstrata, statim illum a daemonibus liberabant. Haec scientia plurimum valuit antiquitus in gente Hebraeorum; ante adventum Christi saepius homines a daemonibus vexabantur," Hugo de Sancto Charo, *Opera* (Venice, 1703), ad II Regum iv. f. 266r. Note Hugh's caution with respect to this "scientia."

12. *Il Convivio,* ed. G. Busnelli and G. Vandelli, 2nd ed. (Florence, 1954), IV, vii, vol. II, pp. 79–80. Cf. Enrico Proto, *L'Apocalissi nella Divina Commedia* (Naples, 1915), pp. 186–87.

13. Aristotle, *De anima,* II, iii, 279–98 (414^a 28–414^b 31); and St. Thomas, *Comm. in Aristotelis lib. de anima,* Lect. 5, 279–98. *Aristotle's De Anima in the Version of William of Moerbeke and the Commentary of St. Thomas Aquinas,* trans. Kenelm Foster, O. P., and Silvester Humphries, O. P. (New Haven, 1951), pp. 196–203.

14. *De Templo Salomonis* Lib. XV (PL 91, col. 770). Of the five senses of the body and those of the heart Bede writes: "corporis videlicet cum per eosdem sensus aliquid pro illo [Domino] agunt; cordis vero, cum sobrie, et iuste, et pie cogitant de iis quae per ipsos corporis sensus agere decernunt."

15. For general discussion of the number five, see Hopper, *Medieval Number Symbolism,* pp. 120 ff., Proto, *L'Apocalissi,* pp. 181–89, and R. E. Kaske, "Dante's 'DXV' and 'Veltro'," *Traditio,* 1961, pp. 197–98.

16. *Rationale divinorum officiorum* (Lyons, 1568). For ritual fives

signifying the senses and the five wounds of Christ see I, vii, 35r, and other "cruces quinque" in index; for his elaborate explanation of the number five as the number of the secular estate as opposed to four, the number of the spiritual estate, based on the historic difference in the number of weeks of Advent, see VI, ii, 255: "Seculares, qui rebus transitoriis student, quae quinque corporis sensibus administrantur, per quinque hebdomadas intelliguntur, iuxta illud Evangelii Joani: *Erant viri quasi quinque millia.* Siquidem quinque millia viri, Deum secuti, designant eos, qui in seculari adhuc habitu positi, exteriorbus, quae posident, bene uti noverant: ipsi namque saturantur quinque panibus, quia legalia instituta eis proponenda sunt, qui per quinarium numerum propter quinque libros Mosi intelliguntur."

17. Ackerman finds Gawain's integrity in his five fingers a natural development of his lack of fault in his five wits; the poet "resorted to the established tradition of allegorizing the five fingers, just as did Chaucer and Langland" ("Penitential Doctrine," p. 263). Earlier, Ackerman had argued that Chaucer's Parson "twice develops allegories on the five fingers . . ." (p. 261). In the passages in question, the five kinds of gluttony are said to be the fingers of the devil's hand by which he draws folk to sin (825–30), and the five steps of luxury are the devil's other hand (850–55); neither figure strikes me as being close to this sign of Gawain's perfection. The Langland figure (C. XX, 109–167) is even more remote: in it the Trinity is elaborately compared to the unity and interdependence of fist, palm and fingers in the human hand.

18. Joannes de Sancto Geminiano, *Summa de exemplis et rerum similitudinibus* (Antwerp, 1630), VI, xlviii, 326–27: "Est enim manus quinque digitis munita in quibus quinque virtutes designantur, quae necessariae sunt homini ut opera eius sint perfecta." In addition to assigning a major virtue to each of the five fingers, Joannes goes on to elucidate three aspects of each virtue as represented by the three bones of each finger. Cf. *De bestiis et aliis rebus,* III, lx (PL 177, col. 124–25), formerly attributed to Hugh of Saint Victor.

19. Piero Valeriano, *Hieroglyphica* (Basel, 1556), pp. 351–52; V. Cartari, *Le Imagini dei Dei de gli Antichi* (Venice, 1587), p. 69; Cornelius a Lapide, *Commentarius in Apoc.* (Lyons, 1732) ad I. 8, p. 18.

20. *Hieroglyph.*, p. 351.

21. John Burrow, "The Two Confession Scenes in *Sir Gawain and the Green Knight,*" cf. Chapter 6 of this volume.

10. STRUCTURE AND SYMMETRY IN *Sir Gawain*

1. Morton W. Bloomfield in *"Sir Gawain and the Green Knight: An Appraisal" (PMLA,* LXXVI [1961], 17), has pointed to the need for detailed analysis of the poem's structure. Some pertinent comments may be found in Charles Moorman, "Myth and Mediaeval Literature: *Sir Gawain and the Green Knight,"* cf. Chapter 11 of this volume, pp. 221–228, and in Francis Berry, *"Sir Gawayne and the Grene Knight,"* in *The Age of Chaucer,* ed. Boris Ford (Pelican Books A290, 1954), pp. 152–155. For further references see the footnotes which follow.

2. With respect to *Sir Gawain,* see Hans Schnyder, *Sir Gawain and the Green Knight: An Essay in Interpretation,* Cooper Monographs, 6 (Bern, 1961). While Schnyder grants (p. 74) that "the poem does not simply consist of a series of allegorical situations pedantically and painstakingly strung together," he treats dozens of recondite symbols in the poem without ever acknowledging the humorous tone, and devotes a chapter to the temptations without ever mentioning the girdle.

3. ll. 2433–36. References are to the edition of J. R. R. Tolkien and E. V. Gordon (Oxford, 1930).

4. See *Anatomy of Criticism* (Princeton, 1957), pp. 82–94. That the shield and girdle stand in relation to each other is recognized by Robert W. Ackerman, "Gawain's Shield: Penitential Doctrine in *Gawain and the Green Knight,"* *Anglia,* LXXVI (1958), 265, and by Richard H. Green, "Gawain's Shield and the Quest for Perfection," cf. Chapter 9 of this volume, p. 192.

5. On the pentangle, see Vincent F. Hopper, *Medieval Number Symbolism . . . ,* Columbia University Studies in English and Comparative Literature, 132 (New York, 1938), pp. 124–125, and Edgar de Bruyne, *Etudes d'esthétique médiévale,* II: *L'époque romane,* Rijksuniversiteit te Gent, Werken uitgegeven door de Faculteit van de Wijsbegeerte en Letteren, 98 (Bruges, 1946), pp. 349–350; also Green, pp. 129–135. On the shield, see Green, pp. 126–129 and Schnyder, pp. 53–54.

6. See line 637.

7. On the symbolism of the knight's garments, see Edgar Prestage, "The Chivalry of Portugal," in *Chivalry: A Series of Studies to Illustrate Its Historical Significance and Civilizing Influence,* ed. Edgar Prestage (New York, 1928), p. 145; A. T. Byles, "Medieval Courtesy

Books and the Prose Romances of Chivalry," ibid., p. 192; Sidney Painter, *French Chivalry: Chivalric Ideas and Practices in Mediaeval France* (Baltimore, 1940), pp. 83–84.

8. See Tolkien and Gordon, p. viii.

9. Ackerman, *(Anglia,* LXXVI, 254–265) suggests that the reference to the five wits would have called up fourteenth-century writings on auricular confession, so that the passage is consistent with the later theme of penitence.

10. George J. Engelhardt, "The Predicament of Gawain," *Modern Language Quarterly,* XVI (1955), 218–225.

11. On the Christian and "otherworldly" aspects of the chivalric code, see Painter, Chap. 3, and F. Warre Cornish, *Chivalry* (London, 1908), pp. 218–219. See also Henry Osborn Taylor, *The Mediaeval Mind: A History of the Development of Thought and Emotion in the Middle Ages,* 2 vols. (London, 1930), I, 545–551.

12. See ll. 1830–33, 2037–39, 2430–32.

13. John Burrow in "The Two Confession Scenes in *Sir Gawain and the Green Knight"* (cf. Chapter 6 of this volume) has pointed out that Gawain twice confesses to covetousness (ll. 2374–86, 2507–08) but his extravagance is corrected and the sin specifically denied (ll. 2366–68, 2429–32).

14. Dale B. J. Randall in "A Note on Structure in *Sir Gawain and the Green Knight"* *(Modern Language Notes,* LXXII [1957], 161–163) points out also that the Green Knight is the fiendish challenger at the beginning and end, but the genial host in the middle. The three parts correspond to those I have outlined—the "prologue," and the two parts of the major action. Such a triple structure was pointed out by Sylvan Barnet ("A Note on the Structure of *Sir Gawain and the Green Knight,"* *MLN,* LXXI [1956], 319), who remarks on its consistency with the pattern hunt-temptation-hunt, with the three temptations, three hunts, three strokes of the ax, and so on.

15. See Laurita Lyttleton Hill, "Madden's Divisions of *Sir Gawain* and the 'Large Initial Capitals' of *Cotton Nero A.x.,"* *Speculum,* XXI (1946), 67–71. Mrs. Hill argues that the size of the capitals is without significance.

16. Randall, pp. 161–163, points out that the frame at the beginning and end reverses the order of the three elements—"þe sege," Brutus, and Arthur's Court.

17. For the principle of description by contrast in this passage, see

Derek A. Pearsall, "Rhetorical 'Descriptio' in *Sir Gawain and the Green Knight,*" *Modern Language Review,* L (1955), 129–134.

18. See Tolkien and Gordon, pp. 94–95.

19. See Robert W. Ackerman, " 'Pared out of Paper': *Gawain* 802 and *Purity* 1408," *Journal of English and Germanic Philology,* LVI (1957), 410–17. Ackerman shows that the line refers to a custom of serving food on festive occasions covered or crowned with paper decorations in such shapes as that of a castle. Cf. Chaucer, *Parson's Tale,* X. 444.

20. For the latter point, see John Speirs, *Medieval English Poetry: The Non-Chaucerian Tradition* (London, 1957), pp. 236–237. On the hunting scenes, see Henry L. Savage, *The Gawain-Poet: Studies in His Personality and Background* (Chapel Hill, 1956), pp. 31–48.

21. On the treatment of the situation here as a reversal of courtly love, see J. F. Kiteley, "The *De Arte Honeste Amandi* of Andreas Capellanus and the Concept of Courtesy in *Sir Gawain and the Green Knight,*" *Anglia,* LXXIX (1961), 7–16.

11. MYTH AND MEDIAEVAL LITERATURE: *Sir Gawain and the Green Knight*

1. The phrase is Stanley Edgar Hyman's: "Myth, Ritual, and Nonsense," *Kenyon Review,* XI, 3 (1949), 455. The reader is directed to this article for a useful critical summary of the currently popular beliefs regarding the place of myth in literature.

2. C. G. Jung and C. Kerenyi, *Essays on a Science of Mythology,* trans. R. F. C. Hull (New York, Bollingen Series XXII, 1949), p. 102.

3. Ibid., p. 104.

4. New York, Bollingen Series XI, 1948.

5. *The King and the Corpse,* p. 76.

6. Ibid., p. 77.

7. Ibid.

8. Note that two pages later the "green girdle of death" mysteriously becomes the "talisman of rebirth" (p. 79).

9. *The King and the Corpse,* pp. 79–80.

10. Ibid., p. 81.

11. "Sir Gawain and the Green Knight," *Scrutiny* XVI, 4 (1949), 274–300.

12. Ibid., 275–6.

13. Ibid., 276.

14. Ibid., 275.

15. Ibid., 277.

16. Ibid.

17. Ibid., 277–8. It is always distressing to note these disagreements among the mythographers. Here Zimmer's death symbol becomes Speirs' life symbol. In the same way, Gawain's ax, a symbol of the primitive, pre-Christian nature of Death in Zimmer's analysis, becomes a fertility symbol in Speirs' discussion.

18. Art. cit., 463.

19. Speirs, art. cit., 278.

20. For example, the lords and ladies of Arthur's court kick the Green Knight's head away as it rolls towards them not out of "cruelty" or "horror," but because the "head of the sacrificed beast in fertility rituals was believed pregnant with magical power" (p. 283). Speirs offers as documentation for this statement a scholarly footnote relating the incident to the origin of football among primitive tribes. Speirs is so eager to connect everything in the poem with specific rituals and village festivals that he claims Gawain's arms are described in great and glittering detail because Greek, Roman, and English dancers were so arrayed in festival dances (p. 285); that mediaeval English knights might have been so arrayed he seems not to have considered. Having stated that the towers of Bercilak's castle are "as innumerable stalks thrust upward from the ground in spring" and that the castle is thus a fertility symbol, close to the "hidden source of life" (p. 287), Speirs adds a footnote remarking that "editors here interpose the red herring of 14th century architecture."

21. Ibid., 289.

22. Ibid., 290.

23. Ibid.

24. Ibid., 297.

25. Ibid., 299.

26. Ibid., 298.

27. The quotations from *Sir Gawain and the Green Knight* which appear in the text of this article are taken from the edition of the poem edited for the Early English Text Society by Sir Israel Gollancz (No. 210 in the Original Series) in 1940. All line references in the text are also to that edition. In quoting from the poem, I have omitted the italics with which Dr. Gollancz designates expansions of abbrevia-

tions. This edition is especially useful for its summary of most of the scholarship devoted to the poem prior to 1940.

28. I accept, as will almost any serious reader, the fact that the initiation, *rite de passage,* withdrawal and return pattern underlies the poem and directs its structure and theme.

29. Art. cit., 299–300.

30. For discussion of mediaeval allegory, the reader is directed to such primary sources as Dante's *Letter to Can Grande,* Boccaccio's *Vita di Dante,* and St. Thomas Aquinas' commentary in *Summa Theologica* I, q.I., a.10, and to such modern works as C. S. Lewis' *The Allegory of Love* (Oxford, 1936), Karl Vossler's *Medieval Culture* (New York, 1929), and T. S. Eliot's familiar study of Dante in *Selected Essays* (New York, 1932).

31. For full discussions of the elements of the basic initiation-quest pattern, the reader is directed to those volumes devoted to defining and analyzing the pattern as it appears in myth, particularly to Van Gennep's *Les Rites des Passages* (Paris, 1909), Lord Raglan's *The Hero* (London, 1949), and Joseph Campbell's *The Hero with a Thousand Faces* (New York, Bollingen Series XVII, 1949).

32. It is interesting to note, however, that even in *The Divine Comedy* some attention to the initiatory aspects of the journey might be profitable. Dante criticism and scholarship has, in devoting itself to an analysis of the journey, neglected the character of the journeyer. Even so eminent a Dante authority as Karl Vossler states that "the poet has sent forth his personality for us monumentally, statically; he has not developed it dynamically *(Mediaeval Culture* II, 216). It is good to see that Francis Fergusson's study of the *Purgatorio, Dante's Drama of the Mind* (Princeton, 1953), treats a development of the hero's character and perception in the second division of the work.

33. "The Significance of the Hunting Scenes in *Sir Gawain and the Green Knight,*" *JEGP,* XXVII (1928), 1–15.

34. *Les Rites des Passage,* chapter iii.

35. Op. cit., pp. 49–59.

36. This is, of course, not the only possible ending of the cycle; the hero may not succeed in convincing his people of the value of his experience. (See Campbell, op. cit., pp. 193–238.)

37. "The Role of Morgan le Fay in *Sir Gawain and the Green Knight,*" *ELH,* XXII, 241–51. It is possible to object to this general line of argument by pointing out that this sort of religious imagery

is usual in the mediaeval romance. However, *Sir Gawain and the Green Knight* is in structure, tone, and imagery far more tightly constructed than the usual romance, so tightly constructed in fact that it would be dangerous to pass off any one of the poem's myriad details as "merely" traditional. What is most apparent in *Sir Gawain and the Green Knight,* even upon the most cursory reading, is that here, as in Chaucer, merely traditional elements become meaningful and functional when set by the author in the new context of the poem. The modest prologue with which Chaucer's Franklin introduces his Breton lay was surely a piece of the mediaeval writer's standard storytelling equipment. Yet Chaucer uses this conventional device to throw light upon the dramatic role of the Franklin. So here, the *Gawain* poet adapts the conventional and largely meaningless religious imagery surrounding the chivalric quest to his own purposes in defining the truly religious nature of Gawain's journey. It seems clear to me also that despite Speirs, Loomis, Weston, *et al.* to the contrary, the *Gawain* poet is a Christian writer, not a Druid in disguise. There is nothing in the poem, aside from the hero pattern which is universal and thus Christian as well as Celtic, which the poet could not have taken directly from the Christian tradition.

38. The general strain of religious imagery which runs throughout the poem serves to reinforce this interpretation of the spiritual nature of Gawain's quest. Mass is heard daily in the castles of both Arthur and Bercilak. Gawain calls three times upon God to aid him in undertaking the quest (ll. 390, 399, 549). Arthur's court commends Gawain to God's protection on his departure (l. 596), and Gawain, having thanked "Jesus & say[n] Gilyan" for his safe arrival at Bercilak's castle (l. 774), blesses the porter who welcomes him there (l. 839). Gawain is said to be the comeliest knight that Christ ever made (l. 869). Bercilak's court rejoices that God has sent Gawain to them to be a model of courtly behavior (ll. 920ff.). Gawain commends Bercilak to God's grace (ll. 1038ff.). The interviews with Bercilak's lady are filled with oaths and commendations to Christ. Upon leaving, Gawain commends Bercilak's castle to Christ (l. 2067) and blesses and is blessed by the porter of Bercilak's castle (ll. 2071ff.). Bercilak and Gawain, after the conclusion of the beheading game, "[bikennen] ayþer oþer / To þe prynce of paradise" (ll. 2472–73).

39. The comparison of Bercilak's lady to Guinevere affords a striking example of the *Gawain* poet's functional use of conventional ma-

terial. Although "fairer than Guinevere" is a perfectly standard compliment in the mediaeval romance, used here in the midst of a comparison of the two courts and in a context involving the queen, the phrase surely constitutes more than a traditional compliment to the Lady. The obvious punning may represent the poet's way of calling special attention to the phrase.

40. It is almost certain that he did. See J. R. Hulbert, "The Name of the Green Knight," *Manly Anniversary Studies in Language and Literature* (Chicago, 1923), pp. 12–19, which demonstrates the *Gawain* poet's knowledge of the Vulgate Cycle.

41. The reason for Morgan's action is, of course, not given in the poem. Most scholars agree, however, that Morgan's action stems from her traditional hatred of Guinevere (see G. L. Kittredge, *A Study of Sir Gawain and the Green Knight* [Cambridge, Mass., 1916], p. 132) and that the introduction of Morgan into the poem represents a last-minute attempt to supply Bercilak with some sort of motivation for initiating the game. John Speirs, as I have said, calls Bercilak's explanation a "bone for the rationalizing mind to play with. . . ." J. R. Hulbert states that Bercilak's explanation is "inherently unreasonable" ("Gawain and the Green Knight," *MP*, XIII [1915-16], 454). Kittredge suggests the explanation which I have adopted and modified here, that the poet was influenced "by that form of the tale of the Magic Horn [from which only the faithful woman might drink] which represents Morgan as sending the talisman to the court with the design of revealing Guinevere's unfaithfulness" (loc. cit.).

42. Op. cit., pp. 129–30.

43. Ibid., p. 118.

44. Ibid.

A selected list of MIDLAND BOOKS

(continued on next page)